LEXICOGRAPHICA Series Maior

LEXICOGRAPHICA

Series Maior

Supplementary Volumes to the International Annual for Lexicography
Suppléments à la Revue Internationale de Lexicographie
Supplementbände zum Internationalen Jahrbuch für Lexikographie

Edited by
Sture Allén, Pierre Corbin, Reinhard R. K. Hartmann,
Franz Josef Hausmann, Hans-Peder Kromann, Oskar Reichmann,
Ladislav Zgusta

17

Published in cooperation with the Dictionary Society of North America
(DSNA) and the European Association for Lexicography (EURALEX)

The Dictionary and the Language Learner

Papers from the EURALEX Seminar
at the University of Leeds, 1–3 April 1985

edited by Anthony Cowie

Max Niemeyer Verlag
Tübingen 1987

CIP-Kurztitelaufnahme der Deutschen Bibliothek

The dictionary and the language learner : papers from the EURALEX seminar
at the Univ. of Leeds, 1 – 3 April 1985 / ed. by Anthony Cowie. – Tübingen :
Niemeyer, 1987.
   (Lexicographica : Series maior ; 17)
NE: Cowie, Anthony P. [Hrsg.]; European Association for Lexicography;
Lexicographica / Series maior

ISBN 3-484-30917-2 ISSN 0175-9264

TABLE OF CONTENTS

Acknowledgements   vii

List of Contributors   ix

Introduction   1

Part I   Research into dictionary use and design   9

R.R.K. Hartmann
    Four perspectives on dictionary use: a critical review
    of research methods   11
Beryl T. Atkins, Hélène Lewis, Della Summers and Janet
    Whitcut
    A research project into the use of learners' dictionaries   29
Barbara Ann Kipfer
    Dictionaries and the intermediate student: communicative
    needs and the development of user reference skills   44
Nicoletta Calzolari, Eugenio Picchi and Antonio Zampolli
    The use of computers in lexicography and lexicology   55
J. Jansen, J.P. Mergeai and J. Vanandroye
    Controlling LDOCE's controlled vocabulary   78

Part II   The dictionary in teaching and translation   95

Henri Béjoint and André Moulin
    The place of the dictionary in an EFL programme   97
Thomas Herbst and Gabriele Stein
    Dictionary-using skills: a plea for a new orientation in
    language teaching   115
Susan Maingay and Michael Rundell
    Anticipating learners' errors - implications for
    dictionary writers   128

vi

Jerzy Tomaszczyk
   FL learners' communication failure: implications for
   pedagogical lexicography   136
Joseph A. Reif
   The development of a dictionary concept: an English
   learner's dictionary and an exotic alphabet   146
Mary Snell-Hornby
   Towards a learner's bilingual dictionary   159

Part III   Progress in dictionary design   171

Rosamund Moon
   Monosemous words and the dictionary   173
A.P. Cowie
   Syntax, the dictionary and the learner's communicative
   needs   183
Robert Ilson
   Illustrations in dictionaries   193
P.D. Drysdale
   The role of examples in a learner's dictionary   213
Carla Marello
   Examples in contemporary Italian bilingual dictionaries   224
Thomas Creamer
   Beyond the definition: some problems with examples in
   recent Chinese-English and English-Chinese bilingual
   dictionaries   238
Ton Broeders
   The treatment of phonological idioms   246

Bibliography   257

ACKNOWLEDGEMENTS

I wish particularly to thank Reinhard Hartmann for encouragement and expert advice at various stages during the editing of this book. Grateful thanks are also due to Mrs. Susan Macdonald for help with Chinese characters and tone markings, and to Mrs. Christine Backhouse for her patient and meticulous work in producing a clear and accurate typescript.

I gratefully acknowledge permission given by the following publishers to reproduce line drawings, diagrams and/or charts from the works specified:

William Collins Sons & Co. Ltd.: *Collins English Learner's Dictionary.*

Librairie Larousse: *Dictionnaire du Français Contemporain; Dictionnaire du Français Langue Etrangère, 1.*

Longman Group UK Ltd.: *Longman Dictionary of Contemporary English; Longman New Universal Dictionary; Longman Active Study Dictionary of English.*

G. & C. Merriam Co.: *Webster's New Collegiate Dictionary, 8th edition.*

Oxford University Press: *Oxford Advanced Learner's Dictionary of Current English.*

Planeta S.A., Barcelona: *Diccionario Planeta de la Lengua Española Usual.*

Routledge and Kegan Paul Ltd.: *The ABC of Basic English; Basic English and its Uses.*

Universal Press International: *The Charlie Brown Dictionary.*

I should also like to thank Macmillan Publishers Ltd. for agreeing to the inclusion in this volume of two diagrams slightly adapted from originals in *The Words You Need.*

APC, Leeds, November 1986.

LIST OF CONTRIBUTORS

Atkins, Ms. Beryl T.   William Collins Sons & Co. Ltd., Glasgow,
    U.K.

Béjoint, Prof. Henri.   Département de Langues Étrangères
    Appliquées, Université de Lyon II, France.

Broeders, Mr. Ton.   Instituut Engels Amerikaans, Katholieke
    Universiteit, Nijmegen, The Netherlands.

Calzolari, Ms. Nicoletta.   Dipartimento di Linguistica, Univer-
    sità di Pisa, Pisa, Italy.

Cowie, Mr. Anthony P.   School of English, University of Leeds,
    Leeds, U.K.

Creamer, Mr. Thomas.   Chinese-English Translation Assistance
    Group, Kensington, Maryland, U.S.A.

Drysdale, Mr. Patrick.   Radley, Abingdon, Oxfordshire, U.K.

Hartmann, Dr. R.R.K.   Dictionary Research Centre, University of
    Exeter, Exeter, U.K.

Herbst, Dr. Thomas.   Lehrstuhl für Angewandte Sprachwissenschaft,
    Universität Augsburg, Augsburg, West Germany.

Ilson, Dr. Robert.   Survey of English Usage, University College,
    London, U.K.

Jansen, Mr. J.   Philologie Germanique, Université de Liège,
    Liège, Belgium.

Kipfer, Ms. Barbara Ann.   Bell Communications Research, Morristown,
    New Jersey, U.S.A.

Lewis, Ms. Hélène.   William Collins Sons & Co. Ltd., Glasgow, U.K.

Maingay, Ms. Susan.   Longman Group Ltd., Harlow, Essex.

Marello, Prof. Carla.   Facoltà di Lettere e Filosofia, Università
    di Torino, Torino, Italy.

Mergeai, Dr. Jean-Paul.   Philologie Germanique, Université de
    Liège, Liège, Belgium.

Moon, Ms. Rosamund.   COBUILD, Birmingham, U.K.

Moulin, Dr. André.   Philologie Germanique, Université de Liège,
    Liège, Belgium.

Picchi, Mr. Eugenio.   Istituto di Linguistica Computazionale,
    Pisa, Italy.

Reif, Dr. Joseph A.   Department of English, Bar-Ilan University, Israel.

Rundell, Mr. Michael.   Longman Group Ltd., Harlow, Essex.

Snell-Hornby, Dr. Mary.   Universität Zürich, Zurich, Switzerland.

Stein, Prof. Gabriele.   Seminar für Englische Sprache, Universität Hamburg, Hamburg, West Germany.

Summers, Ms. Della.   Longman Group Ltd., Harlow, Essex.

Tomaszczyk, Mr. Jerzy.   Institute of English Studies, University of Łódź, Łódź, Poland.

Vanandroye, Ms. Jocelyne.   Philologie Germanique, Université de Liège, Liège, Belgium.

Whitcut, Ms. Janet.   8 The Mount Square, London, U.K.

Zampolli, Prof. Antonio.   Istituto di Linguistica Computazionale, Pisa, Italy.

INTRODUCTION

This volume is evidence of a growing commitment on the part of
teachers, linguists and lexicographers to improving the use of
dictionaries among language learners of all kinds and to enhancing
awareness of the dictionary as a valuable language resource. Its
19 contributions by 28 specialist authors were first given as
papers, or as a stimulus to workshop discussion, at a Seminar on
the *Dictionary and the Language Learner* held under the auspices of the
European Association for Lexicography (EURALEX) at the University
of Leeds in April 1985. Since that meeting, all the contributions
have been revised in the light of discussion at Leeds or later
reflection, and a number have been substantially recast and expanded, updating research findings and incorporating references to
recent published work (e.g. Bergenholtz and Mugdan 1985; Ilson
1985, 1986).

The collection represents three broad and interrelated areas
of concern: current research into the reference needs of the
dictionary user (in particular the foreign learner) and into his
or her reference skills; dictionary use (including training in
use) viewed in the practical context of the classroom; and current
developments in dictionary design in the light of those various
insights and findings. The book confirms the central importance
of the computer, both in investigating dictionary use and in
critically evaluating the dictionary itself.

Reinhard Hartmann, who has played a pioneering role in promoting a user-centred approach to dictionary studies, opens with a
wide-ranging critical survey of published research into dictionary
users, their information needs, their dictionary-related study
activities, and their reference abilities. This four-fold categorization will serve as a valuable framework for future research.
As regards the present state, however, Hartmann cautions the
reader against over-optimism. Evidence still tends to be based
on elicited opinion rather than observed activity, and there are
areas such as user typology where vital questions are only now

being formulated.   Hartmann looks forward to the expansion of research based on controlled direct observation.

The project described by Beryl Atkins and her colleagues is an ambitious attempt to meet the need for more carefully controlled user research called for by Hartmann.   Foreign students of English are being given tests designed to measure their dictionary-using skills and to evaluate the selection and presentation of material in currently available monolingual and bilingual diction-aries.   Computational techniques are employed to record and analyse the results.   The study goes to great lengths to identify the variables inherent in the complex operation of referring to dictionary entries, and the test batteries have already been modified in the light of earlier trials.   The eventual findings are likely to prove of considerable value to teachers and lexico-graphers.

Narrowly focussed studies are needed as much as broadly based research projects.   Barbara Kipfer's study of dictionary use by intermediate-level American students (all native-speakers) shows them to be as unaware of the dictionary as a language-learning resource as the German- or French-speaking students described by other contributors.   Her use of an EFL dictionary with a class of native speakers is a practical application of a view that is gaining ground: that the difference between the language defi-ciencies of foreign and mother-tongue learners is one of degree, not kind.

Nicoletta Calzolari, Eugenio Picchi and Antonio Zampolli pro-vide a comprehensive account of developments in computing which are relevant to lexicography and lexicology.   The use of comput-ers at various stages in the compilation and production of dic-tionaries is well established.   Of greater potential importance for the dictionary researcher and user, however, is the prepara-tion of lexical data bases.   These employ increasingly sophisti-cated technology and have a range of possible applications, in-cluding linguistic analysis, lexicography and language learning. LDBs which draw on the data available in conventional dictionaries, as does the Istituto di Linguistica Computazionale at Pisa, constitute an information resource of immense complexity and rich-ness.

The paper by Jansen, Mergeai and Vanandroye reports one of a series of studies of the Controlled Vocabulary (CV) of the *Longman Dictionary of Contemporary English*, and well illustrates the growing involvement of the computer in research into dictionary design.

The paper is generally critical, not so much of the pedagogical value of a CV, as of the way the *LDOCE* scheme has been implemented in practice. The method is to examine all the entries for CV-items in *LDOCE*, determining in each case the number of senses. Computational methods are then used to find out how often the various senses of a given CV-item appear in a definition environment in the dictionary. Despite editorial claims that only "the most central meanings" of CV-items are used in definitions, analysis of a group of highly polysemous items reveals that a range of meanings is in fact taken up in each case.

Introducing the theme of the dictionary in the classroom, Henri Béjoint and André Moulin argue the case for a handbook designed to show how specific types of dictionary can help the student with particular language-learning tasks.

Béjoint addresses the general question of the value of dictionaries - and dictionary types - in language acquisition. He discusses the preference which is often shown for bilingual dictionaries, whether for encoding or decoding. This is partly explained by the naive view of lexical equivalence which students hold and which appears to be confirmed by the juxtaposition of translation "equivalents" in L1 and L2. Béjoint regards the role of definition metalanguage as important. L2 definitions may be difficult to process. Once processed, however, they may be internalized, by-passing the association of forms in the two languages. It is arguable that, as Hornby claimed, monolingual learners' dictionaries introduce the student directly into the lexical system of the foreign language.

André Moulin considers the kind of advice which the proposed handbook should provide to help the learner with one particular type of dictionary-use situation: writing in the foreign language. Moulin explains that the learner needs to become familiar with a variety of reference works and to develop skill and flexibility in using them. He shows, for example, that uncertainty over

exact meanings of English words may call for the use of a synonym-finder as well as a bilingual dictionary.   He also makes
clear that selection of a word or sense, or checking their closeness of fit, may involve both halves of a bilingual work, or
reference to different information categories in either part.
Moulin is conscious of the dictionary's limitations when it comes
to producing written discourse.   Stereotyped openings or complimentary closes of letters are easily obtained from dictionaries, but highly original uses of language will be more than
the dictionary is able to cope with.

The account by Thomas Herbst and Gabriele Stein of the current
state of training in dictionary use in German universities and
schools is a sober reminder of an almost universal lack of awareness, at grass-roots level, of the dictionary's value as a learning tool.   Teachers in Germany - as elsewhere - often have a
poor knowledge of dictionary conventions and organization and in
consequence are badly placed to explain how various types of
information can be retrieved.   The situation is not helped by
the failure to include dictionary-using skills in public examinations at school level.

Herbst and Stein argue strongly for the provision of systematic
training in dictionary use at school and university.   Apart from
its immediate usefulness, such training would help the learner
acquire the confidence to master other reference systems, including those of the modern working world.

Susan Maingay and Michael Rundell argue that further analytical
research is needed if learners are to be provided with all the
information they need for successful encoding in the foreign
language.   They consider the kinds of errors made by advanced
students in written exercises.   These are often "near misses",
reflecting a grasp of the various properties of words which is
just short of perfect.   The authors go on to argue that individual items present particular sets of problems for the learner.
How can they be identified?   They describe an experiment which
set out to investigate the relative effectiveness of different
types of definition conditions in dictionary entries.   This work
was inconclusive on the point investigated, but it did reveal

significant similarities in the types of error made by different students in the use of given words.   Many pitfalls are in fact predictable, and can be dealt with if the lexicographer has at his disposal a close prior analysis of each headword.

Jerzy Tomaszczyk's experience of working with Polish students of translation, and close examination of the errors they make, suggests that the great majority of errors would not have occurred if dictionaries had been consulted.   However, the translators often fail to refer to dictionaries at all.   Why is this? Tomaszczyk looks for an explanation in the concept of linguistic competence: the foreign learner cannot by definition be aware of all the language deficiencies he has and hence cannot be expected to try to remedy them.   Tomaszczyk is philosophical about formal errors, arguing that perfect accuracy is seldom required for successful communication with native speakers.   He questions, too, the value of insisting that students rely more on reference books, claiming that this tends to undermine confidence in their own ability.

The practical difficulties of teaching English at a university in Israel are uppermost in Joseph Reif's description of the genesis and compilation of a glossed dictionary of English. Reif's particular concern was the difficulty Israeli students have in *reading* English, and especially the formidable obstacle represented by the foreign writing system.   His solution was to add Hebrew glosses to the headwords and examples in an existing monolingual text.   Similar consideration led to the removal of the phonetic transcription, his decision not to add fresh ab-breviations and a policy towards including loanwords which judiciously gives special weight to native Hebrew words.

Mary Snell-Hornby's paper sets out the conditions which a pedagogically designed learner's bilingual dictionary should attempt to meet.   The ideal dictionary, unlike most of those currently available, would take account of the complex network of relations between the two languages and anticipate the learner's problems (some of which are due to Ll interference). Snell-Hornby regards dictionaries of this type as an integral part of an overall language-teaching strategy, in which the learner is successively confronted with items presented naturally in context, the grammatical system of the L2, and finally its lexical system.   Snell-Hornby's teaching concept - like the design of her bilingual dictionary - is governed by a perception of the variety of relations, some simple, some complex, which exist between the lexical systems of different languages.   The sheer diversity of such relations must be matched by variety in the organization of the dictionary entries themselves.

In the first of a group of papers concerned with dictionary design Rosamund Moon discusses a class of word which continues to pose problems of definition for the lexicographer.   These are not strictly monosemous items, as scientific and technical terms typically are; but neither can they be broken down into clearly distinguishable sub-senses.   They are words whose senses characteristically vary with their contexts, so that to represent them in the dictionary as if polysemous would impose an inherent semantic complexity which they do not possess.   The task of the lexicographer, as Moon shows with a wealth of examples (including examples of "heavy-duty" verbs), is to provide some measure of subcategorization (necessary in entries which are typically large) without misrepresenting the semantic simplicity of the headword.

A.P. Cowie argues that although much progress has been made in learners' dictionaries in detailing the syntactic properties of entry-words, we have tended to confine ourselves to those features (e.g. complementation of the verb) which can be explained and illustrated by means of decontextualised sentences.   Discourse analysis and communicative language teaching, however, have made us aware of cohesion across sentence boundaries and of the dis-course function of various syntactic patterns and "grammatical" words.   Such perceptions prompt the question whether points of syntax are best illustrated by sentences or by longer stretches of text.

Robert Ilson's elaborate classification of the uses of pictorial illustrations in dictionaries reveals that much more can be con-veyed to the learner by well-chosen pictures than the referential meanings of single concrete nouns.   The binary sense relation-ships of complementarity and converseness, as within a kinship network, for example, can be effectively presented, with other relationships too, in a family tree diagram. There is scope also for illustrating the positional and directional uses of prepositions, or adjectives in the comparative and superlative degree. Ilson extends his view of illustration to include tables and charts and reminds us of the effectiveness with which purely grammatical contrasts are presented in French monolingual learners' dictionaries.

The ability to select, or in EFL dictionaries more usually compare, suitable examples is an essential though comparatively little understood aspect of the lexicographer's art. Patrick Drysdale has helped to fill this gap by classifying the chief functions of examples, illustrating his categories by reference to children's and foreign learners' dictionaries. His call for a balance between authenticity and the deliberate highlighting of points of meaning or usage is welcome, as is his identification of types of example which take over part of the function of the definition.

The theme of exemplification is also taken up by Carla Marello, who provides a fully illustrated comparison of the forms and uses of examples in Italian bilingual dictionaries. Marello combines an interest in the minutiae of dictionary organization with a concern for the reference problems of the user. She carefully distinguishes between true examples and uses or collocations of the headword presented - often in the same typeface - as part of a definition or grammatical note. She rightly observes that the linguistic status of co-occurrence restrictions as represented in dictionary entries is often far from clear - an important point, since learners may use such indications when writing in the L2.

Thomas Creamer is concerned with the adequacy of dictionary examples from a rather different standpoint, that of the relation-ship between example and definition. Referring to illustrative sentences in a number of English-Chinese and Chinese-English dictionaries, he notes instances where an example lies outside the scope of a definition, or conversely ones in which the definition is too broad, or too general, for the examples subsumed by it. Creamer shows that the citation file is a good servant but a poor master, providing several instances of "authentic" examples which fail to elucidate meaning, structure or usage.

Ton Broeders' subject is the marking of the accentual patterns of English idioms in EFL dictionaries. By applying a Sentence Accent Assignment Rule, Broeders is able to show that in idioms of various syntactic types the position of the accent is often entirely predictable. He also throws interesting light on the perceptions of native speakers regarding idioms. He makes clear in the case of *the bird has flown*, for instance, that the native speaker is aware that *the bird* stands for a person being looked for (the 'quarry'). In other words the native is able to analyse many apparently opaque or figurative sequences in terms of "given" and "new" information. However, the semantic opacity of such expressions makes it difficult for the foreign learner to decide which elements are + or - focus and thus to assign the accent. For him, the accentual patterns need to be consistently shown in the EFL dictionary.

The contributions to this volume testify to the optimism of learner-centred lexicography and to the diversity of current research into dictionary uses and users. Most of the studies reported here focus on specific problems of use or design, though the project launched by Atkins, Lewis, Summers and Whitcut is a welcome move towards carefully-controlled large-scale investigations.

A conviction repeatedly expressed in the book is that teachers should press forward with programmes of training in dictionary use. Underlying calls for such training is an implicit or declared confidence that learners need, and can be brought to value, the wealth of information which present-day dictionaries contain. The same spirit is apparent in the efforts of editors to improve and extend dictionary coverage.

Anthony Cowie, Leeds, November 1986.

P A R T   I

RESEARCH INTO DICTIONARY

USE AND DESIGN

R.R.K. Hartmann

FOUR PERSPECTIVES ON DICTIONARY USE:
A CRITICAL REVIEW OF RESEARCH METHODS

1. Introduction

> "Dictionaries are obviously written for their users. We therefore need
> much more research on the dictionary user, his needs, his expectations, and
> his prejudices."   (Gabriele Stein 1984:4)

The quotation is apt. Ever since the famous 1960 conference
on lexicography at Indiana University, there has been a heightened
feeling that dictionaries do not do enough for their users.
Recommendation No. 1 in the "Summary Report" (Householder & Saporta
1962:279) states: "Dictionaries should be designed with a special
set of users in mind and for their specific needs."

Gabriele Stein's point about the need for more research is well
taken by all of us, even though she does not specify the reasons.
Let me briefly recapitulate four of these:
- dictionary compilers and publishers do not make their purposes
  explicit;
- dictionary reviewers make erratic demands;
- dictionary users do not know what to expect;
- teachers do not know which dictionaries to recommend.

Very often there may be a mis-match, therefore, between the information provided by the dictionary maker and the help required by
the dictionary user. This paper attempts to give a critical
account, under four headings, of some fifteen investigations into
the needs and skills of the dictionary user, of which the language
learner is an important sub-class.

2. Four perspectives on the user

How can we find out about what the learner as dictionary user
requires? What are his/her "needs, expectations and prejudices"?
As far as I know there is no precedent for such a 'survey of surveys'. Although there have been several studies of dictionary
user behaviour, no-one has yet produced an adequate comparison of

their respective assumptions and findings, and certainly there has never been a systematic classification of research methods. (In a field where one opinion is almost as good as any other, it is imperative not only to collect more facts, but also to develop an expertise for judging them.)

Following an earlier introductory paper of mine (Hartmann 1983a), I shall distinguish four groups of research into dictionary use:

(1) research into the information categories presented in dictionaries ('dictionary typology');

(2) research into specific dictionary user groups ('user typology');

(3) research into the contexts of dictionary use ('needs typology');

(4) research into dictionary look-up strategies ('skills typology').

These four orientations are motivated by very different premises and traditions. There are hardly any criteria by which their techniques and results can be properly evaluated and compared, and they tend to be scattered over a wide range of sources and disciplines. I shall first illustrate my four typologies by reference to one model for each, and then elaborate on them more fully in Sections 3 to 6 below.

The four representative studies are, in chronological order, Clarence Barnhart's discussion of the relative usefulness of various information categories to buyers of commercially produced popular dictionaries, Randolph Quirk's survey of university students' attitudes to their dictionaries, Jerzy Tomaszczyk's survey of activity contexts in which monolingual and bilingual dictionaries are used, and Evelyn Mitchell's test of reading strategies of school pupils, with particular reference to dictionary consultation. They span a period of over 20 years and illustrate the whole range of approaches in use.

Clarence Barnhart's paper, first presented at the Bloomington conference and reprinted at least once, starts with the assertion that "it is the function of the popular dictionary to answer the questions that the user of the dictionary asks, and dictionaries on the commercial market will be successful in proportion to the extent to which they answer these questions of the buyer" (1962: 161). To determine what sorts of user questions the editor of a

commercial monolingual dictionary needs to answer, Barnhart had
sent out, as early as 1955, 108 questionnaires to teachers of
English composition classes, asking them to rate six types of
information commonly offered in American college dictionaries
according to the importance attached to them by freshmen students.
It turned out that the most sought-after information was meaning,
followed by spelling and pronunciation, with synonyms, usage and
etymology least important.

As far as I am aware, this was the first attempt at quantifying
our knowledge about the purposes and roles of the dictionary. The
findings, though based on a relatively small sample, have not been
challenged overall by subsequent surveys. They have proved of
considerable interest to lexicographers wishing to decide what
kind of material should be included in the dictionary and how it
should be presented for the benefit of the user. Barnhart also
raised a number of basic issues of dictionary design which have
remained unresolved to this day, e.g. how to separate the different
senses of lexical items and arrange them within the dictionary entry,
or what sort of phonetic transcription might be appropriate for
particular users. Barnhart's treatment of these topics was wide-
ranging and searching, a feature that has influenced a whole generation of user guides and dictionary manuals. Above all, he
gave dictionary typology a new impulse by introducing into the
stale debate the more vital criterion of the user perspective (see
Sections 3 and 4 below).

On the negative side we note that Barnhart did not reproduce
his questionnaire and numerical results in his paper, and in any
case his findings are based not on direct observation of users,
but on indirect reports by their teachers.

Randolph Quirk avoided the pitfall of doubtful data. In the
paper which he first presented at the 1973 New York Academy of
Sciences Colloquium on English Lexicography, he set out to replace
folkloristic beliefs and popular myths about the dictionary by
objective evidence from the users themselves. The instrument
which helped him gather such evidence was a questionnaire issued
to 220 undergraduate students at University College London, half
in the arts, half in the sciences, half men, half women. There

were 30 questions in all, on such things as dictionary ownership, frequency and purposes of use, experience of deficiencies, and suggestions for improvement.

Compared to earlier undifferentiated and highly speculative studies, Quirk's is the first scholarly attempt in Britain to assess the dictionary user's attitudes, expectations and prejudices, if not his or her actual needs and reference skills. The focus is no longer on the producer of the dictionary and its potential usefulness to an anonymous market, but on the opinions of real (if restrictedly academic) users. The most noteworthy findings are the high proportion of students who own (192 out of 220) and regularly use (156 at least monthly) a dictionary, the predominance of 'meaning' as the chief reason for dictionary consultation, and the lack of interest in etymology and pronunciation.

Although factual evidence is still based on reported opinion rather than observed action, Quirk's study has gone a long way towards giving us a more realistic picture of the user. It helped lay the foundations for empirical research, with its embryonic user typology, well before the 'sociological' approach advocated by Wiegand, Dubois and others made itself felt, and sparked off a long line of detailed studies, particularly in relation to the teaching of English to speakers of other languages.

Jerzy Tomaszczyk was one of the first to go beyond the English monolingual context, to investigate the dictionary requirements of the foreign-language learner and translator. He correctly remarked (1979) that while the feeling of dissatisfaction with dictionaries among foreign-language learners has been widespread and criticism of dictionary shortcomings often vociferous, very little is in fact known about the role of monolingual and bilingual dictionaries in the process of language acquisition.

Nearly 450 people completed Tomaszczyk's questionnaire (see Table 1). The most important new vantage point is that of the needs of the language learner. Learners' activity contexts are specified in terms of 'language skills', i.e. listening, reading, speaking, writing and translating, and 'information types', i.e. meaning and synonyms, spelling and pronunciation, usage and etymology.   Dictionary use apparently depends on the nature and extent of the skill practiced and on the proficiency level of the learner, with writing and reading coming top, translating in the middle, and speaking and listening at the bottom.   The order of information types differs from that given by Barnhart and Quirk for obvious reasons, except that here too meaning and spelling predominate.

Tomaszczyk's presentation of numerical evidence is not always clear, the statistical analysis is incomplete, and the question-naire is not reproduced.   More and more the suspicion is gaining ground that indirect surveying of population samples needs to be supplemented or replaced by more carefully controlled direct observation.   On the positive side, the comprehensiveness of the investigation is impressive, which is undoubtedly why it has stimulated further work on the typology of learners' needs and dictionary purposes (see Section 5 below).

The fourth pioneering study to be outlined here is Evelyn Mitchell's (1983).   It formed part of a large-scale research project on reading strategies in secondary schools in Scotland. The objective was to break down the reading process into its con-stituent skills and assess how pupils cope with them.   One of the reading tests was aimed at obtaining data on how information is extracted from a dictionary.   This type of strategy is defined as 'search-do reading', i.e. it consists of first recognising the most relevant piece of information in the dictionary and then utilising it for the purpose of text comprehension (see Table 2). The user group and the user context are given, but the skills needed to achieve the end result are to be elicited from a series of exercise-like tasks, called 'units'.

Thus, as we already know from earlier studies like those of Barnhart, Quirk and Tomaszczyk, the task of finding the meaning of a word is an essential aspect of dictionary use.   Mitchell's study confirms this to be an extremely complex process, with pu-pils experiencing difficulties at every stage.   It involves searching for an appropriate headword, understanding the structure of the entry, identifying the relevant part of the definition, relating the appropriate sense to the context provided, and merging the word, by paraphrase, with the context of the source text. There was virtually no existing procedure the research team could draw on, which makes the findings, tentative though they are, extremely relevant to the job of elaborating a skills typology for the controlled observation of dictionary users in action (see Section 6 below).

After taking a first glance at four ways of studying dictionary use (detailing information types, compiling user profiles, analysing dictionary needs, and testing reference skills), we are now ready to examine these research modes and their limitations in a little more detail. This is done in the next four sections; the typologies will be introduced by quotation titles taken from typical questions in the literature.

3. Dictionary typology: What's in a dictionary?

Discussions of the user often start with or come back to the information categories found in dictionaries. This is why Barnhart's paper is considered a classic in this kind of research. Almost by accident it heralded a change in the approach to dictionary typology itself: the fundamental yardstick for classifying dictionaries is no longer (only) the absolute knowledge of the lexicographer, but rather the relatively varying purposes achieved by the dictionary for the benefit of different groups of users.

Apart from the more theoretical studies of the notion of dictionary typology itself, from Ščerba in the 1930s to Al-Kasimi in the '80s, there are at least two approaches to user-oriented research into dictionary content worth distinguishing, the 'didactic' and the 'critical'. The former is associated with dictionary producers and teachers, and often takes the form of manuals, the latter comes from academics and other self-appointed advisers, in the form of reviews and consumer guides.

Contrary to general belief, the dictionary user handbook is not a recent innovation. My bibliographical data-base lists at least five with similar titles for English alone, not counting the various publishers' workbooks and reference guides for consumers and libraries. It may be worth inspecting just one exemplar here, Roger Lewis' & Martin Pugmire's *How to Use Your Dictionary*, issued (1980) in the Study Skills series of the National Extension College. It starts with a discussion of the various possible uses of the dictionary (the authors admit to being surprised at how many different uses they found themselves), not on the basis of a survey of real users (or real needs), but by reference to the traditional 5 'distinct sorts of information', i.e. meaning, spelling, grammar, etymology and pronunciation. (This, incidentally, is also true of other manuals.) The only thing that comes anywhere near research into user behaviour is a "Pretest" which readers are advised to take before tackling the six units of the course.

Thus Lewis & Pugmire offer us a didactically motivated textbook for adult learners rather than a specification of real needs: guidance on the use of existing dictionaries is given (9 are exemplified, particularly the *Pocket Oxford Dictionary)* rather than understanding of how particular communication problems can be overcome with the aid of reference works.

For that sort of research we have to look hard and far afield, to studies of the appropriateness of dictionary material for particular user groups. Both Quirk and Tomaszczyk had found evidence of dissatisfaction among their respective respondents (e.g. difficulties with the metalanguage of definitions, or requests for names and pictorial illustrations), and had even invited suggestions for improvements. But in practice it is very difficult indeed to measure the suitability of dictionary information for specific users without running the risk of merely treating the episodic or trivial. I can illustrate this problem by reference to a couple of studies of the coverage of vocabulary in certain dictionaries in relation to the allegedly known needs of certain learner-users (cf. also Yorkey 1969).

Given a particular task, a dictionary may be more or less suitable for carrying it out successfully. Želko Bujas (1975) tested the performance of a medium-size general-purpose English-Croatian dictionary against the requirement of reading current topical texts from American and British sources like *Time Magazine* and *The Observer*, aiming for a non-intuitive 'performance coefficient'. Bujas employed 18 student analysts for 2½ years with the brief of going through 34 issues of 9 periodicals to find inadequacies in the dictionary in question, in terms of missing headwords, missing senses, or erroneous equivalents. They recorded 6,272 vocabulary items, of which 78.3% were recommended for insertion in a later revision of the dictionary.

Bujas's work did not yield a generally applicable performance index, but it resulted in a workable procedure for improving an existing bilingual dictionary in an area found wanting (in this case over 2,200 English items essential for understanding modern magazine texts were eventually added to the word-stock covered in its most recent edition).

More limited utility tests, with much more limited results, have been attempted by Kurt Opitz (1979) and Karl Müller (1983) in order to establish whether particular dictionaries are suitable for helping students in English for special purposes with their reading comprehension and vocabulary acquisition practice. Opitz's subjects are students at a nautical college, Müller's are undergraduates in law. Both studies are interesting from the point of view of the dictionary's text coverage of a discipline, but both are inconclusive in the extreme. One cannot help asking questions like: What would have happened if the investigators had used different texts? or different dictionaries? or different groups of students?

Many questions (such as those asked by Barnhart 30 years ago) remain unanswered. For some, not even a suitable empirical research design has been devised. Are the days of the undifferentiated general dictionary numbered? Are there information categories regarded as more important or urgent than the conventional five? Where are the boundaries between the dictionary and other reference works like encyclopaedias and computer databases? Is there a difference between native and foreign users concerning the use of a controlled defining vocabulary? What is the role of grammatical codes and phonetic keys? Does the text structure of dictionary entries impede intelligibility? etc. etc.

4. User typology: Who needs dictionaries?

The upshot of the previous section is that the single undifferentiated user does not exist. The distinctions made in theory between the scholarly-subsidised and the popular-commercial dictionary (Barnhart), the dictionary for university students and that for the family (Quirk), the dictionary for school pupils and that for adults (Mitchell), and the dictionary for native speakers and that for foreign learners (Bujas) are reflected by an increasingly greater specialisation in practical lexicography. Jean Dubois has summarised this trend as follows (1981:236):

"... while until comparatively recently lexicographers had scarcely looked beyond one type of user - persons of cultivated literary tastes, sharing the same educational and linguistic background as themselves - more recently they have been led to acknowledge that the choice of linguistic information in a dictionary, and the means of access provided to it, will vary with the class of user for whom the dictionary is intended."

Yet, a valid user typology still eludes us. But this is not surprising, for while it is relatively easy to correlate a particular information category (e.g. coverage of the vocabulary of a branch of learning) against a particular user group (e.g. students reading texts from that discipline), I know of no comprehensive research project aimed at finding out which dictionary types are actually (and in what proportion) consulted by certain users, and for what reasons. Thus, one of the most basic issues, viz. the relationship between the so-called 'general' and the 'specialised' dictionary and their respective users, remains unresolved for the time being.

It is sometimes claimed that the all-purpose dictionary, because of its broader information content, can cater for a bigger market, while the specialised dictionary can only offer limited material or sectional coverage. However, this view may be misguided in terms of actual instances of use. Tomaszczyk (1979: 115) reported a number of his respondents suggesting "that a wider range of highly specialised dictionaries would be a better solution than the increasingly bulkier general dictionaries". Quite independently, Peter Kühn and Ulrich Püschel (1982) have tested the hypothesis that certain users (like teachers of German - see Table 1) shun general-purpose dictionaries in favour of more re-

stricted ones (like the *Duden* spelling dictionary).   The same
has been observed by Tomaszczyk in a different article with respect
to the so-called general bilingual dictionary: the reference needs
of language learners, translators, scientists, journalists and
other groups "are too diverse and incompatible to be taken care
of efficiently in one type of dictionary"   (1981:288).

If this remarkable finding can be generalised to other areas,
it would have far-reaching implications for dictionary design.
Publishers are of course intuitively aware of ever-changing
markets (cf. Bart Ullstein's discussion of competitive advertis-
ing among British dictionary publishing houses, 1981).   In order
to find out who buys which dictionary for whom and for what
reason and at what price, some have surveyed the general public
by means of opinion polls (Longman/Gallup) and questionnaires
(Brandstetter in Wiesbaden, Elsevier in Amsterdam).   Unfortunately, the results of such enquiries are rarely divulged.
(Alain Rey has sent me a copy of a report about a large-scale
user survey of foreign learners of French carried out by Le
Robert in Paris some years ago;   two more recent questionnaire
surveys have been initiated by the *New Oxford English Dictionary* and
the Australian *Macquarie Dictionary*.)

All this leaves us uncomfortably unsettled.   The only tentative conclusions we seem to be able to reach in the field of
user typology are: a hunch that dictionary users when faced with
a problem tend to tackle only one information category at a time;
a realisation that different users may approach dictionaries in
very different ways;   a suspicion that dictionary reference
behaviour may vary - more than we care to admit - by such parameters
as country, age, education, etc.;   and an overriding feeling that
users do not receive sufficient instruction to enjoy the full
benefit of their dictionaries.   In sum, we could do with more
research into the real needs of real users.

5. Needs typology: What's a dictionary for?

We note with regret that the combined forces of lexicography,
commerce and linguistics have not (yet) produced a satisfactory
account of the reference needs of the dictionary user.   A socio-

logical perspective has been suggested as a solution to this problem by Herbert Ernst Wiegand (1977), who pointed out that the main
purpose of a dictionary is to prevent or at least reduce communication conflicts which may arise from lexical deficit, and that
in order to understand the demands made on the dictionary we need
more detailed empirical descriptions of the many possible contexts
of lexical consultation.

Pedagogical lexicography has embraced this sociological view
of dictionary look-up situations and applied it to the job of analysing learners' needs (indeed 'needs analysis' has become a slogan
in communicative syllabus design, too).   Several contributions to
the thematic issue of the journal *Applied Linguistics* (edited by
A.P. Cowie) reflect some of these insights.   One of these, by
Henri Béjoint (1981), broke new ground by surveying in detail the
dictionary preferences of his students of English at the University
of Lyon (see Table 1).   Béjoint not only clarified the complex
interaction between encoding activities (active production such as
composition) and decoding activities (passive reception such as
reading comprehension), noting the predominance of the latter over
the former, but also commented on the puzzling fact that learners
do not appreciate and utilise the enormous wealth of (e.g. grammatical) information offered in the new generation of EFL learners'
dictionaries.

One of the arguments Béjoint deliberately excluded from his
discussion concerns the point in foreign-language acquisition at
which the use of the bilingual dictionary should be discouraged in
favour of the monolingual target-language dictionary and the
manner in which this could best be achieved.   What little empirical data are available to shed light on this issue are interpreted
by James Baxter (1980) as follows: more encouragement should be
given to the use of monolingual dictionaries because it promotes
fluency by offering definitions in context and vocabulary in
'handfuls', in contrast to bilingual dictionaries which tend to
channel learners towards single-word translation equivalents that
may not be appropriate in the discourse in question.   Baxter
supports this view from his own survey of EFL students in a Japanese university setting (see Table 1) and couples it with a plea

for more instruction in the required reference skills. However, these claims need to be considerably qualified in my opinion before they can replace more established dogma.

According to my investigation of learners of German in South West England (Hartmann 1983b), for instance, the use of bilingual dictionaries is so entrenched within and outside formal language classes - where translation activities still reign supreme - and monolingual learners' dictionaries are so under-developed in languages other than English, that the idea of 'weaning away' the learner from the translation dictionary seems rather unrealistic. (See Snell-Hornby, this volume.) My findings (see Table 1) partly confirm those of Tomaszczyk (1979) and Béjoint (1981). Of the seven categories of activity listed in my questionnaire, by far the most popular is translating (90% of respondents practice it regularly), followed by reading and writing. Of the information categories and types of words consulted, grammar and meaning predominate, while pronunciation, proper names and historical derivations seem relatively unimportant. And one of the questions backs up the point made by Kühn and Püschel (1982) that some specialised dictionaries are at least as much used as general-language dictionaries (67% consult dictionaries of synonyms at least occasionally).

Some of the findings reported in this section need to be supported by further research. Several such studies are in progress, e.g. as postgraduate projects, on similar topics and for other languages (see Atkins et al., this volume). However, we should heed a warning about the inherent limitations of questionnaire-type surveys. Glyn Hatherall has expressed his doubts in these strong words (1984:184):

> "Are subjects saying here what they do, or what they think they do, or what they think they ought to do, or indeed a mixture of all three? ... do we not, on this basis, arrive at a consensus on how subjects are likely to behave when faced with a particular questionnaire, rather than authentic data on what they use the dictionary for?"

Hatherall has also (and in this he is not alone) shown the direction which we can expect future progress to take. This may include closer direct observation by means of protocol, film and audio recordings as well as personal interviews, plus computer tests involving the logging-in and processing of data on video screens (for the latter, cf. Fox et al. 1980).

	Type of User	Size of Sample	Technique	Main Findings
Tomaszczyk (1979)	(various, incl. Polish) foreign-language students and 'Others'	284 & 165	Questionnaire 57 items	use of dictionary depends on nature of activity and proficiency level
Baxter (1980)	Japanese students (of English	342	Questionnaire 6 items	learners rely more on bilingual than monolingual dictionaries
Béjoint (1981)	French students of English	122	Questionnaire 21 items	language learners do not utilise all information offered in dictionary
Kühn and Püschel (1982)	(various) teachers of German	c.50	Questionnaire 21 items	specialised dictionaries used more than general-purpose dictionary
Hartmann (1983b)	British teachers and learners of	67 & 118	Questionnaire 23 items	meaning & grammar most important need (for translation); users receive little dictionary instruction

Table 1: Surveying language learners' dictionary needs

6. Skills typology: How do you find what you need?

We come now to the last, but in many ways most urgent type of research, viz. that concerned with the strategies required from the user to get the most out of dictionary consultation. This is also the most recent and least explored aspect.

Five studies deserve to be singled out for comment (see Table 2). One, by Mitchell (1983), we have already reviewed. Not specifically devoted to language learners and dictionary reference, the research is nevertheless exemplary in providing test items which can elicit data on user skills. The last of Mitchell's 5 units, in particular, manages to simulate the right sort of real-life look-up situations and isolate the right sort of component skills appropriate to extracting problem-related information from the dictionary. If these skills are not present, difficulties may arise. The implication is clear: we must try to understand the strategies that are needed by the learner, and if necessary teach them explicitly (for a seven-step strategy for dictionary-aided reading comprehension in EFL, cf. Scholfield 1982).

Marsha Bensoussan and colleagues in two universities in Israel (1984) came to the rather startling conclusion (see Table 2) that the use of dictionaries does not affect performance in reading comprehension tests for advanced students of English. We must take this claim seriously, as it has been reached on the basis of a rather impressive statistical analysis of a large sample, but it should not stop us from asking a few more critical questions, e.g. whether it is possible to construct test items which can be tackled regardless of whether a dictionary is used in reading a text or not.

Josh Ard (1982) also dealt with foreign learners of English. He was interested in the extent to which the use of bilingual dictionaries helps or hinders progress in essay-writing. To find out, he devised an observational setting from which he obtained a detailed record of what can actually happen (see Table 2). Ard's article documents two composition sessions, one with a Japanese female who used the dictionary a lot and one with an Arabic-speaking male who did not. The technique offers a way of settling some very controversial themes empirically, provided (as Ard himself concedes) the samples are representative for statistical analysis. But even this limited case study reveals interesting facts, e.g. about instances of lexical interference which may or may not be reinforced by the use of a bilingual dictionary.

We still need further numerical information from Hatherall's (1984) observational study of a translation exercise supported by dictionary look-up. From an informal analysis of his experiment he found (see Table 2) that less proficient students use the dictionary less, and reference to the translation dictionary tends to increase the rate of idiomatic errors.

Finally, Wiegand (1985) used the protocol approach with foreign students of German at Heidelberg. He wanted to determine whether a general-purpose monolingual dictionary can help the advanced learner decide points of grammar and other usage problems which may occur in checking the appropriacy of a translation. Predictably there are quite a number of user questions for which the dictionary has no answer. If it were possible to process such records in great numbers, this would seem a sensible way of testing a dictionary's suitability for a particular task while at the same time describing the range of user skills demanded.

7. A critique of research methods

There is yet another way of looking at research: starting not with issues, but with the techniques employed for clarifying them. Has the research reported here made use of all the available tools, and how does it measure up to the general standards of investigation in the social sciences? The answer to the first question is 'no', the answer to the second depends on what criteria one is prepared to use.

This is not the place to enlarge on the classification and description of research techniques. Let us just note that according to one social science manual (Labovitz & Hagedorn 1981); investigative methods can be distinguished by 'research design' into the case study, the survey, and the experiment. Another manual (Selltiz et al. 1976) takes 'data collection' procedures as defining feature, subdividing these into structured and unstructured observation, the questionnaire/interview, and various types of tests.

We recognise most of these research methods from the 15 studies reviewed in this paper. More than half fall into the category of 'survey by questionnaire'; some investigate native speakers (Barnhart 1962, Quirk 1973), some foreign learners (Tomaszczyk 1979, Baxter 1980, Béjoint 1981), some teachers (Kühn & Püschel 1982), some students and teachers (Hartmann 1983b), some poll the

	Main Objective	Size of Sample	Technique	Main Findings
Bensoussan et al. (1984)	measuring reading comprehension in EFL students	c. 700 & 91	9 tests (with comprehension questions on each reading text) & questionnaire	students prefer bilingual dictionaries; no correlation between test scores and dictionary use
Ard (1982)	observing composition strategies in EFL students	2 (of a class, un-specified)	filmed protocol & oral interview	use of bilingual dictionaries can lead to lexical errors; banning them would not prevent such errors
Mitchell (1983)	assessing reading strategies in Scottish school pupils	15 (of 5 groups, total 94)	5 test units	pupils have difficulties locating words and senses in dictionary search for text comprehension
Hatherall (1984)	observing dictionary consultation in German-English translation	22	check-list questionnaire & text analysis	advanced students use dictionary more; unidiomatic literal translation reinforced by reference to bilingual dictionary
Wiegand (1985)	observing dictionary use for checking English-German translation	1 (of seminar of 35)	written protocol	monolingual target-language dictionary does not answer all user questions on grammatical appropriateness

Table 2: Charting language learners' dictionary skills

dictionary buying market at large. Only two of the studies (Quirk 1973, Hartmann 1983b) attempt statistical correlations of their data. A smaller number are case studies using structured observation techniques like protocol (Wiegand 1985) or lexical check-lists (Bujas 1975), others combine unstructured recording with interviewing (Ard 1982). Tests are more difficult to devise and poss-

ibly therefore rarer (Bensoussan et al. 1984, Mitchell 1983).
Even more complex techniques like controlled experiments have not
been used at all.

All this reflects the immature state of the art. Research
into dictionary use still tends to be small-scale, often non-
representative, non-comparable (even contradictory!), non-corre-
lational, and non-replicable. This partly explains the tentative
nature of many of the findings, which frequently have the status
of 'informed opinion' rather than valid generalisation.

The way forward, it seems to me, must be for all of us to
encourage and pursue scholarly studies for the benefit of lexicography, the dictionary user, and the language learner. The
computer may have a more than marginal role to play in this development.

8. Conclusion

The most important conclusion, especially after the critical
remarks in the previous section, is that research into dictionary
use is alive and well, but needs a 'quantum leap' into the realm
of scientific respectability. Of the four approaches distinguished in this paper, the latter two - 'needs analysis' and
'skills analysis' - appear to be the most urgently needed and
promising.

From the point of view of the learner as dictionary user, we
can summarise the position as follows:

(1) The range of dictionary types is greater than ever before,
but knowledge about the information categories offered in them is
still limited. The so-called learner's dictionary is only one
of many dictionary types (underdeveloped for many languages), and
we are far from certain about what its features should be and how
it should be integrated into the language learning/teaching
process.

(2) The range of user types is greater than we care to admit, and
this diversity demands detailed attention. It is not sufficient
to list dichotomies like young/old, lay/professional, student/
family, beginner/advanced, native/foreign etc., for these opposi-

tions are in fact scales, with many intermediate and overlapping characteristics.

(3) The range of individual needs of all these dictionary users is vast. Whether the problem situation is reading comprehension, seeking factual information, translating, or essay writing, the lexicographer's duty is to satisfy these often conflicting requirements as best he can.

(4) The range of skills the learner brings to dictionary use is complex and unpredictable. New observational techniques should be employed to discover their presence and nature.

If the overall impression left by this paper is one of insecurity in the face of multiplicity, it will have achieved one of its objectives. We must do more in research and instruction. EURALEX has an important part to play in fostering the exchange of information and enlarging the range of debate.

Beryl T. Atkins, Hélène Lewis, Della Summers and Janet Whitcut

A RESEARCH PROJECT INTO THE USE OF LEARNERS' DICTIONARIES

1. Introduction

The purpose of this research project is to discover how effective a learner the student of English as a foreign learner is when working with a bilingual and/or monolingual dictionary. We propose to ask students to complete a User Profile Questionnaire in their own language (see Section 2) and to do two sets of tests, the first (Classification Tests) designed to classify them on the basis of their English language skills, and the second (Assessment Tests) intended to assess their dictionary-using skills and to evaluate the selection and presentation of material in the dictionaries used. Samples of the Classification Tests are not included here. For this purpose, we propose to use the set of tests developed by a respected language school in the U.K. Samples of the Assessment Tests are given later in this paper (Section 5).

The research aims to discover how much instruction students receive in the use of dictionaries, and is also designed to provide a comparative eveluation of the effectiveness of bilingual diction- aries and monolingual learners' dictionaries for carrying out vari- ous operations in language use and language learning. By studying work produced by students at various levels using their own dic- tionaries, we hope to learn something about those students' ability to use effectively the dictionaries available to them. We also hope to find out how dictionaries fail students, and hence how dictionaries may be improved, and to identify areas of linguistic analysis and classification which such improvements require, pin- pointing those where academic research would be most helpful for the lexicographer. Our work will also, we hope, offer guidance to teachers who wish to train students in dictionary use, and may suggest classroom work which can serve this purpose.

For practical reasons, we have restricted the scope of this re- search to the learning of English as a *foreign* language (not English as a Second Language, nor English for Special Purposes), and to

monolingual and bilingual dictionaries of the general language
(not of specialist terminology).   We include in this paper samples
of bilingual tests in French, but our research will cover German
and Spanish as well, and also any other language where a "facili-
tator" is available to translate the questionnaire and to compile
additional tests which will yield compatible results.   We hope to
include students in as many parts of the world as possible, at any
level in any educational institution, as long as they have reached
the stage of using a dictionary in their studies.

We should greatly welcome offers of help from teachers of English
in all types of institution at secondary and tertiary level who are
willing to administer the tests.   Names, addresses and type of
institution should be sent, as soon as possible please, to:

> Ms. Beryl T. Atkins,
> 11 South Street,
> Lewes, Sussex, BN7 2BT,
> England.

We have discussed the computing aspects of the project with
Dr. Ian Sedwell of the Dorset Institute of Higher Education and
he has agreed to join our team.   In consultation with him we have
already made some minor adjustments to the format of the tests in
order to make them compatible with the software chosen to record
and analyse the results.   We have now run most of the pilot tests
and are studying the results of these.   In the light of these
analyses we shall wish to make changes to the form of the Questionnaire, and to modify existing tests and add a number of new ones.
In the meantime we are starting to build our network of teachers
and are pleased to report that considerable interest has already
been expressed in helping us.

This research of course depends on our being able to obtain
funding from some outside source.   We have now been able to cost
the project (printing, mailing, computing, keyboarding, etc.) and
have begun our search for funding.   Later, if funds are forthcoming,
we shall log up the results on the computer (answers will be in
tick-box format for ease of logging up), analyse the patterning of
the results, and report the conclusions that can be drawn.

We are aware that our project simply scratches the surface of
the subject: we hope that this research will be taken up and

developed by others, until a clearer picture emerges of how students use dictionaries, and of what dictionaries students need.

2. User profile questionnaire

The following indicates the contents of the draft questionnaire, which will be presented in the student's own language. The form in which it will be laid out for the student will be quite different from the presentation here.

(1) What country are you normally resident in? What is your first language?

(2) How many years have you been learning English?

(3) [Asks for details of English learning: what types of institution? how many lessons a week? Tick-box answers: primary / junior secondary / junior high / senior high schools / vocational-technical college / university / continuing education]

(4) Why are you learning English? [Tick-box answers: school exam /studying English / studying some subject that requires English / improve job prospects / travel / other]

(5) Are you taught in English? [Tick-box answers: always / usually / sometimes / never]

(6) Do you use a textbook in class? ["Yes" & "No" boxes] If so, please give details. [Title / Author / Publisher]

(7) Have you ever been shown in class how to use a dictionary for your English studies? ["Yes" & "No" boxes] If yes, how many lessons have you had in the past year? [Tick-box answers: 0, 1, 5, more than 5]

(8) Are you studying English because it will help you in studying one or more of these subjects? ["Yes" & "No" boxes against each of: English Language / English or American literature / other languages / law / politics / engineering / medicine / science / business studies / teacher training / other]

(9) If you have any dictionaries of your own which you use for your English studies, say here which ones they are. [Space for Publisher / Title / Editor / Date of publication]

(10) How long ago did you get it or them?

(11) Why did you get it or them?   [Tick-box answers: teacher recommended it / bookseller recommended it / parents recommended it / it was good value for money / it looked clear / it had good illustrations / you liked the look of the dictionary / it was given to you / you needed a different dictionary / other reason / (tick more than one if wished)]

(12) Do you use a dictionary or dictionaries that you don't own yourself?   If so, where?   [Tick-box answers: "sometimes", "often", "rarely".   Boxes against each of the following: in the school or university library / in a class set supplied by the school, etc. / at home / somewhere else]

(13) What dictionaries are they?   [Space for Publisher / Title / Editor / Date of publication]

(14) How often do you use a monolingual English dictionary?   [Tick-box answers: one or more a week / once or more a day / less than once a week / never]

(15) How often do you use a bilingual English dictionary?   [Tick-box answers: once or more a week / once or more a day / less than once a week / never]

(16) Which type of dictionary would you normally use for the following operations?   [Tick-box answers: "Bilingual" and "Monolingual" boxes set against the following operations: to find out the meaning of an English word / to find the English word for a word in your own language / to check how to use an English word that you know already / to help you write a letter or an essay in English / something else]

(17) Which of all the dictionaries you use do you find most helpful in your English studies?

3. Rationale behind the sample tests

   We began with the following premises:

(A) tests should be multiple-choice for ease of logging up the results;

(B) every student must complete the User Profile Form and the classification (language skills) tests, but need not complete all the other tests (dictionary skills and dictionary contents), as the value of the individual tests does not depend on a full set having been performed by any one student;

(C) in any specific test, of the principal factors inherent in testing the use of dictionaries (see below) only the factor being tested may be a variable; all the others must be constants.

It is of course impossible to isolate all the factors inherent in such a complex and unstructured operation as the use of a dictionary. We suggest however that the following represent the principal factors involved:

(1) * DICTIONARY TYPE: whether it is monolingual or bilingual.

(2) ACTUAL DICTIONARY USED: the specific dictionary being used and hence the actual content and organization of the entry that the student is consulting.

(3) OPERATOR (A): first factor relating to the user, viz. his/ her intelligence, linguistic ability and knowledge of English.

(4) * OPERATOR (B): second factor, viz. the user's general dictionary-using skills.

(5) OPERATOR (C): third factor, viz. the user's familiarity with the particular dictionary being used.

(6) * OPERATION: the actual operation that the dictionary is being used for, viz. decoding and encoding tasks of various types (comprehension of L2 texts, translation from and into the L2) and language learning activities (work with synonyms, grammatical categories, etc.).

(7) * PRESENTATION: the way in which each dictionary variously presents the information (its classification, layout, metalanguage, etc.).

(8) MATERIAL: the actual type of language material required for the task in hand (vocabulary, grammar, register, etc., information).

(9) TEST: the format and type of the specific test being used.

Items 1, 4, 6 and 7 (marked * in the foregoing list) are those which the sample exercises are designed to test. Of the other items, nos. 2 and 5 are accounted for by the fact that students will be asked to use their accustomed dictionary and to name it; item no. 3 will be covered by the classification tests (not exemplified in this paper); item no. 8 will be controlled by the actual test being undertaken.

To compare monolingual and bilingual dictionaries (no. 1 above) for example, all the other items must be as nearly as possible the same for both the monolingual and bilingual tests. Or again, to assess the individual student's ability to use the dictionary (no. 4 above) all students must do the same tests. Or again, to compare various types of layout (no. 7 above) the type of dictionary, content of entry, type of operation, etc., must be as nearly as possible the same in the various tests.

We can thus identify and control the types of test to be devised (numbers below refer to the foregoing list):

Item to be varied for testing	Factors which must be identical, or as similar as possible
1	2 / 3 / 4 / 5 / 6 / 7 / 8 / 9
4	1 / 2 / 3 / 5 / 6 / 7 / 8 / 9
6	1 / 2 / 3 / 4 / 5 / 7 / 8 / 9
7	1 / 2 / 3 / 4 / 5 / 6 / 8 / 9
8	1 / 2 / 3 / 4 / 5 / 6 / 7 / 9

Fig. 1

The table which appears below (Fig. 2), which is of course incomplete, allows one to pinpoint the items which must remain constant to validate any specific test which might be devised. Such an analysis of variables, when complete, would provide a systematic check-list of the permutations to be tested if one were to attempt to cover every possibility.

The suffixes -A, -B etc. are used to differentiate various sets of the same things or people; thus, assuming several categories of students according to levels of ability in English, STUDENTS-A might be advanced students, STUDENTS-B intermediate, and so on. Or, assuming several possible ways of presenting the same piece of information, LAYOUT-A might be one method, LAYOUT-B another, and

so on.   Again, given the possibility of many different forms of
testing, TEST-A would refer to one particular format of test,
TEST-B another format, TEST-C a third, and so on.

Numbers at the head of the columns relate to the numbered
factors marked with an asterisk in the list given earlier in this
section.   Each number in round brackets down the left side of the
page indicates one single test, with its factors displayed across
the columns.   Thus, conditions for the first test would read:

Monolingual dictionary / 1st group of students/ Writing in L2 /
1st type of presentation / giving vocabulary information / in
1st type of test.

	1 Dict Type	4 Operator	6 Operation	7 Presntatn	8 Materl	9 Test Type
1	MONOLING	STUDENTS-A	WRITING L2	LAYOUT-A	VOCAB	TEST-A
2	BILING	STUDENTS-A	WRITING L2	LAYOUT-A	VOCAB	TEST-A
3	MONOLING	STUDENTS-B	WRITING L2	LAYOUT-A	VOCAB	TEST-A
4	BILING	STUDENTS-B	WRITING L2	LAYOUT-A	VOCAB	TEST-A
5	MONOLING	STUDENTS-A	COMPREHNSN	LAYOUT-A	VOCAB	TEST-A
6	BILING	STUDENTS-A	COMPREHNSN	LAYOUT-A	VOCAB	TEST-A
7	MONOLING	STUDENTS-B	COMPREHNSN	LAYOUT-A	VOCAB	TEST-A
8	BILING	STUDENTS-B	COMPREHNSN	LAYOUT-A	VOCAB	TEST-A
9	MONOLING	STUDENTS-A	TRANSLTN L1	LAYOUT-A	VOCAB	TEST-A
10	BILING	STUDENTS-A	TRANSLTN L1	LAYOUT-A	VOCAB	TEST-A
11	MONOLING	STUDENTS-B	TRANSLTN L1	LAYOUT-A	VOCAB	TEST-A
12	BILING	STUDENTS-B	TRANSLTN L1	LAYOUT-A	VOCAB	TEST-A
13	MONOLING	STUDENTS-A	LANG/LRNING	LAYOUT-A	VOCAB	TEST-A
14	BILING	STUDENTS-A	LANG/LRNING	LAYOUT-A	VOCAB	TEST-A
15	MONOLING	STUDENTS-B	LANG/LRNING	LAYOUT-A	VOCAB	TEST-A
16	BILING	STUDENTS-B	LANG/LRNING	LAYOUT-A	VOCAB	TEST-A
17	MONOLING	STUDENTS-A	COMPREHNSN	LAYOUT-A	VOCAB	TEST-A
18	MONOLING	STUDENTS-A	COMPREHNSN	LAYOUT-B	VOCAB	TEST-A
19	MONOLING	STUDENTS-A	COMPREHNSN	LAYOUT-C	VOCAB	TEST-A
20	MONOLING	STUDENTS-B	COMPREHNSN	LAYOUT-A	VOCAB	TEST-A
21	MONOLING	STUDENTS-B	COMPREHNSN	LAYOUT-B	VOCAB	TEST-A
22	MONOLING	STUDENTS-B	COMPREHNSN	LAYOUT-C	VOCAB	TEST-A

Fig. 2.   Factors to be considered when
          constructing tests of dictionary use.

4. Introduction to the tests

The tests (which all conform to one of the condition patterns in the foregoing table) are designed to allow cross-comparison of results, so that the pairs of tests (1) & (2), (3) & (4), (5) & (6), (7) & (8), and so on, give a comparison of the effectiveness of monolingual and bilingual dictionaries in the same context; tests (1), (5), (9) & (13) when taken together compare the effectiveness of monolingual dictionaries for dealing with different types of operation; tests (17, (18) and (19) taken together will indicate whether one type of presentation is more useful for a particular type of student (say advanced learners); while tests (17) and (20) will show whether a particular presentation is more suited to advanced rather than intermediate learners, and so on.

Not all of the permutations shown as possible in the foregoing table are necessary for our purposes. Some distinctions are superfluous: for instance, that between monolingual and bilingual dictionaries is irrelevant in a test which seeks to elicit where a user would expect to find a compound headword, or similar item. Also, some of the permutations may result in tests which bear no relation to actual language work, for example one which would require the student to translate from L1 to L2 using a monolingual dictionary, without first enabling him or her to find the L2 word in a bilingual dictionary. (To ensure full cooperation from the people administering and those doing the tests, the tests we set must be felt to be realistic, i.e. as close as possible to the way people use dictionaries to work in a foreign language.)

We are asking the student to use the dictionary with which he or she is already familiar. The only alternative to this would seem to be to supply a dictionary entry (or entries) to accompany each test, and this has two disadvantages: (1) some of the students will be familiar with one or more of the dictionaries from which the entries have been taken, but without cumbersome questioning it would be impossible to show which; and (2) this procedure would not reflect normal dictionary use.

We think that it would be valid to include in the tests the following aspects of dictionary use:

(a) points of detail which are the same for both monolingual and bilingual dictionaries, e.g. understanding of grammar and grammar metalanguage; where user expects to find compounds, idiomatic phrases, etc.; morphological variations; subsidiary information about headword, language level, British or American English and so on.

(b) the effectiveness of various methods of presenting information in monolingual dictionaries, for example for decoding (translating from L2 into L1 and comprehension of L2) and encoding (free expression, but not L1-L2 translation without using a bilingual dictionary first).

(c) the effectiveness of various methods of presenting information in bilingual dictionaries, for example for decoding (translating from L2 into L1 and comprehension of L2) and encoding (translating L1-L2, and free expression in L2).

All the instructions in the tests will be in the student's L1. Before starting a batch of exercises, the student will be asked to identify the dictionary he or she is using.

5. Samples of actual tests

SAMPLE A

[Object: to test whether the user can handle polysemy. This test may be done with either monolingual or bilingual dictionaries, but only monolinguals are mentioned in the following sample.]

When you are looking up a word, can you find the *exact meaning* that you need?

Example:

There's a key to the exercises in the back of the grammar book. | KEY |

In this sentence *key* means "an explanation, or set of answers"; but *key* has several other meanings too. In the *Oxford Advanced Learner's Dictionary*, this meaning of *key* is shown under *key* 1 (= the noun; *key* 2 is the verb) and it is sense number 4. In the *Longman Dictionary of Contemporary English* it is *key* 1, sense 3. In the *Chambers Universal Learners' Dictionary* it is *key* sense 6 (because this dictionary does not separate the noun from the verb).

So: if you are using *OALDCE*, you would write   KEY[1] 4

if you are using *LDOCE*, you would write   KEY[1] 3

if you are using *CULD*, you would write   KEY 6

Now, in the same way, using your own dictionary, write in Box 1 (the one that already contains the word itself) the number of the section in which each of these words is explained in your dictionary.   Ignore Boxes 2 and 3 for the moment.

	Box 1	Box 2	Box 3
(1) *The game ended in a draw.*	DRAW		

[... and other similar exercises]

- Did you understand the sentence before you looked in the dictionary?   If you did, then put a cross (X) in Box 2.   Do the same for each sentence.

- Do you understand the sentence now?   If so, then put a cross in Box 3.   Do the same for each sentence.

SAMPLE B

[Object: to test comprehension of parts of speech; to be done without a dictionary.]

Do you know the *part of speech* of the word you want to look up?

Example:

In *I'm going to address the letters*   *address* is a verb.
In *What's her address?*   *address* is a noun.
So in this case you would put a cross in the right box, thus:-

	noun	adjective	verb	preposition
I'm going to address the letters			X	
What's her address?	X			

Now do these questions:

(1) What is the part of speech of *past* in these two sentences?
Put a mark X in the right box:-

	noun	adjective	adverb	preposition
His ancestors lived here in the past.				
We've been here for the past week.				

[... and other similar exercises]

SAMPLE C

[Object: to test comprehension of dictionary conventions and grammatical terms; to be done without a dictionary.]

Example:

You often see in a dictionary something like

> *best   adj superl* of GOOD

Here *superl* is short for "superlative". So *best* means "most good".
(We say *good, better, best*).

So, your answer to this question would be given like this:

best means:

most good	X
least good	
good in a particular way	
rather good	

Now do these questions:

(1) *mice   pl of* MOUSE - *mice* means:

of a mouse	
more than one mouse	
another word for *mouse*	

SAMPLE D

[Object: to compare the effectiveness of various ways of giving the same information. A set of translation exercises will be based on one Ll passage (Passage A below). Exercises of this type make use of bilingual dictionaries only.]

Passage A: Un train rapide reliant Miami à New York a joué de malchance, tant à l'aller qu'au retour, accumulant accidents et retards. Le Silver Meteor a d'abord accroché et tué une grand-mère qui pêchait sur un pont du chemin de fer en Géorgie ...

Passage B [translation of Passage A: basis of exercises] An express train (1) (reliant Miami à New York) was dogged by ill fortune both on the outward journey and the (2) (retour), as accidents and delays followed one upon another. (3) (d'abord), the Silver Meteor (4) (accrocha) and killed a grandmother who was fishing ...

Read Passage A and Passage B. With the help of your dictionary, choose the best English word or phrase to fill each empty space in Passage B. Put a mark X in the box beside the item you choose.

Example: For space (1)   joining Miami to New York   [   ]

                          linking Miami and New York   [X]

                          binding Miami to New York   [   ]

                          hooping Miami to New York   [   ]

(If you think that *linking Miami and New York* is the best translation, you would mark the box like this.)

Now answer the following questions:

(1) For space (2)   both on the way there and the return   [   ]

                     both on the going and the return   [   ]

                     both on the outward journey and the
                                               return   [   ]

                     both on the voyage out and the return   [   ]

[... and other similar exercises]

SAMPLE E

[Object: again, to compare the effectiveness of various ways of giving the same information.   A set of comprehension exercises will be based on one L2 passage (Passage C, below).   Exercises of this type draw upon both monolingual and bilingual dictionaries.]

Passage C: There are hundreds of houses bordering on the suburban stockbroker belt of Edinburgh which have spectacular views over the Forth Estuary, but no one wants to live in them ... At twelve noon, the sound from a stereo system in one flat is deafening.   An hour later it's still blaring away ...

Read Passage C, and with the help of your dictionary answer the following questions by putting a mark X in the "Yes" box or the "No" box:-

Example: Are the houses near
           the stockbroker belt?

| Yes | X |

| No | |

(If you think the answer should be *yes*, put the cross in this box.)

Now answer these questions:

(1) Can you see the Forth Estuary
    from these houses?

| Yes | |

| No | |

SAMPLE F

[Object: to test the effectiveness of various types of dictionaries and ways of presenting information for purposes of vocabulary selection.]

Use your dictionary to mark the right word to fill the space in the following sentences:

Example   *she .... her hair.*

swept	
brushed	X
dusted	
scrubbed	

(If you think *brushed* is the right word, put a mark in this box.)

Now do the following questions:

(1) *It's a bad ...... to bite your nails.*

behaviour	
practice	
custom	
habit	

SAMPLE G

[Object: to discover where the user expects to find such things as compound nouns, nominal and verbal idioms, prepositional and phrasal verbs, plural senses of words, etc. This test is to be done without a dictionary.]

(1) An *electric light bulb* is the part of an electric lamp that gives out light. Where would you expect to find this expression explained in your dictionary? Mark a cross in the appropriate box:

as one sense of *electric* ☐

as one sense of *light* ☐

as one sense of *bulb* ☐

separately, after
electricity and before ☐
electric needle

(2) A *lame duck* means a helpless or injured person, or a business which is in difficulties, not a wounded bird. Where would you expect to find this expression explained? Put a cross in the box:-

as one sense of *lame* ☐

as one sense of *duck* ☐

separately, after *lame*
and before *lamely* ☐

somewhere else ☐

[... and similar exercises on, for example, *to split hairs, to do without, greens* (= "vegetables"), etc.]

6. Conclusion

While the results of the pilot tests are encouraging, we are aware that this is an ambitious project which calls for wide-ranging support from teachers and students and an appropriate level of funding.   We intend to make a further interim report at the EURALEX Congress in September 1986.

Barbara Ann Kipfer

DICTIONARIES AND THE INTERMEDIATE STUDENT:
COMMUNICATIVE NEEDS AND THE DEVELOPMENT
OF USER REFERENCE SKILLS

1. Introduction

I recently conducted an investigation into the acquisition of
dictionary skills and their influence on the language needs and
abilities of intermediate-level students, in particular tenth-,
eleventh-, and twelfth-grade American high-school pupils (Kipfer
1985). The group was chosen for several reasons: first, the students were preparing for college and university studies and/or for
working in the adult world and were presumably more serious-minded
than lower-level students; second, the students had received at
least ten years of language instruction which should have included
help in developing efficient reference skills; third, the students probably had a variety of communicative needs which would tend
to become more specialized later, depending on the direction of
their college study or work activity.

I researched four areas in particular:

(1) the relationship between language needs and dictionary skills
for intermediate students;

(2) the acquisition of dictionary skills and its relationship to
needs and attitudes;

(3) the influence of dictionary skills on reading and writing ability at this level; and

(4) the utilization of three tools for the improvement of reference
skills and communication: more intensive instruction in using
dictionaries, the introduction of learners' dictionaries to native
speakers, and the automated dictionary.

2. Relations between language needs and reference skills

292 students answered a preliminary questionnaire which was intended to reveal the chief uses of dictionaries and student attitudes

to dictionary use. Dictionaries were shown to be used chiefly as a guide to meaning and spelling, and occasionally pronunciation. My assumption that dictionaries are used more for writing than reading (cf. Béjoint 1981, Tomaszczyk 1979) was borne out.

The students answering my questionnaire did not indicate that they had much difficulty in finding the information they needed from dictionaries. Seventy-two per cent of the students (Q.19) agreed that people are lazy about looking information up and, sadly, many of those respondents called dictionaries "boring" (Q.15) and claimed to use them only when absolutely necessary.[1] The answers to two questions were contradictory: many said they actually "read" reference books and yet when asked specifically which and how often, responded that encyclopedias were used "once or twice a year" (the answer from more than half - see Q.12) and that dictionary use takes more time than they are willing to give.

The respondents understood the need to spell words correctly and claimed this to be the main reason for dictionary use when writing, though seventy-three per cent also said they used dictionaries to check meanings while writing (Q.6). A large group ticked thesauruses as their main reference source. Many, when asked which dictionaries they owned, listed titles of thesauruses, which suggested that some students may not even know the difference between major types of reference work.

3. Acquisition of reference skills: the influence of attitudes and needs

If students have difficulty in understanding the metalanguage in which definitions are expressed, it could be caused by the unfamiliarity that results from infrequent dictionary use. Fifty-two per cent of those answering my questionnaire admitted they did not know their dictionary well. The only explanatory matter students felt a need to refer to was the pronunciation key (Q.9). Not one student had read about lexicography or been taught about dictionary-making in school and none said they had been given information about

---

1 Q.1, Q.2, etc., refer to numbered blocks of questions appearing in the Appendix - ed.

differences between the available commercial dictionaries. Many
dictionary users continue blindly to accept whatever titles are
available, assuming that they are of equal quality, that any will
meet their needs, and that the structure of each is the same (cf.
Herbst and Stein, this volume). Only thirty per cent of those
answering the questionnaire even knew the title of the dictionary
they used, and, of those, more than half said simply that it was
"Webster's".

Few of the students covered by the survey could explain differences between the major types of dictionaries (Q.14). The descriptions given of learners' dictionaries were usually "beginners'", and
"children's". Definitions offered of college/desk editions were
dictionaries of "everyday words" and dictionaries "for students going
to college." Historical dictionaries were mainly thought to describe
"old words" or the "facts of history." Unabridged works could "contain full meanings," "list every word that exists," or "contain every
word." Pocket dictionaries, obviously the most familiar to those
questioned, were said to "contain the most-used words," "common
expressions," or, simply, "shortened meanings."

The section of the questionnaire relating to attitude (Q.15) did
not always receive very serious answers, but I can report that students most often marked "easy to use", "worthwhile", "requires
little effort", and "informative" as indications of how they regard
dictionaries. A few students said that using the dictionary was
"not worth the trouble" or "not fulfilling needs." "I'd rather
figure out a meaning by how it is used," one respondent answered.
"It is much easier to use a thesaurus," a few others said, and
several commented, "It is easier to ask someone else what a definition is." When students do consult dictionaries, they seem to
do so without question or comparison with other sources of information. So, there may be two problems: those who do not use dictionaries may be lazy, which is difficult to determine and may be
even more difficult to treat; and those who do use dictionaries
may regard them as unquestionable authorities which do not require
checking or further corroboration (cf. Tomaszczyk, this volume).

4. Skills instruction and the use of learners' dictionaries

I was able to interest a group of 30 students in working with learners' dictionaries. I prepared them by setting two tests on dictionaries and their features (one for which students could use a dictionary and one for which they could not), teaching two classes and providing an introduction to learners' dictionaries. Students were then given a third test. This was a set of exercises taken from the *Longman Dictionary of Contemporary English (LDOCE)* companion workbook, *Learning with LDOCE* (1979). Rather than write new questions, I decided that using exercises from the workbook would give the best indication of what the students had learned from working with it and with *LDOCE*. The point was to find out what effects direct instruction in the use of learners' dictionaries would have. The *Learning with LDOCE* questions were altered and shortened somewhat; I substituted American English for some British English expressions and selected those exercises I thought would be most interesting for my group.

The group had difficulties with only four of 20 questions and agreed afterwards that looking up so many details in the time allowed was tiresome. However, they did not have any difficulty in finding answers. There was also much praise for *LDOCE* itself (for typography, illustrations, and clarity of explanations).

5. The automated dictionary and students' communicative needs

Computerized "dictionaries" already exist in the form of spelling "checkers" for word processing systems, but they do not provide definitions. These dictionaries simply give information on spelling but they may be accompanied by hyphenation programs and synonym lists which are offered as automatic hyphenators and thesauri respectively. However, many complete dictionaries are available in machine-readable form and publishers could develop automated versions of printed products. The automated dictionary is a tool which might not only be amusing for intermediate users but might also be used to teach the advantages of effective reference skills and improve language proficiency. The automated version will not necessarily replace the printed dictionary; it may in fact have the effect of increasing demand for the conventional product (Fox, Bebel and Parker 1980).

Certain attributes of the computer may affect the ways students benefit from the automated dictionary. Some processes may be

grasped more fully by a learner because of the speed of operation
of the computer; the learner may fully grasp the implications of
an extended process in less time than that taken by a manual operation.   Most learning mechanisms are geared to the average student, but the automated dictionary, through its adaptable software
and variety of possible access points, might be adjusted to meet
individual learner needs.   A key attribute is the computer's ease
of use: for example, the task of searching through an alphabetical
listing is one that machines can perform much faster than humans.
One reason students do not use hand-held dictionaries as often as
they might is because referring to them interrupts study activity.
The student has to find the dictionary, and within it locate the
entry word and the desired information.   Few students can continually sustain an attention span to bridge such interruptions in
reading and writing.   Ease and speed of use are features which
render the automated dictionary of great benefit to students.

In addition, an automated dictionary keyed to particular textbooks and editable by teachers is possible, as well as its modifi-
cation to suit various levels of attainment.   It might be desirable to modify the automated dictionary for a certain group by.
simplifying definitions, giving more examples, or deleting etymologies.

In its basic form, the automated dictionary contains an alphabetized word list and a data-base.   The user asks for a word and
receives a definition.   This would be a relatively simple task on
a large or networked machine, and various other language aids might
then be available: a spelling checker, an electronic thesaurus, a
grammar correction device, or word games.   These functions would
enhance the dictionary's value as an educational tool while sus-
taining the curiosity of most of its users.   Menu systems are
probably the simplest and clearest means of access to all these
functions.

Several alternatives for structure and access are available.
An automated dictionary which has access to larger dictionary databases could be constructed.   By plugging into (or dialling) a network, one could have the dictionary's memory act as storage, re-
trieving entries by demand only.   On the other hand, stand-alone

devices are capable of supporting useful dictionaries today.
Personal computers are becoming less expensive while their power
and memory capacities are increasing; the 10- to 30-megabyte hard
disk is an example of larger storage which is quickly coming within
the reach of more users. The word processor/dictionary set-up is
one which could utilize such a machine to help such groups as intermediate-level students.

6. Utilization of tools: findings and suggestions

I suggest that the three tools discussed above should be developed for intermediate-level students and offered together with a
solid background in lexicography. In particular, students should
be taught what information may be collected for dictionaries and in
what different forms it may be represented. The tools have their
various advantages, but the student also needs a background understanding of the different dictionary types available and of their
respective advantages.

The results of the tests supported my initial hypothesis that
direct teaching of dictionary reference skills can be an effective
means of improving language understanding. But it can also open
up the range of information to which students gain access. Students who earlier had not grasped much beyond the fact that meanings, spellings, and pronunciations were available, were able after
instruction to answer rather advanced questions about dictionary
organization and perform exercises requiring difficult look-up procedures.

The learner's dictionary differs from general dictionaries both
in its range of grammatical information and in the number of examples of usage, making it a good learning tool for native-language
intermediate-level users. In addition to help with meaning, pronunciation, and spelling, students are offered grammatical and
usage information not available in many college/desk dictionaries.
"Coding" is the device enabling the lexicographer to give students
access to special features while using a minimal amount of space.
At the same time, the learner's dictionary should be regarded as a
supplement to the standard native-speaker's for this group; because
of its special orientation, the EFL dictionary may lack the cover-

age of specialist vocabulary needed to meet the native English speaker's vocabulary needs (Cowie 1983).

The automated dictionary is extremely attractive as a tool for the intermediate-level student, though it is essential that the technology of the automated dictionary be matched to the learning processes of its users. Among the processes the automated dictionary could support are:

(a) the acquisition of reference skills and procedures (e.g. the ability to recognize lexicographical conventions used to represent meaning, pronunciation, grammar, etc.);

(b) the acquisition of established word-senses e.g. through a repetitive visual display of dictionary metalanguage used in the description of senses, often by genus and differentiae);

(c) the embedding of facts (through feedback-oriented exercises and word games) and skills; and

(d) the integration of facts (the student attacks a problem in his own way, makes choices, and manipulates the way the dictionary structure is presented to him).

7. Conclusion

Neither a poor understanding of compilers' intentions and methods nor the text structure of most dictionaries seems to inhibit the students' acquisition of reference skills. Problems that exist probably stem from a lack of dictionary instruction in schools and homes and a low level of enthusiasm for dictionary use. Lexicographers are partly to blame for not promoting materials to improve reference skills - though an exception has been noted in Whitcut's guide (1979). However, lexicographers can take comfort in the fact that they produce learning-aids whose usefulness is recognized by most ordinary language users. Intermediate-level students are not having problems for which the dictionaries can be held responsible: they are simply not using them efficiently or fully.

Pupils are taught a little in their early school years about dictionaries and are expected to maintain that knowledge on their own. It is rarely reinforced at the intermediate level (cf. Herbst and Stein, this volume). The results of the tests I administered to students, after minimal reinforcement through my introduction, make clear the benefits of teaching dictionary reference skills later in a student's educational career. We should not expect limited early teaching to make students self-sufficient in dictionary skills. Since their information needs change, their reference skills require adjustment also.

I have suggested that a diversity of pedagogic devices are necessary for accomplishing our goals. The diversity of the three tools - intensive teaching of reference skills, the promotion of learners' dictionaries, and the introduction of the automated dictionary - can take on aspects of a portfolio, a collection of techniques gathered together for a purpose. At the moment we have only an imperfect idea of how to put such a portfolio together and implement its use on a large scale. Further testing of the three techniques is the only reasonable way to find out which means or combination of means best serve the needs of intermediate students. An eventual training programme will only be as effective as they are shown to be.

8. Appendix: questionnaire responses

(1) Dictionaries at home .. .. YES 277 NO 13
    Owner   .. .. SHARE 162 OWN 119
    Know title (and date)   .. .. YES 89 NO 204
    Answered "Webster(s)"   52

(2) Carry dictionary .. .. YES 3 NO 280
    Keep dictionary at school   .. .. YES 21 NO 255

(3) Dictionaries in classrooms   .. .. YES 249 NO 22

(4) Purposes:
    Spelling 190
    Hyphenation 16
    Definition/meaning   264
    Word history 32

    Uses:
    Reading   .. .. YES 44 NO 110

Writing .. ..   YES 230   NO 31

(5) Kinds of reading:
Non-fiction   150
Fiction   161
Reference (entry rdg, referrals)   209
Magazines   90
Newspapers   89
None   31

(6) Kinds of writing:
Short answers   157
Short essays   254
Papers/reports   202
Stories   172
Poems   53
Research   5
Homework (i.e. only use)   22

Use of dictionary for writing:
Spelling   267
Pronunciation   14
Definition   213
Part of speech   3
Synonyms   11
No use   40

(7) Find what you need? .. ..   YES 252   NO 21
                        .. ..   Most of time   16 Don't look   3

(8) Some formal instruction .. ..   YES 71   NO 102
    Self-taught .. ..   YES 86   NO 44

(9) Have read:
Preface/introduction .. ..   YES 15   NO 67
Explanatory notes .. ..   YES 18   NO 66
Abbreviation table .. ..   YES 48   NO 80
Pronunciation key .. ..   YES 103   NO 28

(10) Read: encyclopedic and back matter .. .. YES 26 NO 59

(11) Dictionary: main reference source .. .. YES 17 NO 56

(12) Frequency reference book use (most frequent answers):

Specialized dictionaries (very often) ..   77

Encyclopedias (once or twice a year) ..   142

Thesauri (often/fairly often)   170

Word books (never)   41

Bad spellers' dictionaries (never)   110

Almanacs (fairly often/sometimes   61

(13) Familiarity with dictionary .. ..   GOOD 160

.. .. NOT GOOD 152

.. .. .. FAIRLY WELL/OK 101

(14) Knowledge of dictionary

Has anyone told you differences between available
dictionaries? .. .. YES O NO 207

Correct or close answers to "What is a ...":
Learners' dictionary   3
College/desk dictionary   71
Historical dictionary   1
Unabridged   7
Pocket   52

Have read about dictionaries .. .. .. YES O NO 84

(15) Attitude (ticked by respondents):
Easy   97
Exciting/fun   17
Requiring little effort   50
Worthwhile   47
Informative   125
Difficult   10
Tedious   22
Time-consuming   3
Not worth the trouble   28
Cumbersome; not fulfilling needs   24

54

(16) Friends' attitudes:
    Worthwhile   10
    Don't know   71

(17) Family's attitudes:
    Favorable comment   29

(18) Like books in general .. .. YES 52 NO 117

(19) People lazy in look-ups .. .. YES 212 NO 24
    Unpopular to use reference books .. .. YES 18 NO 47

Nicoletta Calzolari, Eugenio Picchi and Antonio Zampolli

THE USE OF COMPUTERS IN LEXICOGRAPHY AND LEXICOLOGY

A commonly accepted classification of the uses of computers in lexicology and lexicography does not yet exist. For practical reasons, we shall divide these uses into two main groups:

(A) The use of computers in dictionary making.

(B) Lexicographical data bases.

A. Dictionary making

The uses of computers as an aid in dictionary making are usually subdivided into three main groups, which correspond to three operational stages:

(1) data collection;
(2) lexical entry preparation;
(3) editing and printing.

A.1. Data Collection

Two main types of data are collected as documentary sources:

A.1.1. Pre-existing dictionaries

Some lexicographical enterprises have decided to convert into machine-readable form appropriately chosen printed lexicographical resources (general or technical dictionaries, lexicons, etc.), as an aid for the creation of new dictionaries. Once in machine-readable form (MRF) these resources, as well as dictionaries already independently available in MRF, may be consulted and exploited, during the editing of a new dictionary, by using multiple-access techniques, as described later in section B.

A.1.2. Citations excerpted from a corpus

Traditionally, human excerptors were set to read through various texts, selecting what they noted as unusual or particularly informative examples and copying each textual citation onto a paper citation slip.

As far as historical dictionaries are concerned, the "excerption density" was usually very low (1%). Only a small fraction of the corpus, which is often called the "basic archive", "could be read at a much higher excerption density, say 25 or 30%, so as to take in not only the more unusual and special - if you like, lexico-graphically interesting - examples, but also a large representation of the more common-place uses of common words" (Aitken 1983:34).

Even so, those collections may contain several hundred thousands of quotation-slips (for example, the OED in its present form con-tains about 1,820,000 quotations, selected from nearly six million quotation slips).

The use of computers to produce different kinds of indexes, con-cordances and quotation-slips from a text or a corpus is today a routine task, at least in those cases in which the researcher has access to already available software. Relevant software packages at present exist both for mainframes and for personal computers. Although different, the various procedures prepared by academic or commercial specialized centres follow a common logical scheme, which consists of three main steps:

- acquisition of texts in machine-readable form;
- lemmatization;
- production of textual documentation.

A.1.2.1. Acquisition of texts in machine-readable form

There are several alternatives when converting textual material into MRF: key-punch; key to paper tape; on-line typewriter; key to disk; selectric typewriter; keyboarding on visual display terminals; etc. All these require that someone types the text on a keyboard, and until recently this manual operation was a major obstacle, owing to its cost.

Nowadays, the need to type a text manually is obviated by the existence of four major sources of texts in MRF:

omni-font scanners: devices able to recognize graphic characters and to record them on magnetic support;

textual archives: in many countries specialized centres are collect-ing texts in MRF, and copies are often distributed on request, under particular conditions;

photocomposition: many texts (books, newspapers, etc.) are now re-corded for photocomposition by publishing-houses in MRF, as input for photocomposition;

word-processing: "the airwaves and cables of the information society are already filled with electronic digital texts" (Amsler 1983), and in the office automation framework the majority of texts are electronically digited for word processing purposes.

If these sources are to be utilized, a number of problems must be solved:

organizational: how to arrange the exchange of information and data between different textual archives;

legal: how to deal with the copyright of the different "owners": authors, publishing houses, those responsible for textual archives, etc.;

scientific: some minimal norms are needed, the adoption of which will guarantee that the representation of a text in MRF contains all the minimal information requested by linguistic, lexicographical or philological processing.

The availability of corpora in MRF varies with different languages. Some academic/historical dictionary projects are collecting and processing large textual corpora. Well-known examples are the "Trésor de la langue française" (Nancy), "Tesoro italiano delle origini" (Firenze, Pisa), "The Dictionary of Hebrew" (Jerusalem), "Old Spanish" (Madison, Illinois), "Old English" (Toronto), etc.

Corpora collected to provide statistical information for "frequency dictionaries" may also be considered. However, they are usually rather small and sometimes selected according to sampling criteria rather unsuitable for lexicographical use.[1]

It seems worthwhile to consider the feasibility of promoting action, at a national[2] or international level, for the creation for each language of corpora in MRF, which may serve as a reference

---

1 See for example the Brown Corpus, the LIF Corpus, etc.
2 The Swedish Språkdata may be cited as a model (Allen 1983).

corpus for a variety of research tasks, including lexicographical
projects.   Two major problems are obviously to be taken into account:

- responsibility for the maintenance and updating of a corpus, once
  it has been created;

- the copyright problem for different uses, at an academic and commercial level.

A.1.2.2.   Lemmatization

After a text has been converted into MRF, it is possible to ask
the computer to produce immediately the documentation (concordances,
frequencies, citation slips, etc.) regarding graphic forms, which
are the only linguistic units explicitly represented in the printed
text.   If this documentation is instead to take account of other
linguistic units (lemmas, collocations, syntagms, etc.), it is
necessary to introduce the explicit representation of these units
in the text, before the production of concordances, indices, etc.,
can begin.

The dilemma "to lemmatize or not to lemmatize" the concordances
and indexes dates back to the very beginnings of the use of computers in linguistic and philological text-processing.

The answer depends on various factors.   The decision to lemmatize is usually taken for highly inflected languages, and for linguistic or lexicographic analysis rather than for philological or
literary applications.   Two of the main obstacles to lemmatization
are:

- the lack of precise, widely accepted, linguistic norms, ensuring
  comparability and reutilization of lemmatizations performed by
  different researchers (Tombeur 1983);

- the high cost of lemmatization, especially if performed entirely
  manually.

Although lemmatization is in most cases still completely manual,
various semi-automatic systems have been experimented with.   They
are usually based on the distinction between word-forms which are
considered univocal (i.e. pertaining to only one lemma) in a given
lexical system, and forms which are considered homographic.   The

former are directly lemmatized by the program. The latter are submitted to the analysis of the lemmatizer. (For a description, see Zampolli 1983).

Disambiguation of homographs is a very time-consuming task. However, so far only few attempts have been made with regard to (semi-)automatic disambiguation. These can be subdivided into two basic approaches:

(1) Local disambiguation

Algorithms usually try to solve homography between forms belonging to different parts of speech. For each possible pair of parts of speech, rules are formulated which examine the context immediately surrounding the homograph, up to a certain number of contiguous words. Specific elements (words or grammatical categories) or sequences of elements are searched for. The formulation of these rules is essentially based on the concept of "impossibility" or "possibility" of co-occurrence of a pair of given words and/or word-classes in a specified "span" of context. These rules are often aided by statistical algorithms which use quantitative information, obtained by examining previously lemmatized texts, on the frequency distribution of words and grammatical categories in the immediate context of the homographs in a sample corpus. At present, an estimated 80-90% of words in a text can be successfully analyzed in certain systems (Ratti 1982). The remaining 10-20% are submitted to an interactive manual disambiguation process.

(2) Disambiguation via syntactic-semantic parsers

Automatic parsing of natural language texts has always been the main interest of computational linguists. By contrast, until now lexicographers have never shown any particular interest in parsing systems. In computational lexicology and lexicography, parsers could be used for different purposes: e.g. to study collocations, to identify particular syntactic-semantic patterns for the choice of "lexicographically interesting" quotations, to analyze the definitions given in a dictionary, etc. Here we shall focus on the possible use of a parser as a homograph disambiguator. If the sentence is not in itself ambiguous and its overall syntactic structure is recognized, the parser will obviously accept only one of the possible grammatical "analyses" of a homographic form.

The problem is that the presently existing parsers are unable - to our knowledge - to treat exhaustively the large variety and quantity of phenomena present in the types of corpora which usually constitute the basic documentation of the lexicographer. It would be interesting to explore the feasibility of creating less ambitious parsers able only to identify surface constituents, and to quantatively evaluate their efficiency for the disambiguation of homographs in the process of lemmatization.

A.1.2.3. Production of textual documentation

Each specialized Centre has its own procedures to produce the results usually requested:[3]   direct and reverse indexes, various types of frequency distribution, rhyme-indexes, index locorum, concordances, quotation slips, etc. Some software packages are parametrized, i.e. they enable their users to specify a number of "processing options", which may look at the nature and ordering of the entries, selectivity versus completeness, different contextualization criteria, etc.

With regard to data collection for dictionary making, it is not yet clear which type of documentation is more convenient. Some are of the opinion that the best solution is to continue to produce contexts printed separately onto citation-slips, or in the form of concordances. Others prefer the possibility of displaying selected contexts on the screen on request.

Some academic projects, which accurately lemmatize the texts during the data collection phase, pre-select particularly significant examples, so that the editor, when compiling a lexical entry, works on contexts which have already been strongly reduced in number, and are grouped under their own lemma. In other projects, the editor is presented with all the contexts of the corpus. He has to accomplish at the same time both the task of selecting the examples and of grouping together the different graphic forms, separating the

---

3 Very well known are for example COCOA of the Oxford Computing Centre. In Italy, almost all ongoing projects use the "procedure di spoglio" of the Institute for Computational Linguistics of CNR (National Research Council).

homographs, etc.[4] The experimental data presently available still seem to be insufficient as a basis for a final choice between the two alternatives.

A.2. Preparation of Dictionary Entries

It is useful, in our opinion, to distinguish between two different frameworks:

A.2.1. First framework

The dictionary is centred around the descriptive content: definitions, syntactic information, etc. Some methodology and software tools are already being used, mainly in a commercial context.

In particular, they assist the lexicographer by:

- reducing the work connected with the handling of the graphic conventions, usually so bulky in dictionaries;

- making it easier to retrieve previously stored information;

- ensuring automatically the formal coherence of the information.

As a typical example we may quote the *Compulexis* dictionary system.[5]

A common interesting feature consists in allowing the data to be entered in typographically neutral form. A system of tags is used to store the data-type of each lexicographical entity of the dictionary: examples, idioms, translations, parts of speech, syntactic information, etc. Those systems automatically assign a specific typographical representation to each data-type, generate separators (commas, semicolons, etc.) between the various elements, and generate fixed repetitive text elements.

---

4 The arguments involved are both economic (time and cost: does the time gained by the editor compensate for the lemmatization pre-editing work?) and scientific (is it possible for the "lemmatizing" researcher, often performing text-by-text work, to select the quotations to be retained compatibly with the interests of the editor when writing the lexical entry?)

5 "The system is designed as a complete set of tools for the development and handling of monolingual as well as bilingual dictionaries. It serves three different but related purposes, namely:
   - Editorial tools for the compiler/editor
   - Data bases for further lexicographical development
   - Type-setting tools
   (...) The principle of the system is to allow the user to input, output and retrieve the exact data in the dictionary."

Furthermore, the tags may direct the system to form a data base from which other products may be retrieved, either as complete products or as the basis for further (strongly reduced) editing. A system of this type requires the development of a fairly generalized taxonomy of the type of information that can appear in dictionaries. Within this framework, however, the computer assists the compiler only in the formal part of his work.

A.2.2. Second framework

The second framework concerns dictionaries strongly based on the classification and ordering of a very large number of quotations from a corpus, as for example large historical academic dictionaries.

The editorial analysis consists of a "rapid shuffling and re-shuffling of examples" (Aitken 1983:41), in an iterative process in which the editor selects from the archive "significant" quotations and tentatively arranges them into senses with provisional definitions, thus progressively constructing the microstructure of the entry. Furthermore, he may wish to consult different types of complementary sources of information, ranging from bibliographic references to relevant entries of pre-existing dictionaries.

Computing facilities are not yet widely used in this editing stage, and much work is still necessary to take full advantage of the potential benefits offered by computational linguistic know-how and methodology.

A.2.2.1. Selection of quotations

Given the quantity of contexts produced by computational text processing, the problem of reducing the number of quotations to be treated editorially, by a process of representative selection, appears in certain cases to be very urgent. In other words, there are often far too many computer-produced quotations for the lexicographer to go through manually, and strategies are needed to (semi-)automatically screen the material.

Among the solutions suggested for words of high frequency, the simplest is to instruct the computer to select only one context in every n (where n grows progressively (10, 20 ... 100) with the frequency of the word).

A more refined system consists in making the computer select significant collocations.

There are several possible statistical aids.   One of these is
to "start from the observed frequency between node and collocate,
compare it to an expected one (based on the frequency of both elements in the corpus) and .then to evaluate the possible difference
between observed and expected values by means of a standard deviation" (Martin et al 1983:85).

Another possibility is to search systematically in the archive
for a predetermined construction for a given word.

> "Par exemple, pour la rédaction de *debout* disposer des exemples de *debout* en
> emploi interjectif *debout!*;   pour la rédaction d'*homme* explorer les con-
> structions du type *homme à* + infinitif" (Gorcy 1983:122).

This type of interactive question-answering obviously requires a
well constructed interrogation language, operating both on word
forms and on grammatical taggings.   The ultimate goal would obviously
be to have at one's disposal a parser capable of producing automatically a description of the syntactic-semantic structure of the text.
In this case it would be possible to identify quotations which exemplify in the corpus occurrences of particular syntactic and semantic
patterns.   Unfortunately, as already noted above, the existing
parsers are not yet capable of exhaustively treating the variety and
quantity of phenomena present in a corpus.   However something new
is now moving in this sector.   Examples are the DEREDEC system
(Montréal) (Plante 1983) and research at the Institute for Computational Linguistics in Pisa.

A.2.2.2.   Towards a lexicographical workstation

A major challenge is to develop a "lexicographic workstation",
by which the lexicographer "preparing" the description of dictionary
entries can interact with a lexical data base, conceived as a set
of different knowledge sources (text corpus, old lexicographical
archives/deposits, pre-existing dictionaries, bibliographical references, etc.) made available on-line and accessible by means of
appropriately designed software tools.

According to some scholars, the publication of a dictionary of
the future will represent a design decision made at an editor's
workstation, in which components of an underlying lexical data base
are "sculpted" together in an attractive visual form, without chang-

ing any of the underlying computer data.

This prospect may not be so far away for the updating of existing traditional dictionaries. The lexicographer could effectively examine and characterize newly found citations automatically extracted from an incoming text stream, modifying and creating lexical entries in an existing data base, thus continually updating the dictionary to remain contemporary with the use of the language (Amsler 1983).

Far more complex is the situation where one devises an integrated system for the compilation of new dictionaries, in which the gap between data collection via electronic text processing and final photocomposition is filled by computer-assisted editing of the entries. Some experimental projects aim essentially at facilitating access to a corpus and to a dictionary, and the storing of preliminary versions of lexical entries for further processing (Lentz 1981, Zampolli 1983).

A software component ensures quick access to the data, thus enabling the lexicographer to use the corpora interactively via the terminal. For example, the lexicographer can search for specific word forms, word forms matching (beginning, containing or ending with) a specified string of graphemes, co-occurrences of word forms and/or grapheme strings in a given span of text (if the texts are already lemmatized, the lexicographer may operate on lemmas and/or word forms). The component provides the lexicographer with information on the frequencies of distribution, in different sections of the corpus, of the searched elements. The lexicographer may then request the contexts to be displayed on the video screen or to be output in printed form. Each context, which is algorithmically "cut out" by the computer, may be interactively modified by the addition or exclusion of selected syntagms (Picchi 1983).

Another component enables the lexicographer to consult existing dictionaries in the database. The lexicographer will obviously benefit from the multiple dictionary access techniques described in B, may search for different types of information in the entries both of existing dictionaries and of the dictionary which is being constructed.

Specific functions permit the insertion and cyclic reordering of the selected contexts in the different sections of the microstructure, thus producing a preliminary version of the new dictionary entry.   All stored information can be altered, expanded and corrected at any time and consulted immediately for comparison within the new dictionary, in order to ensure homogeneity and coherence.

We feel that a greater cooperative effort between lexicographers and computational linguists is needed if a complete procedure is to be constructed.   In particular, the operations which the lexicographer performs when preparing a dictionary entry must be analysed and described accurately.

The objection of many lexicographers is that "no computer system offers a way for the editor to shuffle and re-shuffle examples, of which the editor's work so largely consists" (Kipfer 1982).   They think that the "traditional dictionary-slips-on-the-table method" is still the best because "the computer is limited in the number of slips one can see on one video-screen" (Kipfer 1982).   They suggest that editors continue to produce concordances or, even better, citation slips, which can be used in the traditional manner.   In order to avoid retyping the selected citations, they suggest that the citations stored in the computer's memory should be numbered. The editor then keys in only the microstructure (headword, etymologies, grammatical information, definitions, etc.) and for each section keys in the code numbers of the citations he wants.

The first explicit and general discussion of this problem was probably held during a round-table meeting between computational linguists and lexicographers from more than ten countries, held in Pisa in 1972.

The situation today is probably somewhat different due to the evolution of data-base methodologies and of workstation technology, which seem to offer the opportunity of "simulating" on the video the games of "solitaire" which the lexicographer has always played, ordering and reordering the traditional slips. .

A.3 Editing and Printing

Photocomposition techniques are now commonly used by most publishing houses.   A variety of editorial controls and readjustments to the text of the dictionary prepared in MRF for photocomposition

are thus possible before the final printing. Quémada (1983:27)
provides some examples.[6]   Other examples are given by Knowles
(1983:186-87), Howlett (1983:157) Petersen (1983) and Pfister
(1983).

Even more effective controls are obviously possible if the dictionary is prepared directly in MRF (as in the frameworks described
in A.2.), following a tagging scheme. This might cover: control
of different types of cross-references; print-out of lists of words
and expressions with specialized meaning to be submitted to experts;
automatic verification of the coherence of the typographical conventions, etc.   In historical dictionaries, it is possible to retrieve exhaustive lists of the citations of a given author from a
work, so as to re-control them in the original text, or to replace
them in the case of availability of new critical editions.

The advantages of working on a dictionary in MRF are obvious
when revising or updating a pre-existing dictionary.

B.   Lexical data bases

B.1.   Typology of MRDs

The expression "Machine Readable Dictionary" (MRD) is increasingly
employed nowadays in the field of Computational Linguistics.   The
expression is however employed within different frameworks, and with
different meanings according to different objects, and is applied
either to different approaches to an identical underlying generic
notion or to notions which are distinct one from the other.

In order to clarify the terminology, we first wish to draw up a
tentative typology of MRDs, listing at least the principal types
which are usually denoted by this expression.   We should however

---

6 "Citons en particulier, pour la mise au point de la nomenclature: les inven-
   taires cumulatifs des entrées figurant dans de nombreux dictionnaires, en
   parallèle à l'index de formes dans les corpus; les résolutions des variantes
   graphiques; l'élimination des mots cachés (oubliés) dans le texte du dictionnaire; pour la gestion des exemples et des citations retenus, leur analyse,
   sélection et classement et les aménagements textuels, etc., qui en découlent;
   pour le traitement des définitions, la normalisation des définisseurs,
   l'homogénéisation du métalangage, etc....; pour les corrections et les con-
   trôles divers du texte en cours d'élaboration et, avant son achèvement, les
   renvois, l'équilibrage des exemples, la normalisation et homogénéisation des
   informations, etc."

bear in mind that these categories are by no means rigid and separate.

(1) *Machine Readable Lexicons*, which are extracted from a corpus of electronically processed texts and which refer to single authors;

(2) *Machine Readable Dictionaries*, prepared for photocomposition, simply with typesetting codes and without supplementary information;

(3) *Machine Readable Dictionaries plus codes* explicitly classifying linguistic information. In other words, information on the nature and structure of the data is recorded not only implicitly via changes in type-faces (as a side-effect of photocomposition commands) but also via codes explicitly intended for future access and retrieval.

(4) *Machine Dictionaries*, classified, encoded, and with selected information (the Italian Machine Dictionary on tape can be considered a prototype);

(5) *Lexical Data Bases (LDB)*, with structured and formalized information, both at the entry level and particularly at the level of relations between entries, finalized for interactive utilization by many categories of potential users, and associated with specialized software modules for access, interrogation and on-line processing.

The last type of MRD is the specific subject which will be discussed below.

B.2. Sources and types of information

Traditional standard printed dictionaries are certainly one of the most suitable starting points for MDs since they provide a large quantity of important data. Furthermore, they are an invaluable source of information if appropriately structured both from a linguistic and computational point of view. Practically all the new printed dictionaries nowadays are prepared in machine-readable form for simple printing, i.e. for photocomposition. This is a sector in which the publishing "world" is strongly involved.

Thus an increasing number of dictionary projects are now relying on computer techniques, and the *New Oxford English Dictionary* is certainly an example worth mentioning of the considerable effort presently being made in the area of conversion into machine readable form (Hultin and Logan 1984).

However, the conversion of a simple dictionary in machine readable form into a true MD or even more into a complex and structured
LDB is really a major undertaking both from the linguistic and the
computational point of view.   A dictionary on its surface is an
elaborately formatted object, and its computerization is a complicated and difficult matter, specially if one wishes to discover
the information underlying the surface data.

An important aspect we wish to underline is that the lexicon can
be considered as lying at the crossroads between the traditional
levels of linguistic analysis: graphic, phonetic, morphological,
syntactic and semantic.   However, cognitive, pragmatic, psychological and sociological issues are also important with regard to
the lexicon, and are often strongly connected.

Information concerning each of these levels can and must be codified (according to different theories) in a lexicon, especially in
the case of computerized lexicons.   The following are some examples
of the range of information which a computerized lexicon can contain:

lemma-word, written according to its usual orthography, plus phonetic
codes;

morphosyntactic labels: parts of speech, gender, etc.;

homograph codes, with a distinction between "lexical" and "grammatical"
homography;

semantic explanation: a very brief definition (synonyms, paraphrases)
to distinguish between homographic lemmas which pertain to the same
part of speech;

usage status: archaic, dialectal, popular, literary, etc.;

paradigms: grammatical codes specifying the type of morphological
inflection;

forms, written in their usual orthography;

morphosyntactic labels of those forms: number, gender, tense, etc.;

definitions : the definitions of the reference dictionaries;

taxonomy: a numbering system is used for classifying the different
meanings of a polysemous lemma;

semantic procedure codes, e.g. metaphor, metonymy, extension, etc.

A particular domain of research can thus be shared by various separate sectors, which can be approached within different perspectives.

One of the main goals to be pursued is to reach a lexical description crossing the specific boundaries of each area, and which is sufficiently general and neutral to allow the different theories to select and pick up only the basic elements from the amount of shared knowledge which are relevant to the specific application or research.

Again this is the direction in which LDBs should move in the near future, and efforts should be made, on a theoretical basis, to establish up to which point a set of structures and formats compatible with different applications, or with different theories, can be envisaged, defined, and implemented.

B.3. Uses and users

Within linguistics, interest over the past few years has gradually moved from syntax to the lexicon, so that an increasing number of well structured and comprehensive lexicons have been developed and created for users. In this respect, a large number of systems, which range from parsing to machine-translation, lexicon-drivers, and large computerized lexicons, are being employed in a wide variety of natural language processing applications.

The aim of LDBs is also to achieve structured and finalized information at many descriptive levels by extending and developing the scope of early machine dictionary projects intended mainly for lemmatizing purposes. They employ increasingly sophisticated computational technology, and the variety of application areas is such that they may be considered as one of the most promising fields of research.

The potential users of LDBs may be classified as follows:

(1) human users (specialists and lexicographers, lexicologists, linguists, or normal users for everyday dictionary look-up);

(2) "procedural users" (i.e. other programs or complex systems for which the LDB is one of the components).

Therefore, a LDB must be as flexible as possible, both from a computational and a linguistic point of view.

LDBs may be used in a wide variety of cases ranging from lemmatization to spelling verification, and from lexicological research and lexicographical practice (e.g. to improve coherence and consistency in dictionary-making) to a number of computational linguistic applications, such as parsers, question-answering systems, man-machine communication, machine (aided) translation, language teaching, etc. They are used within the field of the "language industry" for all applications requiring the use of a lexicon, i.e. in practically all cases, since the problem of lexical access arises whenever we are dealing with words, and wherever the issue of natural language is involved. Consequently LDBs should be considered as the repositories of all the information to which any natural language processing system must have access: morphological, syntactic, semantic, pragmatic, conceptual.

B.4. A prototype of the lexicographical workstation

At Pisa, we are currently working on the design and development of a prototype system of a multifunctional lexical database. We wish to underline the following aspects:

- the source of the data;

- the computational and logical organization of the data in a database structure;

- the results achieved or achievable using this database organization in terms of new information obtained from the original data of a machine-readable dictionary;

- the characteristics, considered from the end-user's perspective, of a lexical database of the type envisaged;

- the link between the lexical and the textual database;

- the relevance of this new concept of integrated linguistic database (lexical plus textual database) when the end-user is the lexicographer himself.

B.4.1. Source of our data

A number of Italian standard printed dictionaries, either trans-

cribed in machine-readable form or already available from the
publishers for photocomposition were used as data sources for our
lexical data base.

Machine-readable dictionaries are nowadays acknowledged to be
invaluable sources of information on the lexical system of a language.   However, if left in simple sequential alphabetical form,
with only the codes necessary for photocomposition, and in text or
string format (as provided by publishing houses) they are of
little interest.   They must instead undergo a complex process of
transformation so as to exploit their enormous information potential.   Dictionaries are in fact a relatively structured type of
text, and this facilitates their organization into a database.
However, there is in particular one type of information which is
not explicitly structured for itself, namely definitions and examples or citations, but which is nonetheless of great value when
trying to extract new types of information from a machine-readable
dictionary.

B.4.2. The database organization

It was decided to re-structure the dictionary data according to
the methods of database structuring, and in particular to select
the relational data model in which relations are used to describe
connections between data items.

Our dictionary database comprises a number of relations.   Each
relation is a table in which each column corresponds to a different
attribute (e.g. the morphological codes), and each row to a distinct
entity tuple (e.g. a lemma).   The lemma relation was obviously
the first relation to be implemented.

The new database organization gives us direct access to all those
information categories which in a normal dictionary are already
present in coded form.   Lemmas can obviously be used for a normal
search in the automatic as well as in the printed dictionary, but
other new means of consultation are also available.   It is thus
possible to consult the dictionary not only by lemmas, but also by
grammatical category, or by usage code, or by inflectional codes,
etc.   The creation of inverted files on the fields corresponding
to these attributes makes it possible to obtain immediately the
entire set of lemmas with a common value for a specific attribute.

Thus a list, for example, of all the adverbs, or all the intransitive verbs, or all the dialectal words recorded in the dictionary, or all the words with a given ending, etc., can be obtained interactively.

Furthermore, the possibility of using natural language definitions to extract semantic information on the lexical entries is particularly interesting. With this in view, a number of linguistically relevant relations has been set up with regard to which it is possible to obtain significant data by running appropriate procedures on the dictionary definitions. It is moreover important that these relationships are defined over the entire lexicon. Information can be obtained, for example, with regard to the relations of synonymy, hyponymy and hyperonymy, antonymy, morphological derivation, co-occurrence, case-frames, etc. These relations can be recognized and stated on the basis of several patterns which occur repeatedly in the definitions and which can often be directly connected with certain types of semantic features or semantic relations or functions.

B.4.3. Relations among words

Once relationships of these types have been defined in the whole lexicon, structures of the lexicon are easily traced along a number of different paths, depending on the relation chosen. For instance, one can ask for all the hyponyms of a word, thus obtaining a semantically coherent cluster with certain properties in common. One can query all the verbs of movement, or all the names of sounds, or all the types of furniture, and so on. Within the lexicon a number of hierarchical structures are thus created and we can work on them in order to formalize, for example, the property of inheritance of relevant features.

It is possible to ask for all the lemmas ending with a certain substring, and connect them with all their definitions. Queries of this type are very useful when analyzing the phenomenon of word-formation. In fact we can obtain very interesting data concerning the interaction between morphology and semantics, and we can evaluate extensively the meaning changes effected by the addition of given suffixes to bases, with the aim of coding regular morphological and semantic behaviour.

Our dictionary is completely cross-indexed according to the above-listed relations, and it is evident that a computerized dictionary organized according to these semantic relations becomes a first nucleus of a knowledge base, from which a great deal of encyclopaedic information is also retrievable.

One of the effects of this restructuring will also be that of reducing the amount of explicit information on each lexical entry by handling with rules all the information which is predictable on the basis of what is already present (e.g. by inheriting properties from superordinates in the hierarchic arrangement of entries which are available in our dictionary).

B.4.4. The end-user's perspectives

In order to meet the needs of the user, one of our principle aims was to create a system particularly suitable for the "linguist" user, who need not be obliged to learn special computer techniques.

If the term "data model" is used to indicate the entire lexical data universe, i.e. the complete set of relations stored in the system, and if a "schema" is a set of declarations describing the data model, then the set of the relations available for particular users is known as the "data sub-model" and the set of declarations for the data sub-model is called a "subschema".

Tables are temporarily created to give the meaning of, for example, "the superlatives of (Italian) adjectives ending in -o, -a", or of "archaic adverbs", etc., as required by the user.   This is very similar to the database interrogation process, as each query operates on the resident relations to build or to define new relations.   A requirement may be a subset formed by only one relation, aimed for example at supplying the meaning of "all the lemmas ending in -$it\grave{a}$ which have archaic graphic variants".   Or one's view may extend over more than one relation as with "join" operations, to obtain information of the following type: "all the word-forms of certain irregular verbs of the 3rd conjugation".

Until now we have implemented a query language in an interactive environment.   This language - which is very useful at this stage of the project - enables the user to access the primary and secondary keys in transparent mode.   The resulting information is essential if the present structure is to be extended into a logically more complex structure.

User/database interaction must be possible on various levels:

(1) *Standard queries*, e.g. all the word-forms which belong to a lemma;

(2) *Complex queries* which were not always envisaged when the database was created, e.g. a phonetician could be interested in selecting all or some of the words in which a voiced consonant is followed by the vowel *a*;

(3) *Complex processing* of the information; e.g. statistical surveys of the distribution of the forms in the various inflexional classes, or of occurrences of homography in the various parts-of-speech;

(4) *Modifications to the schema* with the definition of additional relations.

A more complex non-procedural language is now being designed. With this language the database can also be accessed by a number of users concurrently.

B.4.5.   Integration of the LDB with a textual DB

The dictionary can function in a stand-alone mode for human users, or as a module within larger systems, thus providing different possibilities of lexical access for a number of other applications. The application which is of interest here is the connection with an Information Retrieval System for large textual corpora. The two systems are directly compatible and they work as an integrated system to query texts by means of the database dictionary.

The modes of querying texts are defined by the user, and the dictionary is allowed interface to the texts.

Each lemma is expanded into its full inflectional paradigm, and the original input word is replaced in the query by a cluster composed of all the members of the inflectional paradigm. This cluster is produced without any intervention by the user, in a perfectly transparent way, and its members are used by the query program as access keys to the textual corpus.

Obviously every possible query that can be put to the dictionary alone can also be used as a "filter" to make enquiries to textual corpora. We can therefore make very "precise" searches of texts, where the search-key is no longer a simple word-form or a lemma, but for example a word acting as a "semantic marker". The dictionary in fact extends this "semantic marker" to all the lexical items which are coded as its hyponyms. It becomes possible, for instance, to ask the dictionary for all the registered names of colours, and then to go to the texts with this semantically homogeneous subset to find all the contexts where a colour name is used.

The same is obviously possible for synonyms, derivatives, grammatical categories, and so on. It is clear that the dictionary is used in connection with an information retrieval system on texts as a powerful tool for making linguistic generalizations on the lexical level, and for using the detected regularities with a filtering function in the retrieval operation. It can be conceived as an automatic guide to the human user in the investigation, in texts, of the use of particular sets of lexical elements interrelated according to one or the other of certain dimensions of relatedness.

This prototype workstation can therefore be conceived as a central nucleus of basic data (lexical and textual), organized according to suitable structures, plus a set of software mdoules which render these data available at different levels for different users.

B.5. General characteristics of a LDB

The LDBs we have described above should have two important properties, which are those of "multi-functionalism" and "multi-dimensionalism".

By the term "multi-functional" we mean the possibility of using LDBs in various applications, by different categories of users. The availability of a single central repository of "neutral" dictionary data would enable access by many different interfaces, according to the needs of the whole range of possible applications (dictionary server). It should be possible for different external procedures to use different parts of the dictionary content in specific applications. The user (human or procedural) virtually ignores the internal physical structure of the LDB, considering only the data which are useful to his/its own purposes.

The concept of multi-dimensionalism is strongly linked to that of multiple access. By following different paths within the DB it is possible to search different word aspects. When the original data can be viewed within a variety of different perspectives, the important effect of "multiplying" the information offered by the same set of source data is obtained.

Moreover, it is possible to create, as by-products, many virtual secondary sub-lexicons, containing specifically selected parts of the dictionary, such as terminological sub-dictionaries, synonym dictionaries, thesauri, etc. In a well-structured and comprehensive LDB, they only differ in the way the original data are selected, sorted and interrelated.

We can imagine a multi-access dictionary with all the properties described so far, and possibly more, as recorded on a diskette or a compact disc and accessible to the ordinary user in his own home. We are here envisaging the "dictionary of the future" or "tele-dictionary" for general consultation, which will become the "diction-ary of the present" in a few years. Modern technology will cer-tainly be able to produce the kinds of facilities we have described so far.

C. Conclusions

A lexical data base also offers new possibilities to publishing houses, since they will be able to produce from a LDB a variety of different lexicographical products in the most favourable circum-stances.

> "From the very numbers of dictionaries of varying shapes and sizes that follow in the wake of the major ones, it is clear that different levels of detail are appropriate to different people and to different kinds of use (...) The amount of information that these editions contain is clearly chosen for largely economic reasons and from the point of view of any dictionary user" (Kay 1983:163).

If appropriately coded, however, the information structured in a LDB could allow editors to produce, (semi-)automatically, different kinds of dictionaries (printed or sold on magnetic support).

In this framework, the relevance of a standard taxonomy of lexi-cographical data must be stressed. This would facilitate not only the non-ambiguous description of the content of dictionaries, but also the totally or partially automatic exchange of lexicographical data between different dictionaries.

The creation of a lexical DB, in our opinion, should directly involve dictionary publishers. These are still, nowadays, the "owners" of the major repositories of lexicographical information.

Because their collection is very expensive and their economic value very high, there is certainly good reason to protect the data, and to exploit its potential value for new products required by the so-called information society: spelling checkers, translation aids, text-editing aids, automatic indexing, etc.

These utilizations require that the present lexicographical collections be transformed into data bases structured according to models which take into account the linguistic nature of the lexicographical information independently of its various possible applications, according to the principles indicated above at B.

We can consider these data bases as intermediate products which are necessary - among other reasons - to optimize the production costs of printed dictionaries; to integrate the lexicographical data within the information systems previously mentioned; and to create new lexicographical products, as for example mono- and plurilingual dictionaries on CD-ROM.

J. Jansen, J.P. Mergeai and J. Vanandroye

CONTROLLING LDOCE'S CONTROLLED VOCABULARY

1. Introduction

One of the main reasons put forward by EFL learners for not using monolingual dictionaries is that the defining vocabulary of some headwords is not easily understandable (MacFarquhar and Richards 1983).   In order to counter this problem the editors of the *Longman Dictionary of Contemporary English (LDOCE)* made use of a Controlled Vocabulary (CV), in which "only the most 'central' meanings of these 2,000 words, and only easily understood derivatives, were used" (1978:ix).   Small capitals are used in definitions for cross-referring the user to the entry for any defining word which is not part of the CV.   Despite its obvious advantages, the use made by the *LDOCE* editors of a CV in all their definitions and examples presents a number of problems, particularly for the foreign learner. This paper concentrates on various critical aspects of *LDOCE's* CV, specifically on ambiguities due to the use of polysemous words, phrasal verbs and idioms in the defining vocabulary, and on how these types of ambiguities might be remedied.   Finally, we will examine ways of producing computer-assisted language learning (CALL) exercises for EFL learners.

2. Computational tools

In order to analyse the CV, we developed various computational tools from the *LDOCE* file made available to us for research purposes under contract with the publishers.   First, we created a CV-subfile which contained all the entries describing *LDOCE's* CV-items used in isolation: all the *LDOCE* headwords were printed, then all the CV-items were tagged manually.   Second, we adapted the CV-subfile to STAIRS (Storage And Information Retrieval System), an information retrieval package produced by IBM, which has turned out to be a most useful tool for our investigations and for exploitation of the database.   As can be seen from Fig. 1, STAIRS provides an impressive range of operators for querying any field in a database. STAIRS accepts any query, not only in the form of isolated words but also Boolean combinations of these, as well as concatenations, i.e. strings of adjacent words (see Fig. 2). Furthermore, we can use a so-called mask, allowing us to search for "word-stems" (see Fig. 3) to obtain all occurrences of the queried strings of characters irrespective of what follows. It answers these queries instantaneously, providing all the relevant documents together with frequency data and statistics about them.

ADJ	strict adjacency
SYN	synonymy relationship in a given query
WITH	same sentence
SAME	same paragraph
NOT - AND - OR - XOR (exclusive or): boolean operators	

Fig. 1.   STAIRS operators

```
*** DATABASE:  LDCX   DOCUMENT:  REC=   1  PRIVACY:  O  PAGE 0001
SEARCH - QUERY
00002 (BREAK$ BROK$) ADJ DOWN
*** DATABASE:  LDCX   DOCUMENT:  REC=   1  PRIVACY:  O
     HEADNUM:   S0085000
     HEADHOMO:  01
     HEADFORM:
     HEADTYPE:
     RUNONNBR:
     DEFINUM:   23
     SUBJECT:
     RULE:      1234567890
     SEMAN:     L

HEADWORD   see
POS        V
INFLEX     saw:/sC:/:, seen:/si:n/
DEFITEXT   you see not fml (used with rather weak meaning in ex-
           planations) ""Why are you so late?'' ""Well, you see,
           the bus broke down.'':  I've got to stay with my mother,
           you see, so I can't come along
USAGE      <USAGE 1 To see is to experience with the eyes, and it
           does not depend on the will.  In this meaning, one can
           say Can you see anything? but not *Are you seeing any-
           thing?  When one uses the eyes on purpose and with at-
           tention, one is looking at something:  Stop looking at
           me like that!  To watch is to look at something that is
           moving:  one
```

Fig. 2.   Extract from a STAIRS query using the mask

($) and the "adjacency" operator

A by-product of STAIRS is the dictionary and word count of all the word-forms in all the documents (see Fig. 4). Such a STAIRS CV-subfile dictionary was most useful for checking to what extent the constraints in the CV had been adhered to and for detecting certain weak points.

```
AQUARIUS - SEARCH MODE - BEGIN YOUR QUERY AFTER THE STATEMENT NUMBER
00002 hand✿.defitext.
HAND✿                       480 OCCURRENCES
HAND                        248 OCCURRENCES        163 DOCUMENTS
HAND''                        1 OCCURRENCE           1 DOCUMENT
HAND'S                        1 OCCURRENCE           1 DOCUMENT
HANDBOOK                      1 OCCURRENCE           1 DOCUMENT
HANDED                        6 OCCURRENCES          6 DOCUMENTS
HANDFUL                      10 OCCURRENCES         10 DOCUMENTS
HANDHOLD                      1 OCCURRENCE           1 DOCUMENT
HANDKERCHIEF                 10 OCCURRENCES         10 DOCUMENTS
HANDLE                       55 OCCURRENCES         49 DOCUMENTS
HANDLEABLE                    5 OCCURRENCES          5 DOCUMENTS
HANDLED                       2 OCCURRENCES          1 DOCUMENT
HANDLES                       2 OCCURRENCES          2 DOCUMENTS
HANDLING                      4 OCCURRENCES          4 DOCUMENTS
HANDS                       128 OCCURRENCES        108 DOCUMENTS
HANDSOME                      3 OCCURRENCES          3 DOCUMENTS
HANDWRITING                   3 OCCURRENCES          3 DOCUMENTS


1=SEARCH  2=SEL  3=OFF  4=BRWSE  5=HELP  6=COPY  7=DOC-1  10=P-1
11=P*   <LDCX
```

Fig. 3.

WORD	DATA BASE 1	DATA BASE 2	DATA BASE 3	DATA BASE 4
ACCIDENTALLY	5	-	-	-
ACCIDENTS	5	-	-	-
ACCL	1	-	-	-
ACCOMMODATION	1	-	-	-
ACCOMPANY	1	-	-	-
ACCORDANCE	21	-	-	-
ACCORDING	135	-	-	-
ACCOUNT	54	-	-	-
ACCOUNTED	2	-	-	-
ACCOUNTS	11	-	-	-
ACCUSE	1	-	-	-
ACCUSTOM	2	-	-	-
ACCUSTOMED	4	-	-	-
ACE	4	-	-	-
ACEN	1	-	-	-
ACGO	2	-	-	-
ACH	3	-	-	-
ACHE	7	-	-	-
ACHES	3	-	-	-
ACHIEVE	12	-	-	-
ACHING	5	-	-	-
ACID	13	-	-	-
ACID-LIKE	1	-	-	-
ACIDS	1	-	-	-
ACQUIRE	1	-	-	-
ACRONYM	1	-	-	-
ACROSS	132	-	-	-
ACROSS-THE-BOARD	1	-	-	-
ACT	355	-	-	-
ACTED	12	-	-	-
ACTING	19	-	-	-
ACTION	310	-	-	-
ACTIONS	59	-	-	-
ACTIVATE	1	-	-	-
ACTIVE	53	-	-	-
ACTIVELY	2	-	-	-
ACTIVELY)	1	-	-	-
ACTIVITIES	26	-	-	-
ACTIVITY	118	-	-	-
ACTOR	28	-	-	-
ACTORS	10	-	-	-
ACTRESS	14	-	-	-
ACTRESSES	1	-	-	-
ACTS	21	-	-	-
ACTUAL	32	-	-	-
ACTUALITY	1	-	-	-
ACTUALLY	54	-	-	-
ACUPUNCTURE	1	-	-	-
ACUTE	1	-	-	-
ACXX	1	-	-	-
ACZB	4	-	-	-
AD	44	-	-	-
ADAM	1	-	-	-
ADD	42	-	-	-
ADDED	32	-	-	-

Fig. 4.   DICTIONARY PRINTOUT

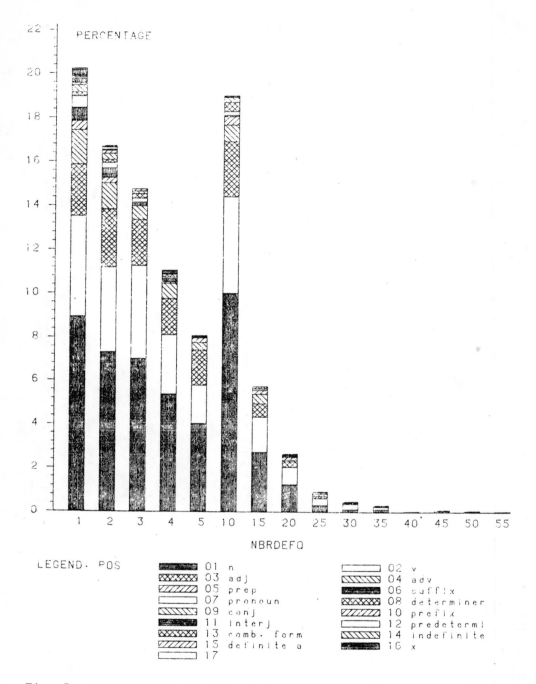

Fig. 5. LDOCE Controlled Vocabulary: senses/headword according
to POS

3. Critical comments

The presentation of the CV lacks consistency:

(1) The parts of speech (POS) are not systematically mentioned, so that we could not check the relevant POS for many items. By default we entered all possible headwords corresponding to a given word form. Note:

> *but* may be conjunction, preposition, adverb, pronoun or noun
> *church* may be noun, adjective or verb
> *left* may be adjective, noun, adverb or past participle

(2) Strangely enough, some words are listed in the CV but are not entered in the dictionary itself as headwords:

> *amusing* (21 occurrences in our subfile)
> *anyone* (43 occurrences)
> *rid* (10 occurrences)
> *someone* (1016 occurrences)

(3) The list does not include some words which are actually used in the definitions and examples:

> *business* (176 occurrences in our subfile)
> *forth* (2 occurrences)
> *hole* (58 occurrences)
> *unless* (1 occurrence)
> *whose* (44 occurrences)

These words have a high degree of frequency in Michael West's *General Service List of English Words* (1953).

(4) As a result of excessive reliance on affixation, some words, like *free-dom* do not appear in the list. Others are:

> *busi-ness*
> *for-th*
> *un-less*

(5) The only phrasal verb entered in the CV list is *to wrap (up)*, which implies that the dictionary makers consider all other occurrences of phrasal verbs in definitions as combinations of verbs + adverbs/prepositions.

After manual clean-up operations, we arrived at a total number

of 3,135 CV-items.   The difference between the number given by
the editors and ours can be explained as follows:

2,100 corresponds to the number of lexemes,
3,135 corresponds to the number of dictionary entries including
homographs differentiated by superscript numbers, but leaving aside
any combinations like compounds, affixed words or phrasal verbs
entered in *LDOCE*. [1]

4. Statistical data regarding the CV-corpus

Thanks to a statistical package (SAS) we were able to analyse
the population of our subfile.   Among the most significant findings were these: [2]

(1) Only 632 CV-items (20.19%) are monosemous.   Among these words
only 144 are verbs: this means that fractionally less than 80% of
the verbs which can be used in the defining vocabulary are polysemous and thus to some extent ambiguous. [3]

(2) Verbs and nouns represent 72.05% of the total population of the
CV.

(3) If we simply take the first sense of a headword into account,
which is a mistake students tend to make, we obtain only 40% of the
possible definitions.   We also have evidence that the first sense
does not always refer to the central meaning of a word, hence the
difficulty for the learner in finding the exact meaning of a defining word.

(4) The occurrence of so many polysemous words in the CV led us to
analyse some examples of ambiguity within the definitions and to
try to qualify the editors' claim to use only the "most central
meanings" of the CV-items.   We define the degree of ambiguity as
the number of possible senses and idioms that are attributed to an

---

1 It appears from a count made by Engels et al (1981) that there are no less
   than 16,000 word-forms in the definitions and examples of *LDOCE*.
2 The headwords with combined POS have not been taken into account.
3 This figure is likely to be larger because we had to enter in our subfile
   words which we felt were not attested in the defining vocabulary: e.g.
   to up, *to leg*, etc.
   For obvious reasons, it was impossible to check the POS usage of these
   homographs.

entry in *LDOCE*. For verbs the number of possible phrasal verbs and their various definitions have also been taken into account.

(5) The internal dictionary confirmed our hypothesis that there exists a correlation between the degree of ambiguity/polysemy and the frequency of use in the CV-subfile. As shown in the table, polysemous verbs occur much more frequently than monosemous verbs: we get 1,114 occurrences of *take* or any morphological variant in the subfile, but only 8 occurrences of monosemous *subtract*.

Word form	Degree of ambiguity	Number of occurrences in internal dictionary
go	162	3,084
run	93	448
take	90	1,114
break	71	320
play	70	585
cut	70	282
–	–	–
–	–	–
–	–	–
accustom	1	6
educate	1	4
enquire	1	8
inform	1	17
subtract	1	8

4.1. Homography

The first problem we analysed was homography:

Number of forms	Number of homographs	Mean per form	Total number of senses	Mean of senses per form
150	324	2.16	1,208	8.1

The item *bank* for example has 2 possible parts of speech (POS) and 5 entries in *LDOCE*. Its use is attested 83 times in our subfile and only as a noun: 76 of these uses refer to the fourth entry and 7 refer to the first. So two homographs are used in the definitions although there is no typographical means of differentiating those homographs in the definitions.

4.2. Polysemy

The second problem we analysed was polysemy. We chose a series of highly polysemous nouns and analysed their usage (*hand*, because it has the largest number of definitions, and all nouns with a degree of ambiguity of 20: *front*, *service*, *sight*, *water*).

hand n: degree of ambiguity: 52 (12 definitions + 40 idioms)

number of occurrences: 134

```
                       sense  1 : 110
                              2 :   5
                              3 :   1
                              4 :   4
                              7 :   1
                              8 :   1
                             10 :   1
                             12 :   1
                             18 :   6
                             28 :   1
                             33 :   1
                             38 :   2
```

v: degree of ambiguity: 14 (1 definition + 1 idiom + 12 phrasal verbs)

number of occurrences: 7

```
                    simple verb : 2
                    phrasal verbs :  hand over  : 4
                                     hand round : 1
```

Comments:

- The compound *hand gun* is given and labelled   *AmE.*
- It can be assumed that intermediate French-speaking learners would have difficulties understanding *hand* 2 (needle), 7 (workman), 8 (performer), 10 (quality of touch), 12 (control).
- There are twice as many occurrences of *hand over, v. adv.,* as of *hand, v.*

front n: degree of ambiguity: 20 (14 definitions + 6 idioms)

number of occurrences: 59

```
                       sense  1 :  5
                              2 : 10
                              3 : 16
                              4 :  3
                              5 :  2
                    idiom 15 :  2
                          16 : 21
```

Comments:

- Out of the 14 different senses entered for *front,* 5 are used, the third definition ("the most forward or import-ant position") being the most frequent.
- No less than 39% of its uses are idiomatic.

service n: degree of ambiguity: 20 (16 definitions + 4 idioms)

number of occurrences: 55

	sense		
	1	:	5
	2	:	11
	3	:	1
	5	:	3
	6	:	1
	7	:	4
	9	:	15
	10	:	8
	11	:	6
	14	:	1

Comments:

- 10 out its 16 possible senses are attested.
- None of the 4 idioms entered under *service* is used, but the phrases "a boy in service to a person of high rank", under *page,* and "have at one's service", under *command,* are not considered as idioms.
- The use of *service* in the seventh definition of *bar* ("a narrow band of metal or cloth worn on a military uniform or medal esp. to show rank, service, or good performance") is ambiguous in that it is difficult to make out to which sense it is related.

sight n: degree of ambiguity: 20 (9 definitions + 11 idioms)

number of occurrences: 43

	sense		
	1	:	15
	2	:	14
	3	:	4
	6	:	1
idiom	13	:	1
	14	:	1
	15	:	1
	16	:	1
	18	:	5

Comments:

- Out of the 9 different senses for *sight*, 4 meanings of the simple noun are used, the first definition being the most frequent.
- About 23% of the uses of *sight* are idiomatic.

water n: degree of ambiguity: 20 (8 definitions + 12 idioms)

number of occurrences: 248

	sense		
	1	:	114
	2	:	22
	3	:	99

```
                                    6  :   4
                                    7  :   8
                     idiom        15  :   1
```

Comments:
- 5 of its 8 senses and 1 of its 12 idioms are used,
  the first definition being duly represented in about
  46% of its occurrences.

4.3. Phrasal verbs

Another major problem for the learner of English is that of
phrasal verbs.   We analysed their frequency and use by considering
the occurrences of 5 of the most polysemous verbs in their definition context (all have more than 35 senses and a large number of
possible phrasal verbs cross-referred in small capitals at the end
of the main entry).   Only the idiomatic uses were counted: for
obvious reasons we could not consider *run out of* as a phrasal verb
in: *She jumped to her feet and ran out of the room.*   (s.v. *jump*).

```
run v:        degree of ambiguity:     109
              number of occurrences:   109
                              run v:    93
                              sense     1 : 69
                                        3 :  5
                                        4a:  1
                                        4b:  1
                                        6a:  3
                                        7a:  1
                                        8a:  3
                                        9 :  3
                                       12 :  1
                                       14 :  3
                                       15 :  1
                                       18 :  2
                         run v adv/prep  : 16
                         about           :  1
                         away            :  9
                         into            :  2
                         off             :  2
                         on              :  1
                         through         :  1
```

Comments:
- 12 different meanings of *run* as a simple verb are
  attested.
- 74 occurrences refer to the act of "moving fast",
  all other uses (19) being to a certain extent idiomatic.

- In 16 cases *run* is used idiomatically as part of a phrasal verb.
- The phrasal verb *run about*, in the entry *quite*, is not entered in *LDOCE*.

break v: degree of ambiguity: 70

number of occurrences: 73

break v	:	55
v adv/prep	:	18

across	:	1
down	:	6
into	:	1
loose	:	1
off	:	3
open	:	2
up	:	4

Comments:
- *break* in the following occurrences is idiomatic and as such should be cross referred or given in small capitals:
- *break the habit* (under ALCOHOLIC); *break the law* (under CHARGE); *break the flow* (under INTERRUPT); *the rules* (under ORDER); *break a record* (under RECORD).
- About 25% of the occurrences of *break* are of phrasal verbs, 2 of these not being entered in *LDOCE*: *break loose* (under *some*) *break across* (under *surface*).

get v: degree of ambiguity: 131

number of occurrences: 523

get v	:	459
v adv/prep	:	64

ahead	:	1
along	:	1
at	:	1
away	:	1
away with	:	1
back	:	3
in	:	2
into	:	16
off	:	4
on	:	10
out	:	8
through	:	3
up	:	13

Comments:

- More than half of *get*'s 25 senses are exemplified at least once.
- One out of 9 uses of *get* is a phrasal verb.

take v: degree of ambiguity: 97
number of occurrences: 571

take v	:	497
v adv/prep	:	74
apart	:	1
away	:	18
away from	:	5
back	:	4
down	:	1
in	:	8
off	:	16
on	:	2
out	:	6
out of	:	5
up	:	8

Comments:

- The treatment of phrasal verbs is not consistent: 16 phrasal verbs appear as main entries whereas 3 *(away/down/up)* appear within the entry for *take*.
- Excluding idiomatic definitions, there are 43 different definitions for *take*. Such a large number of senses very often discourages students from consulting the dictionary.

5. Ways of improving *LDOCE's* CV

(1) Ideally, definitions should consist of words with annotations, cross-referring the defining word to its appropriate sense in the dictionary. This can be done by means of superscripts. The absence of a cross-reference would imply reference to the first sense of the item in question. The problem of homographs could be dealt with by means of double cross-references, the first digit referring to the entry number and the second to the definition number.

(2) The order of the definitions should as far as possible be based on some principle of gradation, for example progression from the most general and/or common meaning to the more idiomatic uses.

(3) Idiomatic phrases, including phrasal verbs, should be avoided, whenever possible, in the defining vocabulary. If their use cannot be avoided, a cross-reference should make clear that the word-combination is used in an idiomatic way.

6. CALL exercises

Research into EFL dictionary design has stimulated the production of automatic or semi-automatic English language exercises, and this is one of the ultimate goals of a project now being developed at the University of Liège. These exercises are based on *LDOCE's* CV for three reasons:

(1) for practical reasons: we had to restrict our adaptations to small subfiles to avoid exceeding the memory capacity allotted to us on the University mainframe computer;

(2) because of the very nature of a controlled vocabulary: high-load lexical and grammatical words are the most difficult for EFL learners to cope with;

(3) because of the variety of readily accessible types of information housed in the *LDOCE* formatted fields (register and field labels, grammatical codes, etc.) which provide us with a wide range of possible exercises.

We first adapted a set of exercises produced by Laplanche, Michiels and Moulin (1982). Very briefly, these were Cloze tests based on headword deletion and the replacement within the lexical field examined (definition, example, idiomatic expressions or any combination of these) of the headword or any of its morphological variants by some arbitrary symbol (∿ for example). In this pilot experiment, students were provided with a list of words from which they had to choose an appropriate filler for the slot.

We devised a series of similar, but fully automatic, exercises based on the Lancaster-Oslo-Bergen text corpus (Johansson 1981):

(1) every nth word is deleted: the choice of the deletion interval is left open to the teacher (see Fig. 6).

(2) The various types of information provided in *LDOCE* are all accessible and as such can serve as deletion criteria:

- morphological information: derivatives, compounds and variants
  are generated by a program devised by J. Jansen;
- syntactic and stylistic information: parts of speech, grammatical
  codes, register labels, geographical labels, subject codes, semantic codes, or any combination of these. Examples include:
  verbs coded [V4], nouns with the subject code "sport", and
  Americanisms.

In addition, the teacher is free to use a stoplist, which contains
the words which should not be deleted (see Fig. 7).

   This type of exercise can also be applied to any text that the
teacher wishes to enter. In addition, we are now developing on-
line versions so as to give students access to help functions on
the deleted item. These include: definition(s); example(s);
idiomatic expression(s); the whole entry. These exercises are
most useful in that they test lexical proficiency, familiarize students with monolingual dictionaries and give lexicographers information on how to improve definitions and examples.

[157 TEXT F14]
*<*6THE REGISTRAR-GENERAL FORECASTS...*>
*<*6ONE OF THESE ∿ WILL FAIL*>
*<*4But four happy ∿ say he's talking nonsense*>
*<*0by *2 ∿ NORMAN*>

   *4P*2EOPLE *0disapprove of teenagers ∿.   They shake their heads
and ∿: *"They're too young.**"

   They point to ∿ statistics which show that one out of ∿ girls who
marry between 16 and 18 ∿ up in the divorce court.   And they ∿:
*"That proves it.**"   But does it?

   To ∿ out, I travelled all over the ∿, meeting couples who married
very ∿.   None of them was newly ∿.   Most had been married for ∿ two
to six years.

   I am ∿ to tell you the stories of ∿ such couples.   If the Regis-
trar ∿, who compiles national statistics of ∿, deaths and marriages
is right, one of them will be in the ∿ court within the next 20
years.

   All of them have ∿ greater hardship than most couples who ∿ until
they are older before ∿.   Almost all have had to ∿ the suspicion
that they *lhad *0to ∿ married, although it was untrue.

They have ∿ up against parental disapproval, and ∿ who wanted to see their ∿ lines before offering them accommodation. They have all had to ∿ children on small wages.

Take, for ∿, the case of the Annandales who were ∿ six and a half years ago, when ∿ was 17, and Pam 16. Now they have a ∿ home in Germany, where 23-year-old ∿, a regular in the {ORAF}, is ∿. They have a car and Pat has a ∿ coat.

But less than four ∿ ago they went hungry in ∿ that their baby, David, would have ∿.

They told me about it ∿ when Brian was on leave and they were ∿ with Pam's parents in Francis-road, ∿, Kent.

Brian was then a National ∿, getting just under *+5 a week.

He ∿ that, because he was under 21, the {O ∿} would not give him and ∿ married quarters.

Nor*- again because he was a ∿ *- would they grant him the ∿ a week extra normally given to ∿ men in the {ORAF} who have to ∿ their own rent.

*"It was a ∿ bad time,**" said Brian. *"It could have ∿ a split between us. But, luckily, it ∿ us closer together.**"

He added: *"We ∿ now that we took a terrific ∿, marrying so young. But when our ∿ pointed this out to us ∿ we married, we thought they were ∿.**"

1. ASHFORD	20. FOUR	39. ORDER
2. BEFORE	20. FOUR	40. PAM
3. BETWEEN	22. FUR	41. PARENTS
4. BIRTHS	23. GENERAL	42. PAY
5. BRIAN	24. GET	43. RAF
5. BRIAN	25. GOING	44. RAISE
7. BROUGHT	26. GUINEA	45. REALISE
8. CAUSED	27. INSTANCE	46. RECENTLY
9. COME	28. LANDLADIES	47. RISK
10. COUNTRY	29. MARRIAGE	48. SAY
11. COUPLES	30. MARRIAGES	48. SAY
12. DIANA	31. MARRIED	50. SERVICEMAN
13. DIVORCE	31. MARRIED	51. STATIONED
14. ENCOUNTERED	31. MARRIED	52. STAYING
15. ENDS	34. MARRYING	53. VERY
16. FACE	35. MARRYING	54. WAIT
17. FIND	36. MINOR	55. WRONG
18. FOOD	37. NICE	56. YEARS
19. FOUND	38. OFFICIAL	57. YOUNG

Fig. 6.   F14   LOB

'S	DONE	ME	THAN
A	DOWN	MIGHT	THAT
ABOUT	EACH	MIGHTN'T	THE
AFTER	FEW	MORE	THEIR
ALL	FOR	MOST	THEM
ALTHOUGH	FROM	MUCH	THEMSELVES
AM	HAD	MUST	THERE
AN	HADN'T	MUSTN'T	THESE
AND	HAS	MY	THEY
ANY	HASN'T	MYSELF	THIS
ARE	HAVE	NEVER	THOSE
AREN'T	HAVEN'T	NO	THOUGH
AS	HAVING	NOT	TO
AT	HE	OF	UP
BACK	HER	OFF	US
BE	HERSELF	ON	WAS
BECAUSE	HIM	ONE	WASN'T
BEEN	HIMSELF	OR	WE
BOTH	HIS	OUGHT	WERE
BUT	HOW	OUGHTN'T	WEREN'T
BY	HOWEVER	OUR	WHAT
CAN	I	OURSELVES	WHEN
CAN'T	IF	OUT	WHERE
CANNOT	IN	OVER	WHICH
COULD	INTO	SHALL	WHO
COULDN'T	IS	SHAN'T	WHOM
DID	ISN'T	SHE	WHOSE
DIDN'T	IT	SHOULD	WHY
DO	ITS	SHOULDN'T	WILL
DOES	ITSELF	SOME	WITH
DOESN'T	MANY		
DOING	MAY		
DON'T			

Fig. 7.   Stoplist

P A R T   I I

THE DICTIONARY IN TEACHING

AND TRANSLATION

Henri Béjoint and André Moulin

THE PLACE OF THE DICTIONARY IN AN EFL PROGRAMME

Part I   (Henri Béjoint)

THE VALUE OF THE DICTIONARY IN VOCABULARY ACQUISITION

1. Introduction

We propose to write a handbook that will introduce foreign learners to the wealth of existing dictionaries in English, to the variety of information that each type can offer, and to the ways in
which they can be used to solve language-learning problems.

Any proposal to write such a book requires some justification.
The first reason that comes to mind, of course, is the absence of
a guide of precisely this type.   Admittedly, there are booklets
produced by dictionary compilers or publishers which aim at helping
the users of particular dictionaries (Whitcut 1979, Underhill 1983).
Also, current research may well result in other publications in the
near future (for a guide with slightly broader aims than those just
mentioned see Burridge and Adam (1985), and cf. Reif, this volume).
What we have in mind would be comprehensive, yet short and simple to
use.   It would be tailored to the needs of the foreign learner of
English (specifically the French-speaking learner, but we think a
wider appeal is possible) and would include an introduction to the
use of bilingual dictionaries.   Finally, it would be based on a
tentative typology of situations and difficulties of dictionary use.

The fact that we have nothing quite like the handbook we have in
mind, however, is not a sufficient reason for its publication.   Our
guide must also be useful to the people it is intended for.   Our
project rests on the following assumptions:

(1) Dictionaries (monolingual and bilingual) are actually useful to
learners of English as a foreign language.

(2) Dictionaries would be still more helpful if learners made full
use of the wealth of information that they contain - which is obviously not the case.

(3) It is possible to help those learners by improving their consultation skills, and a guide such as ours is intended to do precisely that.

However, the ways in which dictionaries are used, and the part they play in the process of language learning are by no means altogether clear. Several investigations into the use of dictionaries have been carried out recently (see the references in Béjoint 1981, to which should be added Hartmann 1982, Mitchell 1983, Galisson 1983, Hatherall 1984, Bensoussan 1984 and Wiegand 1985). Those studies tell us a great deal about such matters as the types of lexical units students look up most (or least) often in their dictionaries, the types of information they find most (or least) useful, and the dictionaries and dictionary types they prefer. At the same time, Hatherall is right to point out that studies based on questionnaires are open to criticism:

> "Are subjects saying what they do, or what they think they do, or what they think they ought to do, or indeed a mixture of all three?" (1984:184)

These objections do not totally invalidate studies based on questionnaires. After all, the weaknesses that Hatherall underlines have been known to scientists for some time (for a discussion of "The Observer's Paradox" in dialectology and sociolinguistics, see Labov 1972:90), and a piece of research, even though not totally reliable, is still better than no research at all. But the reservations are well worth considering. Galisson (1983), whilst also using a questionnaire, devised it so as to be able to juxtapose the real (or, rather, declared) use of dictionaries and the "image" of the dictionary among his student population. The results are interesting:

> "... the 'image' is in no way determined by usage ... it is linked to the perception of the dictionary as an inexhaustible source of information, and not as a tool to be used ..." (1983:84)

In other words, the dictionary is useful because it is within easy reach of our desk, and because we know it has all the answers, not necessarily because we actually use it. And we simply must have one, because it is a "concrete sign that we belong to the class of those who know" (1983:85). Such conclusions not only compound the weaknesses of studies based on questionnaires; they also provide rather discouraging feedback to lexicographers. The reasons why people buy dictionaries are not totally rational or functional and in this context all dictionaries are equal, any dictionary goes, the idea being to have one rather than use it. But in fairness to Galisson, it must be said that he also shows that his student population really use their dictionaries. There are in fact good reasons why lexicographers should work to improve their products and why language teachers should give thought to the role of dictionaries in language acquisition.

One line of enquiry concerns the characteristic structure of the dictionary. It has often been observed that dictionaries, with their macrostructure composed of separate articles, each being centered on one lexical unit and containing a fixed arrangement of information, are particularly well suited to consultation (as opposed to reading). They are normally referred to when the user has a specific problem of linguistic communication that he or she thinks can be solved by looking up a word. The dictionary is consulted for help with both decoding or encoding tasks, but especially when the user is not excessively pressed for time (hence it is mostly used in written communication). More often than not in such situations, though this does not always appear clearly in the studies just mentioned, the students tend to turn to a bilingual rather than to a monolingual dictionary (Snell-Hornby, this volume, Baxter 1980:333).

Now many people, including lexicographers and foreign language teachers, tend to dismiss the bilingual dictionary as a makeshift device, a tool that at best can only serve to solve minor problems of comprehension, and at worst should hardly be tolerated. This attitude, which seems to assume different forms in different countries, can be explained by different factors, among which are the principles underlying foreign language teaching for the past decades. (Those principles we tend to accept as proven truths rather than as the hypotheses they actually are). In the same way, the superiority of the monolingual over the bilingual dictionary is not as obvious as many people think. According to Ellegård (1978:240-241) the main advantage of the monolingual dictionary is that, being commercially more profitable, it can offer more for the same price: more entries and more information in each entry. But no researcher has yet tried to establish how each dictionary type "works", that is, how it helps the user solve specific problems of expression or comprehension, and what part it plays in the acquisition of lexical competence.   That is what I shall try to do in the remainder of this part of our joint paper.   I shall concentrate on semantic information, first because the treatment of meaning is the area where bilingual and monolingual dictionaries differ most, and second because the differences that can be observed in other areas (syntactic, morphological, collocational, phonetic, etc.) are more accidental than fundamental (Baxter 1980:330).   I shall also focus on the use of the dictionary for decoding.   My underlying aim will be to identify those areas of strength and weakness in the dictionary types which can be usefully treated in the students' guide.

2.   For and against the bilingual dictionary

The preference which students show for the bilingual dictionary in tackling encoding tasks is easily explained: they would not know what to look up in their monolingual L2 dictionaries, since an L2 translation equivalent is precisely what they are looking for (cf. Moulin, below).   In decoding tasks, the reasons are more complex.   When we tend to prefer one type to another in a situation like this, it is probably because we find it quicker and easier to use.   The advantage of the bilingual dictionary in terms of rapidity can be explained, however lamely, by the fact that it generally gives one word (an L1 equivalent) whereas the monolingual dictionary provides a sentence (a definition).   But how can one say it is easier?   No psychologist can tell us what happens in learners' minds when they come across lexical units in the L2 that they have never encountered before.   One can only formulate a hypothesis: learners tend to assume that the lexicon of the mother tongue reflects a fixed categorization of reality, and that consequently every lexical unit in the L2 has an equivalent in the L1 (Lyons 1977, Meara 1983, Snell-Hornby, this volume).   To put it differently, when a student comes across an unknown lexical form in the L2, he assumes that it corresponds to a sense that he already knows. Hence the tendency to turn to the bilingual dictionary to find merely a form in the L1, by-passing the question of the content of both lexical units.

This assumption is, of course, wrong in the following cases (among others):

(1) when comparable items in the two languages belong to different semantic networks (i.e. are what Zgusta (1971) calls "anisomorphous"). Consider, for example, Eng *solicitor, barrister* and Fr *avocat, avoué notaire;*

(2) with common, highly polysemous words (for example, Eng *get, hand, green,* etc.), whose extension is so rich and complicated that there are many equivalents in the L1 according to the contexts in which they occur;

(3) when the student does not know the referent at all, and consequently not even the item in the L1.

In all these cases, the bilingual dictionary is more or less inadequate. In (3), it can do nothing at all to help the learner. In (1), it can add a gloss to explain what the L2 item means in the context of the foreign culture (in fact, it does so very often and, some would say, better than the monolingual dictionary, since it can contrast L1 and L2). But it cannot give an equivalent. In (2), it can provide translations of example phrases or even sentences rather than simply of individual words, but here again experience shows that students sometimes find it difficult to recognize that it is impossible to provide an equivalent for the headword in every context in which it could occur.

Of course, the fact that the bilingual dictionary is sometimes an inadequate tool does not automatically mean that the monolingual dictionary is ideally suited to decoding an L2 text. But to throw further light on the problem, one must ask what lexical competence is, and how it is acquired.

3.   The dictionary and the acquisition of lexical competence

Lexical competence can be defined as the ability to associate forms and referents. In foreign language learning, the conceptual framework is already "there", and we do not know what happens to L2 lexemes (Tomaszczyk, this volume). Broadly speaking, there are two possibilities: either they join the pre-existing conceptual framework, thus creating "an association not of two elements, but of

three: an L2 form joined to a complete L1 sign (form + content)"
(Cherchi 1985:39). In that hypothesis, what happens to the cases
mentioned in (1) above remains a mystery. Alternatively, the L2
items form a second framework, stored elsewhere and accessed separately. What evidence we have is inconclusive. Even research
on bilingualism does not seem to be able to give a definite answer.
Le Dorze and Nespoulos, among others, suggest that the second hypothesis is to be taken seriously, but can by no means be considered
proven:

> "Miller and Johnson-Laird's model make us wonder, considering the processes
> of translation, whether there is a separate semantic representation for each
> of the two languages or whether there is only one semantic organization to
> which two sets of lexical units (L1 and L2) are attached. The data we have
> at our disposal does not allow us to answer that question. However, since
> two languages rarely analyze human experience in completely identical ways,
> it is perhaps more logical to suppose that the semantic representations of
> two different languages are distinct." (1984:78)

All this is extremely relevant for lexicographers and language
teachers. If we could prove that one theory is right and the other
wrong, we could understand rather better how dictionaries help the
student, while our advice as to which dictionaries to use and how to
use them would rest on sounder foundations.

However, the issue is complicated by additional factors. (For
a survey of relevant research, see Meara 1983). The mode of storage
of the foreign lexis in the brain, and access to it, may vary with
the age of the learner, with his or her level of proficiency in the
L1 and the L2; and it may vary with different types of lexical unit.
Furthermore, it may be possible to modify what happens in the learner's brain by changing the mode of introduction to new vocabulary.
This has been one of the major preoccupations of foreign language
teaching for the past decades. Cherchi claims that it is possible
to by-pass the direct association of L2 to L1 forms by "using objects
or representations of objects ... or by modifying the signifié: if
one evokes a red double-decker, a strangely green pea, a table laid
for breakfast in an English home, one can hope that only the signifi-
ants *bus, pea, breakfast* will stick to those signifiés" (1985:39).

A further question that is particularly intriguing, and very
important if one wants to understand better how dictionaries help
the learner, is what role can be played by L2 metalanguage in the

teaching and acquisition of L2 lexis.

4.   The role of metalanguage

Metalanguage plays a part in the early development of native language lexical competence, as witness such questions as "Mummy, what's a reptile?"   One notes that metalanguage is only present in the acquisition of the more infrequent words;   a question like "Mummy, what's a cat?" would indicate something unusual in the child's background.   Apart from those cases, most lexical units in the L1 are acquired "linguistically", that is by being met and interpreted in stretches of discourse.   In foreign language learning, especially in the early stages, most words are also acquired linguistically.   For more advanced learners, metalanguage is present when it occurs naturally in a text and when, needing help in decoding, the student turns to a dictionary (or to a teacher, for whom the use of metalanguage is a possible way of dealing with the difficulty).   What happens then is not fully understood.   User surveys have shown that learners are often dissatisfied with L2 definitions, finding them either too simple or too complex (Béjoint 1981:217, Galisson 1983:56).   Observation of students using monolingual dictionaries confirms that they do indeed find definitions difficult to process, even though they usually somehow manage to understand.   But after that stage, one may wonder whether the definition is internalized and stored in the reader's mind as a set of semantic features corresponding to the form in the L2.   (If such was the case, we could say that metalanguage was one way to by-pass the association of an L2 with an L1 form, and a much stronger case could be made out for the monolingual dictionary.)

Or, alternatively, does the L2 definition not merely send the learner "back" to an item in the L1 that most closely corresponds to the referent described?   Thus, to quote an example used by Wiegand (1984), a French learner of English hearing or reading the definition of Eng *barracks* as "a set of buildings used for the permanent housing of troops" will switch very quickly to *caserne*, perhaps even before finishing the definition. Observation shows this to be a very common process.

5. Conclusions

What conclusions can be drawn from this brief survey? Clearly, that bilingual dictionaries are ideal for quick consultation in many cases, and that monolingual dictionaries, though more difficult to use, have the extra merit of introducing the user right into the lexical system of the L2 (Tomaszczyk 1981:291), thereby contributing to the development of lexical competence - provided, of course that definitions are clearly, precisely and fully written (Jain 1981). Students have to be convinced, however, that frequent and careful consultation of the dictionary can lead to a better command of the language. Evidence that students still need to be convinced is provided by Galisson's study. When asked which function the dictionary serves best, the students answered as follows: learning 47%, decoding 43%, encoding 15%. When asked to define the word *dictionary*, though, they mentioned only decoding and encoding, not learning (Galisson 1983:71-83). The difference in the responses is no doubt due to the fact that in the first question "learning" was offered to the students as a possible answer; in the second, they were given no cues, and the crucial additional function does not seem to have occurred to them.

In addition, of course, students are ignorant of the important differences between their bilingual and monolingual dictionaries that this part of our paper has attempted to elucidate. They must therefore be shown the limits and weaknesses of particular dictionaries and of the major types. This represents a formidable task for the teacher wishing to improve the consultation skills of his students. This is why we believe that teachers would appreciate the help which could be provided by a well-designed students' handbook.

Part II   (André Moulin)

THE DICTIONARY AND ENCODING TASKS

1. Introduction

   While the first part of our contribution endeavoured to define
the scope of our project and explain its rationale, the second part
will deal in some detail with a particular and often neglected type
of dictionary-use situation: encoding a message.   It will also
examine what kind of advice a guidebook could offer to help the
dictionary-user cope with different cases.

   Although encoding an *aural* message in a foreign language -finding
the syntactic patterns, words and phrases necessary to embody it-
can be a particularly complex operation, the very circumstances
under which it takes place are such that they seldom allow any consultation of the dictionary.   If we turn our attention to the encoding of a *written* message, we have to take another type of difficulty into account: whereas the average individual seems to possess an innate capacity to express himself orally, and naturally
tends to use and develop it, the writing skill, even in the mother
tongue, is only acquired through conscious, deliberate and sustained
effort.

   Teaching the EFL learner how to solve the numerous problems associated with writing in a foreign language is beyond the scope of the
present paper.   It is however our contention that (a) knowing when
and how to use the dictionary is a major asset when it comes to
developing the writing skill; (b) this kind of knowledge can and
should be taught as an integral part of the curriculum (cf. Herbst
and Stein, this volume).   Incidentally, one of the reasons why so
many learners never use the dictionary -or use it wrongly- for writing tasks is simply that they have not received the right prepara-
tion.   We are by no means trying to minimize the difficulties.   We
realize that once he tries to articulate his discourse, to select
the proper level of formality, etc, the learner very rapidly comes
up against the limitations of the dictionary.   Although trying to
lay down strict rules concerning dictionary consultation would be
absurd, we think a few suggestions can be made.

Writing should precede dictionary consultation. In other words, the result will be better if the learner first tries to express his thoughts by using the words and phrases which come spontaneously to mind, probably because they are part of what is often called his active vocabulary. This will enable him to concentrate on such crucial matters as global meaning and discourse structure. When, at a later stage, the author re-reads his first draft and examines it critically, dictionary consultation will naturally fit into the process of reorganization and more particularly of clarification and correction. Unfortunately, although the dictionary may supply valuable information concerning the various dimensions of words, phrases and possibly -via the verb patterns and examples- of clauses, it will provide very little help when it comes to improving the logical or stylistic coherence of a sentence or paragraph, let alone of the whole discourse: the author will have to receive specific training in the writing skill (with all the related sub-skills this requires).

The moment has come to say a few words concerning that type of exercise which the French call "thème" -translation from the mother tongue into the foreign language. Confronted with a text written in his mother tongue but by someone else, the learner must, before attempting to render it in the target language, make sure he understands the full meaning of the original. We thus have two operations here: decoding (i.e. interpreting in the source language, in this case the learner's mother tongue) and encoding (in the target language). Incidentally, this transfer from one language into another often brings to light the ambiguities -or the richness- of the original. The translator's art consists in rendering this original richness without depreciating or possibly overvaluing it. The teacher's art consists in choosing a source text adapted to his students' proficiency in both decoding and encoding. He should also draw their attention to the specific difficulties and hazards of the task: word-for-word translation, for instance, is probably one of the worst ways of using a dictionary.

Equally injudicious is the attempt to replace writing by translating. This can take several forms. The beginner finds writing directly in English too difficult, writes in his mother tongue instead and then tries to translate into English a text which is far above his capacities. Perhaps not so surprisingly, the same attitude can be found among more advanced learners, who assume that the dictionary's richness will compensate for the indigence of their written English or conceal their lack of imagination or their reluctance to make the necessary efforts of concentration.

Let us now examine various situations in which dictionary consultation may help the writer of a text, whether he works directly in English or translates from his mother tongue.

2. Difficulties with single words

2.1. Uncertainty over the exact meaning of a word

When the French learner thinks he knows the word to be used but is not quite sure whether it is correct, he can of course consult the English-French part of his bilingual dictionary or turn directly to an explaining (learner's, concise or standard) dictionary. If he wants to be absolutely sure that his choice is not only correct, but appropriate or even felicitous, or if he wants to avoid repetition he can turn to a dictionary of synonyms. If he "knows" what the right word is but simply has difficulty in remembering it, consulting first a *synonym-finder* may be the most efficient -and economical- way of jogging his memory. Having found the elusive term, he can double-check by returning to his translating or explaining dictionary. As his familiarity with the foreign language increases, he will turn more and more to an explaining rather than to a translating dictionary. Similarly, he will feel a need for ever greater accuracy and probably make a habit of consulting a standard rather than a concise monolingual dictionary.

2.2. Unknown English words

While writing an English sentence, the learner is stopped in his tracks by a gap in his vocabulary -an English word he does not know. Racking his brain produces nothing except a native-tongue concept or item. Actually, the latter may turn out to be the ideal starting-point for a word search. Take for instance the following incomplete sentence produced by a French writer: *While writing an English sentence, the learner ... a difficulty.* Looking for the right completion, all the French writer can think of is *rencontrer, buter sur, achopper sur une difficulté.* As he personally prefers *buter sur,* he

decides to look up the phrase in his French-English dictionary
(e.g. the *Collins-Robert French Dictionary*). Although *buter* has
several senses, selecting the right one is easy because the phrase
buter sur une difficulté is mentioned and even rendered by two equivalents: *to come up against a difficulty, hit a snag**. The former equivalent seems semantically adequate and syntactically very convenient:
the learner only has to insert *comes up against* into the empty slot.
The asterisk after *snag* is a warning to the user: this is a rather
informal item. Needless to say the importance of this stylistic
marker will be obvious to the user if and only if he has been warn-
ed about stylistic factors.

How can he check the validity of his choice? (a) By examining
carefully the examples supplied for the sense in question; (b) by
looking up in the English-French part of his bilingual dictionary
the equivalent he has chosen; (c) by consulting a monolingual
dictionary. In the present case, procedure (a) is already very
informative, as the whole phrase is translated. If the learner
wants to dig a little deeper (which he should be encouraged to do
as often as possible) he can apply procedure (b) to the second
equivalent, *snag*. This will confirm that the phrase *to hit a snag*
(alternatively, *to run into a snag*) does exist and belongs to a rather
familiar style (hence the French rendering: *tomber sur un os*/sur un
bec**). Procedure (c) requires consultation of a learner's dictionary. *The Oxford Advanced Learner's Dictionary (OALDCE)* gives the
following explanation:

> snag ... 2 (colloq): hidden, unknown or unexpected difficulty
> or obstacle: *strike/come upon a snag*. *There is a snag in it
> somewhere.*

The Longman Dictionary of Contemporary English (LDOCE) explains the meaning of *snag* but provides neither a stylistic label nor an example
sentence.

2.3. Handling idioms

The preceding section has already illustrated some of the syntactic and stylistic problems posed by idioms. (Note again: *run into
a snag*). Let us now examine more closely the steps which the
writer is likely to take when, looking for the best way to express
an idea, he remembers (or finds in his translating dictionary) an

idiomatic phrase.   First, he may have to check the idiom's exact
make-up by looking up what he considers to be the key word.   Dictionaries like the *Oxford Dictionary of Current Idiomatic English (ODCIE)*
provide an index which lists the verbs, adverbs, nouns, etc., which
appear in the headphrases contained in it.   This is a great help
for learners whose memories tend to play tricks on them.

Then the user will verify the meaning of the idiom and make sure
it really corresponds to what he wants to say.   This should be
done with care, as idioms often express delicate shades of meaning,
may be entirely fixed in form (so that changing or leaving out just
one word may prove fatal) and tend to be stylistically marked (see
above).   Next comes the problem of knowing how to handle the idiom.
Learners' dictionaries may help with the syntax but at this juncture
a dictionary such as *ODCIE* will again prove to be a far more sophisticated tool.   Not only does it provide indications of the words
which collocate with a given idiom, but it also explains in detail
the several transformations which a particular idiom can or cannot
undergo (emphatic, relative, passive, etc., transforms).   Again,
to be able to make the most of this information, the user must have
been made aware of these grammatical problems.   This can be done
in simple terms (see e.g. the Introduction to *ODCIE*, Vol. 1).

3.   Difficulty with sentences

Suppose the learner wants to render the idea expressed by the
French sentence: *Que voulez-vous que je fasse?*   The verb *to want*
immediately comes to mind and, associated with it, a vague memory
that, syntactically speaking, this is a tricky customer.   Incidentally, the learner may also ask himself how he is to render this
French subjunctive.   If he consults a translating dictionary,
several examples under the entry *vouloir* are likely to put him on the
right track:

vouloir que qn fasse/qch se fasse to want sb to do/sth to be done

il ne veut pas qu'elle y aille he doesn't want her to go

Learners' dictionaries will confirm that in this case *want* requires
a particular syntactic pattern (VP17 in *OALDCE*; V3 in *LDOCE*).

We realize that we may seem to be equating the correctness of compound and complex sentences with the syntactic acceptability of simple (one-clause) sentences. Although dictionaries may provide, e.g. in the entries for subordinating conjunctions, interesting information concerning the various types of compound sentence, we think that the ideal place to discuss such complex problems is a grammar or even a handbook on writing. On the other hand, contact with secondary-school teachers during in-service refresher courses confirms that most of them never use the simple and yet detailed syntactic information offered by learners' dictionaries and consequently never tell their pupils about it. We therefore think that a guide that could persuade both teachers and learners to draw on this rich syntactic information would already achieve a great deal.

At this juncture, the learner who has been made aware of all the aspects of the problem of encoding may remember that he must also think of stylistic appropriacy. He may remember -or find in a dictionary of synonyms- other possible exponents of the notion he is trying to express. What about using *wish* as distinct from *require* or *demand*? In *LDOCE* (in the entry for *wish*, 5) he will find the label *polite* associated with an example such as: *Do you wish me to come back later?* Perhaps this corresponds best to the level of formality he requires, particularly if he intends to use the sentence in writing.

Finally, let us say a few words about the problem of pragmatic adequacy. To take an example from the field of LSP we can turn our attention to the difficulties encountered by numerous non-English speaking scientific authors writing articles or papers in English. Most of them know a few set phrases traditionally used to introduce a paper or draw conclusions but are rather at a loss when it comes to conceding a minor point or raising an objection in nuanced terms. Can the dictionary help them? Again, the translating dictionary may be able to do so provided that (a) the rhetorical function exists in both languages and (b) it is realized by comparable linguistic means. Take the French sentence: *"Ce phénomène est certes un cas isolé. Néanmoins, on peut se demander si ..."*. The *Collins-Robert* entry reads:

certes ... *adv* (a) *(de concession) (sans doute):* certainly, admittedly

Il est certes le plus fort, mais ... he is admittedly *ou* certainly the strongest, but ...

Although this entry says nothing about the subtle nuances which the choice of either *certainly* or *admittedly* can introduce (not even the best monolingual dictionary goes that far), this remains a fairly easy problem: in his translation the scientific author can keep the same syntactic pattern as in French and render the adverb *certes* through its equivalent: *This phenomenon is, admittedly, an isolated case.* More often than not, though, the dictionary will provide no help. Start from the sentence: *Il est plutôt décevant de constater que l'auteur ne dit mot du problème.* The French scientific author can of course translate almost word for word and will probably be understood. The chances are, however, that no dictionary will suggest the more idiomatic form which a native writer would, in such a case, probably use instinctively: *The author, rather disappointingly, says nothing about ... .* In fact *Collins-Robert* does not list this attitudinal disjunct. *LDOCE* and *Webster's Third* mention it but provide neither definition nor explanation. Given the usefulness of attitudinal disjuncts to signal certain rhetorical functions it seems to us that they should be (a) studied in any course concerned with writing scientific English and (b) dealt with very explicitly in both translating and explaining dictionaries. This brings us back to our main theme: the dictionary consulting skill should be taught and integrated into the normal EFL program. While on the subject, we may also add that too many dictionaries are rather anaemic when it comes to illustrating or explaining rhetorical functions.

4. Difficulties with particular types of discourse

Let us suppose that a Frenchman wants to write a letter in English. If he has not been prepared for this kind of exercise, the best thing he can do is quite frankly to consult a bilingual (and later possibly an English monolingual) guide to or handbook of correspondence. This will provide him with model letters and traditional phrases and formulas adapted to different needs and circumstances (commercial dealings, social life, etc.) and will remind him to take into account such aspects as the genre (letter, telegram, etc.) or level of formality.

.Let us now suppose that the learner does not have access to this kind of reference work. Again he will probably try to start from his mother tongue experience and find equivalents for traditional salutations and complimentary closes such as: *Monsieur, ... J'ai l'honneur de ... Veuillez agréer, Monsieur, l'expression de mes sentiments ...*

Already the salutation looks deceptively easy. In English you do not normally begin a letter with *Sir* but with *Dear Sir*. A translating dictionary such as *Collins-Robert* will supply this information, provided the user takes the trouble to run through the *monsieur* entry until he reaches sense (d), which will tell him all he needs to know concerning formality:

(d) *(en-tête de lettre) Monsieur (gén)* Dear Sir; *(personne connue)* Dear Mr. X;

The *honneur* entry reads:

(c) *(Admin: formule épistolaire) J'ai l'honneur de vous informer que ...* I am writing to inform you that, I beg to inform you that *(formal) ...*

Provided one knows where to look, it is also possible to find the right formula by consulting a monolingual dictionary. In the *honour* entry, *OALDCE* suggests 3 ... *I have the honour to inform you that* ... but does not say anything about formality. In a very interesting appendix called "A Handbook of Style", *Webster's New Collegiate Dictionary* gives quite useful technical details about style in business correspondence but provides no examples.

The above remarks are in no way meant to put off the potential dictionary user but simply to teach him the virtues of prudence and discrimination. Our example illustrates the nature of the help which a dictionary can provide for the writer. It also makes apparent the dictionary's limitations when it comes to producing written discourse: as already indicated, grammatical, stylistic and pragmatic cohesion remain under the entire responsibility of the writer. The example in fact illustrates a very small proportion of the difficulties encountered by the producer of written discourse. The salutation and complimentary close of a fairly formal letter have been codified by usage; but the more original the style and content of the discourse the more difficult is it for the author (or translator) to use the dictionary profitably.

Delisle (1980:62) remarks that a translator may very well string together in impeccable syntactic order lexemes or syntagms which are perfect equivalents of their source language counterparts and nevertheless end up with a target text which is unacceptable because it sounds unnatural, is unidiomatic, etc. While re-reading and re-writing his first draft, the experienced translator will very often try to ignore the formulations (not the meaning) of the original. Parenthetically, he may, while re-writing his draft, again consult a monolingual dictionary or a dictionary of synonyms -as he might do if he was writing directly in the target language or, mutatis mutandis, in his mother tongue. What the translator is in fact aiming for is discourse equivalence, which often has little to do with outward discourse resemblance or parallelism. This explains why it is so much more difficult to assess the faithfulness of a whole chunk of translated discourse than to establish the accuracy of the translation of separate lexical items in relation to their immediate context.

I may appear to have cut the ground from under my lexicographic feet. Although the words found in the dictionary may not be the exact ones the author will finally keep, dictionary consultation, provided it is integrated within the whole language learning approach, remains nevertheless the safest way of making sure that the writer at least gets his word senses right. It is only when he reaches the level of the sentence or paragraph and encounters complex syntactic, stylistic or pragmatic problems that he comes up against the limitations of the dictionary. Those considerations cannot be taken as an excuse to skip those stages of the writing process where dictionaries, when used discriminatingly, prove to be such informative and reliable guides.

It is precisely this intelligent use that we would like to develop and make more widespread. We hope we have made it abundantly clear that to achieve this aim at least two conditions must be met:

- intelligent dictionary consultation needs to be taught and integrated in the FL program (cf. Herbst and Stein, this volume);
- the development of this skill requires that learners be made aware of the existence and nature of various linguistic problems

(transformational potential, style and cultural differences - among others).   This can and should be achieved by using simple words (a minimum of specialist terms but no jargon) and simple examples.

As we both believe in early skills development, we think that linguistic awareness and skill in (monolingual) dictionary consultation should first be developed in relation to the learning of the mother tongue at primary school level.   This would not only facilitate the task of the FL teacher but, more importantly, enable him to build on a much firmer foundation.

Thomas Herbst and Gabriele Stein

DICTIONARY-USING SKILLS:
A PLEA FOR A NEW ORIENTATION IN LANGUAGE TEACHING

1. Introduction

   Research in various countries into the use of monolingual English
learners' dictionaries has shown quite clearly that the majority of
school pupils and university students are not able to make full use
of the different types of information which those dictionaries provide.[1] In view of the considerable progress that has been made in
recent years with regard to layout, presentation of information,
transparency of codes etc., especially in learners' dictionaries of
English, it would be entirely unjustified to put all the blame on
the dictionaries, although there is certainly room for further improvement.   The problem appears to be, rather, that successful use
of EFL dictionaries such as the *Oxford Advanced Learner's Dictionary*
(OALDCE) or the *Longman Dictionary of Contemporary English (LDOCE)* presupposes
a specific competence because of the wide range of information they
contain, and that students lack this competence.   Tests with advanced students of English at the University of Hamburg have shown
that the situation is similar for bilingual English-German, German-
English dictionaries.   Though the students were used to consulting
bilingual dictionaries, they were - sad to say - totally uniformed
about the bilingual English-German, German-English dictionary market,
and quite unaware of the fact that the particular dictionary they
were using was either completely outdated or so small in coverage
that it could not meet their encoding and decoding language needs.
A bilingual dictionary presupposes a different competence from that
needed to consult a monolingual learner's dictionary, just as a
non-alphabetical dictionary, such as Roget's *Thesaurus*, for instance,
requires a different competence again.   In each case competence
consists in making the best possible use of a specific type of dictionary.   We might call the general capacity "dictionary-using

---

[1] See especially Tomaszczyk (1979), Béjoint (1981), Heath and Herbst (1985),
    and cf. Hartmann (this volume - ed.).

competence". Dictionaries are reference books and any reference system requires its users to apply specific reference skills. These need to be learnt and mastered by repeated and constant exercise. Otherwise they will not be remembered and will have to be reactivated or relearnt. The same principle holds for what we might term "dictionary-using skills" or "dictionary reference skills".

It is clear also that these skills must be implanted by deliberate teaching, and where else, or where better, than in language classes at school or university? Let us therefore look at the role played by the dictionary in these two educational institutions. Since we have both gone through the educational system in the Federal Republic of Germany and are both now teachers at German universities our brief account is based on personal experience.

2. The dictionary in universities and schools in the Federal Republic of Germany

2.1. The situation in university language departments

Future foreign language teachers in the Federal Republic, as state civil servants, have to complete two courses. They have to graduate in the language(s) of their choice at university, and they then have to follow a teacher training course with a strong pedagogical orientation.

In recent years, quite a number of much-needed changes have taken place, leading to better overall professional qualifications and greater staff flexibility within the university system in the Federal Republic. Bearing these developments in mind we would characterize a typical foreign language department in a German university as follows. The in-service teaching staff is both native and non-native. The subject fields to be taught and the weekly teaching load depend on the specific language background and the actual position held. The usual job description for native speakers of German is that they have to teach either the literature of the foreign language in question or linguistics. Non-native speakers, on the other hand, are usually expected to give practical language courses in their mother tongue. English staff in an English department in Germany will thus teach English because

they are assumed to know their mother tongue better than native
speakers of German.   Until some ten or fifteen years ago, the
non-native staff of English departments, according to German
university tradition, were recruited from foreign students or
graduates in German who wished to improve their knowledge of
German in the country itself.   Foreign students of German did not
typically possess a qualification to teach English nor indeed any
training in linguistics or applied linguistics, since those subjects were not normally part of courses in German at British universities.[2]   Such students turned teachers therefore had to fall
back on memories of their own school days and the teaching they had
received in their mother tongue.   They would not have had any training in dictionary use in their English classes because teaching of
the mother tongue in British schools rarely includes instruction
and practice in how to use a dictionary.   For obvious reasons it
has always been assumed that native speakers know their mother
tongue.   The same holds for the teaching of German in Germany, and
as many colleagues from Holland and France assure us, for mother-
tongue teaching in those countries also.   An Englishman teaching
English at a German university, with no professional qualification
in teaching English as a foreign language, will even now seldom
have more than a superficial knowledge of such monolingual English
dictionaries as the *Concise Oxford Dictionary*, the *Chambers 20th Century
Dictionary* or the *Collins English Dictionary*.   He will have had some
experience and practice in using a bilingual English-German, German-
English dictionary, but he may never have heard of such monolingual
learners' dictionaries as the *OALDCE* and *LDOCE*.   He will thus not be
in a position to teach German students how to use dictionaries which
have been compiled especially for foreign students of English.
The practical language courses traditionally given by non-native
staff at German universities thus do not include the substantial
dictionary education component so urgently needed in foreign
language teaching.

   Although some universities still appoint as lektors students of

---

2 Some British universities (including Bradford, Leeds and Oxford) now offer
   modern language programmes which include, or can be combined with, courses
   in modern linguistics.

German who have just graduated at a British university, the situation is changing gradually. In many university foreign language departments there is nowadays a requirement that foreigners must have a qualification to teach their mother tongue if they are to find employment at a German university. On the whole, the role of the lektor in Germany (as compared with that of his opposite number in language departments in Britain) is no longer seen as that of a native speaker who - simply by virtue of that fact - can hold conversation classes and provide "first-hand" information about his country. On the contrary, the job of lektor is increasingly regarded as that of a highly professional language teacher. This welcome change does not, however, seem to have resulted in the teaching of dictionary use becoming an integral part of language courses at university.

Let us now turn to the native staff in a foreign language department, and especially those with an interest in linguistics. For their own research these teachers all rely, often quite heavily, on dictionaries of the foreign language whether monolingual or bilingual. They use them as valuable, indispensable linguistic tools, but they would not think of teaching their students how to use them to their best advantage. They usually have not had any longer-term instruction in how to use a dictionary because of the widespread traditional neglect of dictionary education. Moreover, they feel little urge to teach something that they themselves were not taught and thus something that apparently does not constitute a basic component of foreign language teaching. They therefore expect their students to acquire dictionary reference skills on their own while working at home - much as they themselves did many years previously. In addition, they may assume that these skills fall within the domain of colleagues who teach the practical language courses, for they themselves are concerned with linguistic issues and the associated teaching problems. With the exception of a few dictionary addicts, an exception which confirms the rule, they will not offer courses on lexicography or dictionary use. This situation is undoubtedly also related to the present state of linguistic theory and research. Lexicography has only recently started to attract the attention of linguists. It does not yet figure in those textbooks that are commonly used for introductory

courses in linguistics.[3]   It goes without saying, however, that
a chapter on dictionaries should become as traditional and normal
a feature of such books as chapters on phonetics/phonology, syntax
or semantics.

With respect to the teaching of dictionary reference skills
then, the prospect facing future foreign language teachers at
universities in the Federal Republic is anything but encouraging.

2.2.   The dictionary in schools

What role does the dictionary play in the classroom in German
schools?   Judging from enquiries conducted among teachers and
students with experience of English teaching in *Gymnasien* in
Bavaria, it seems reasonable to describe the current position in
schools as follows:[4]

(1) When the monolingual English dictionary is first introduced in
class, this is accompanied by a systematic initial treatment of
dictionary-using skills.   However, on average, no more than two
to three lessons are devoted to the dictionary at this stage.

(2) In most cases this introduction is the only experience of the
systematic teaching of dictionary-using skills which students have.
Some teachers practise the use of the dictionary regularly after
this phase, but this seems to be exceptional.   Often the dictionary is discussed in connection with texts or student errors which
could have been avoided by consulting a dictionary.   According to
students' statements, however, many teachers simply refer them to
the dictionary at such times rather than explaining in detail how
the information could actually have been retrieved.

(3) As far as the major types of dictionary use are concerned, it
is the value of the dictionary as an instrument for decoding that
tends to be emphasized rather than its usefulness in encoding.
More importance is attached to meanings and idioms than to infor-

---

3 There is, for example, only limited coverage in Bolinger (1968) and Dineen
   (1967).
4 These generalisations are based on a large number of conversations with teachers and students about dictionary use at school, and on replies to questionnaires distributed to 71 first-year students of English at Augsburg University,
   to 23 English teachers at a teacher training seminar at the Dillingen Teachers'
   Academy of Further Training and to 37 English teachers at Bavarian *Gymnasien*.

mation on syntax, and there too it seems that example sentences and prepositions in bold type[5] are given more attention than verb patterns or other codes (such as C or U). This means that more emphasis is put on the teaching of the less difficult reference skills.

(4) Most teachers seem rather sceptical about their students' ability to use the dictionary appropriately. It is interesting to note, however, that many teachers do not blame this supposed inability on the quality of the dictionaries but attribute it to laziness or a general lack of interest on the part of the students.

Scepticism about the value of teaching dictionary-using skills at school may be justified. It is significant that in a survey carried out amongst 160 students at the universities of Augsburg and Erlangen-Nürnberg only 70 knew that the *OALDCE* (which is the dictionary they used at school) contained syntactic information in the form of verb patterns and of these only 26 stated that they had actually learnt this information at school.

One of the main barriers to the learning of dictionary-using skills at school seems to be the limited amount of time spent on the teaching of those skills. It is difficult to imagine the teaching of a grammatical problem such as the use of the past tense and the present perfect in English, which is hardly more complex than the mastering of the full range of dictionary-using skills, being restricted to two or three lessons of explanations and occasional hints thereafter. If only limited time is spent on the dictionary, then this is a clear indication that it is seen as playing only a marginal role in foreign language teaching.

This general attitude is also reflected in the English curricula of the German *Bundesländer*, which while at least explicitly mentioning the appropriate use of the dictionary as a teaching objective, often do so in such very general terms as "the proper use of works of reference".[6] Considering the backwash effect of examinations on teaching it is also significant that dictionary-using skills as

---

5 i.e. prepositions which, with their objects, function as complements after verbs, adjectives or nouns (Herbst 1984a).
6 For a detailed discussion of these curricula, see Heath and Herbst (1985).

such do not form part of examinations.   Although it is encouraging
that the regulations for the final state school examination *(Abitur-
prüfung)* in all German *Länder* permit the use of a dictionary, it is
merely seen as an instrument for tackling particular problems of
the language in such examinations.   While this is of course precisely the normal role of the dictionary, it could be argued that
in school the various possible uses of the dictionary ought to be
tested in order to force the student to acquire the full range of
dictionary-using skills (and also to oblige the teacher to teach
and practise them).

3.   The relation to trends in language teaching

Other problems are closely tied to present-day attitudes and
fashions in language teaching.   We shall highlight the following:

(1) The view is still widely held and propagated that communication
in the limited sense of getting one's message across is in itself
an adequate linguistic achievement.   A corollary of this approach
is the overemphasis on speaking to the detriment of writing.
Semantic precision, situational appropriateness and grammatical
correctness have all too often and too readily been set aside and
even discredited.   The result of much "communicative" teaching
has been a rather superficial language knowledge rather than a
sound and consciously internalized language command.   Why consult
a dictionary to find the appropriate item, one might ask, if a
vague message suffices for one's interlocutor to guess the meaning
from the context of situation?   It thus seems that much of the
present-day emphasis in foreign language teaching not only discourages dictionary training but actually runs counter to it.

(2) Such superficially acquired language knowledge represents a
danger if it is not recognized as such.   A survey of essays written
for the *Schülerwettbewerb Fremdsprachen* (a junior linguists' competi-
tion) has revealed that some 30% of the mistakes made could have
been avoided through appropriate use of a dictionary.   Some of
these mistakes, especially at the levels of orthography and word
formation (e.g. *pattern pupil*, *criminal novel* or *right consciousness)*, can
probably be explained by the fact that students saw no need to look
anything up.   This false sense of security, the misleading feeling

of "knowing the language", may at least partly have been caused by
a teaching methodology based on the so-called communicative approach (Herbst forthcoming).   Without wishing to question the
merits of this approach, it seems important in view of the large
number of such errors that students should also develop a feeling
for possible mistakes in order to know when they should consult a
dictionary.   Swan (1985:81), in a critical appraisal of the communicative approach, remarks: "Students not only have to learn
how information is conveyed or elicited, or how requests are made;
they also have to learn the words and expressions which are used
to refer to the things in the world they want to talk about, ask
about or request."   From the lexicographer's point of view one
might add that they also have to learn where to find information
about these words.

(3) Another, more respectable, attitude is that it is sometimes
better for the student to solve linguistic problems without consulting a dictionary.   Using a dictionary is often seen as "not
knowing something" and finding the solution to a problem in this
way is regarded as "second best".   For certain study purposes,
indeed - skimming or scanning a text - it may not be necessary to
have a full understanding of the individual words, and constant
use of the dictionary may be an actual hindrance (Kruse 1979).
While this is undoubtedly true, it is equally true that for purposes of accurate *encoding* (i.e. writing in, or translating into,
the foreign language) the dictionary is indispensable.   It is also
true that in many cases where foreign languages are used outside
school (e.g. in commerce or industry) reference to dictionaries is
unavoidable.   It would be illusory to suppose that schools could
achieve the standard of near-nativeness in their teaching of foreign
languages that would enable people to write business letters or
read articles on technical or scientific subjects without consulting dictionaries.   Thus the dictionary will no doubt continue to
be referred to in many situations where the foreign language is
being used for a practical purpose.

(4) A very important additional factor in the German context is the
teaching of the mother tongue.   Many years' experience of teaching
and testing leave us in no doubt that a great number of German

students of English - that is language students - have a very poor
knowledge of grammar. They are not familiar with basic grammatical
terms, not even the most traditional ones, and they cannot analyse
simple sentences of the types *Sie ist in der Küche*, *Er ist Lehrer*. One
has the impression that students have never acquired the rudiments
of grammar, either in the foreign language they are being taught, or
in the mother tongue they learnt much earlier. Learners' dictionaries such as the *OALDCE* and *LDOCE* are and will be wasted on pupils
and students who do not have even a basic framework of grammatical
knowledge.

4. The need for a new orientation

What all these points bring home is that we need a new orientation in language teaching. This reorientation should start with
more in-depth teaching of the mother tongue. The better the language teaching in the mother tongue, the better the preparation of
the linguistic ground for foreign language teaching. This holds
for grammar as well as dictionary-using skills. Teaching objectives in foreign language teaching should not be solely oriented
to the ideal of native-speaker-like competence nor be defined as a
more or less degenerate form of full native-speaker competence.
They should reflect the situations in which foreign learners use
the language and be defined on the basis of the skills required
of them there, realistically taking account of limits to the L2-
competence of the learners. With regard to the spoken language,
this approach means that students will have to be prepared for
situations in which they do not understand their interlocutors and
will have to acquire the necessary strategies to master such situations (cf. Götz 1984). With respect to the written language it
means that for many purposes competence in the foreign language
should be seen as comprising linguistic skills as well as dictionary-using skills.

It is obviously not enough to keep repeating that there should
be better training in dictionary use at school and university.
The weight of tradition is against us. We will therefore outline
what the functions of dictionary education are and how they fit in
with general educational principles. The ordering of these functions does not imply a hierarchical structure.

4.1. Acquisition of general reference skills

Successful consultation of an alphabetical dictionary presupposes familiarity with

(1) the general introduction (to understand the structural arrangement in the dictionary);

(2) alphabetical order (and its problematic areas, e.g. the place of English *Saint* abbreviated to *St*, or of German umlauts represented as vowel followed by *e* (e.g. *ae*) or as vowel + umlaut (e.g. *ä*));

(3) the function and working of cross-references.

These three components (information on the reference system, its order of arrangement, and its interrelations) are basic to any reference system. A pupil or student who has internalized this abstract structure and acquired these general reference skills by constant practice in one particular area will feel confident to approach, use and master other reference systems. Learning at school or university is always exemplary: it enables us to open up other areas of knowledge by transferring the methods applied in the exemplary case.

Developing general reference skills through the use of dictionaries agrees with this basic tenet of all teaching and will help our students to find their way in a modern world of constantly developing data-banks.

4.2. Development of discriminating faculties and skills

The consultation of a reference system presupposes also that one has isolated and identified for oneself the particular item or area of interest about which one seeks further information. The formulation of one's information needs obliges one constantly to review and check one's own knowledge. The information provided by the reference system, on the other hand, will also have to be assessed for its usefulness. Users have to employ their cognitive faculties and discriminating skills to single out from the information offered the items they need. The use of a reference system such as a dictionary will therefore develop and sharpen the users' discriminating faculties and skills. In doing so, it will prepare the users for, and train them in, one of the main tasks of a teacher: the critical assessment of texts.

4.3. Language achievement control

In all learning there is a very subtle and gradual process of acquisition. There are many phases of insecurity characterized by a kind of half-knowledge before this in turn becomes completely internalized, permanent knowledge. The dictionary is an institution which enables language learners to check their own knowledge, and to eliminate weaknesses in spelling, pronunciation, grammar and meaning. Dictionary education thus provides them with a tool of achievement control. The more effective their handling of this tool, the better their command of the language and the greater their self-confidence. Language learners who are put in the position, and who develop the habit, of checking their personal achievement will become more and more independent. The dictionary is a tool that will wean learners away from the classroom teacher and guide them towards further independent study. Development of, and training in, achievement control skills are not only indispensable for the teaching profession. These skills are needed in the exercise of any profession, as are the two other skills outlined above.

4.4. Guide for self-study and self-education

This function of the dictionary follows from the function discussed in 4.3, control over one's language achievement. The emphasis in 4.3 is on the control of learning matter that has not yet been completely mastered or has been partially forgotten. In recognizing a fourth function, we stress the fact that the dictionary also helps the users to acquire new knowledge, to educate them further. In doing so, it equips the users, again in an exemplary way, for a task that they will be faced by for the whole of their lifetime.

The demand for more dictionary work in the classroom cannot be regarded simply as a plea to add still one more teaching item to the foreign language syllabus, alongside areas of study such as literature or cultural background. It must be seen as an integral part of teaching the language itself - if foreign language teaching at school is to result in the ability to master foreign language situations. Students must learn that if, for example, they are looking for the antonyms of such adjectives as *credible*, *secure* or

just, it is wrong simply to use forms such as **uncredible*, **unsecure*
or **injust* – these are examples from the essays of the *Schülerwett-*
bewerb Fremdsprachen. They must be brought to realize -- especially·
when ignorant of the right word in the foreign language, which in
the material analyzed accounts for a considerable proportion of the
errors – that the bilingual dictionary (used in combination with
a monolingual dictionary) often provides the answer.[7]

An equally important area is that of syntax. Errors such as
*ability at doing, **example for sth* or **advices*, which also occur relatively frequently, could be avoided by making use of the relevant
information provided in learners' dictionaries such as *OALDCE* or
LDOCE. The reference skills needed to gain this information from
the dictionaries can be practised relatively easily in class, as
for instance within the framework of the comprehension exercise
(a common test form at German schools), by setting tasks explicitly
involving the use of a dictionary. Almost any text provides ample
opportunity for questions involving the use of a dictionary. Thus
a text such as the following passage, chosen at random from *The*
Guardian Weekly (November 24, 1985) could be taken as the basis for
questions concerning the two problems mentioned above – antonyms
and syntax:

> " ... The overwhelming response to the agreement on this side of the water
> has been of approval and.encouragement. That is not, as Unionists might
> maintain, because the mainland is unfamiliar with the difficulties of
> ·governing Northern Ireland but because it is all too familiar with them.
> It knows that the province cannot be governed without a degree of national-
> ist consent. One way to secure that consent would have been in a power-
> sharing government. ..."

(1) Find out – with the help of a dictionary – what the antonyms
of the nouns *agreement*, *approval* and *encouragement* are. Which of these
nouns can be used in the plural (with the same meaning as in the
text)? How does your dictionary tell you?

---

7 Obviously, the amount of dictionary work to be done in particular language
classes depends to a considerable extent on the type of course, the type of
learner, etc. The teaching of dictionary-using skills must have consequences for the broader methodology adopted since one important benefit is
an improved insight into the limits of one's own L2-competence; some 40%
of the errors that could have been avoided through the appropriate use of a
dictionary in the essays of the *Schülerwettbewerb* analyzed concern meaning,
collocation and style.

(2) Illustrate all the patterns given in your dictionary for the verb *maintain* when it is used with the same meaning as in the text.

(3) Find out from your dictionary whether *to secure* in 1.6 could be replaced by *of securing*.   How is this indicated in your dictionary?

Similar questions can be set for dictionary-using skills directed at such features as orthography, or geographical or stylistic variants (British/American English, formal/informal, etc.) (cf. Heath and Herbst 1985).[8]   Obviously, such questions should always be designed in such a way that the learners cannot be expected to solve them without the dictionary - otherwise they become pointless. The great advantage of this type of exercise is that while it requires students to learn what kinds of information their dictionaries contain (e.g. verb patterns) and to acquire the appropriate dictionary-using skills, it is not alien to language work proper but an integral part of it.

Thus what is needed to improve the dictionary competence of learners is not so much the development of special methods of teaching dictionary use, as the recognition that for foreign learners competence in dictionary use is part of their wider competence as speakers, readers or writers of the foreign language.

---

8 Obviously, such questions are to a certain extent artificial but this is equally true of other exercises (such as "Find synonyms for ..." or "Paraphrase") used in the comprehension piece.   To emphasize the communicative value of such exercises, students could also be asked to use the words or constructions found in the dictionary when answering questions on the text.

Susan Maingay and Michael Rundell

ANTICIPATING LEARNERS' ERRORS -
IMPLICATIONS FOR DICTIONARY WRITERS

1. Introduction

   Although dictionaries have for some years been rather out of
fashion in the field of English Language Teaching, there now
appears to be a new and growing awareness on the part of teachers
that dictionaries can provide a valuable teaching/learning resource.[1]   Along with this comes a growing need for ELT lexicographers to look closely at the demands made on their dictionaries
and to examine the ways in which these demands can be met.   The
range of uses to which ELT dictionaries are put is very wide.   At
one end of the scale students will look up a new word they have met
in a text in order to confirm a guess or just to get a sufficient
idea of its meaning to be able to read on; at the other end (and
this occurs particularly in writing tasks) they will use a dictionary in order to build up a detailed picture of the meaning and use
of a word.   It is, of course, this end of the scale which presents
the biggest challenge to lexicographers, for it is in this area
that the necessary scope and delicacy of the information contained
in a dictionary entry are both crucial and difficult to achieve.

2. Students' errors and the ELT dictionary

   To get some idea of the type of information students need it is
illuminating to look at examples of students' writing where the
hypotheses they have made about a particular word have let them
down and to attempt some kind of classification of the resulting
errors.   The following examples are drawn from three sources:
the work of Indian students at the Indian Institute of Technology
in New Delhi,[2] essays by Japanese students at the Senior High

---

1 This renewed interest is reflected in recent ELT publications, e.g. Ilson
   (1985).
2 These were from papers kindly supplied by Professor Mahavir Jain of the
   Indian Institute of Technology.

School in Hiroshima, and samples of essays by students who took the Cambridge Proficiency Exam in 1982.[3]

(1) She caught a cold because of her moist socks.

(2) Don't put that old cock and bull story over to me.

(3) She puts on those tears when her wishes are not fulfilled.

(4) You have to be on the alert that a marriage is a living thing.

(5) My mother is fond of gathering stamps.

(6) My mother wants to be a lean woman.

(7) My family is a very joyous group.

(8) All my family are putting on glasses.

(9) He uses false teeth.

(10) I wanna become a novelist of Science Fiction.

(11) My sister will marry a man whom I very hate. The man is very impudent.

(12) My grandmother suggested us to go on a trip.

(13) We found some very cheap and moreover nice rice cakes.

We classified the errors in these sentences using four main categories: semantic, syntactic, collocational, and stylistic. This is of course a fairly crude procedure, partly because some of the sentences exhibit more than one type of problem, but more importantly because our inferences about the writers' intentions may sometimes be entirely wrong. But despite these limitations, it has nevertheless proved a fairly useful method of analysis. (Note that some of the sentences have been assigned to more than one category.)

semantic	1, 5, 6, 8, 9, 10, 11
collocational	1, 2, 5, 6
stylistic	7, 13
syntactic	2, 4, 12

What characterises these errors is not that they are hopelessly· off-target but, on the contrary, that the writers are in each case in very much the right area, but have failed - though only just - to hit the exact spot. And it must be one of the more discour-

---

3 For other analyses of students' errors which have been undertaken to determine how far the ELT dictionary does, or might, help the learner, see Jain (1978, 1981) and Huang (1985).

aging aspects of language-learning that even the nearest of near-
misses has - to the native speaker - a dissonant quality that
immediately marks it down as an "error".   The reasons for these
failures are no doubt very complex, but it is probably a reasonable generalisation to say that when advanced learners select the
"wrong" word it is usually because they have *some* information
about it, but not as much as they need.   They have, in other
words, a one- or two-dimensional picture.   By contrast, the native speaker's ability intuitively to make the right selection
results from having a full, three-dimensional picture of the word
and its precise place in the lexicon.   Mastery of the selection
procedures, therefore, must entail a process whereby learners are
led from the one-dimensional, minimally-adequate understanding of
a word - just enough, say, to get them through a reading passage
in which the word occurs - to a full appreciation of all its
features and of what makes it different from other words that are
semantically, syntactically and/or stylistically close to it.
The question that arises here is what contribution, if any, the
ELT dictionary can make to helping this process along.

   Put very simply, the native speaker's competence in this area
comes from repeated exposure to a word in all its characteristic
contexts and grammatical frames.   Now the native-speaker dictionary has the luxury of being able to take this process largely for
granted, and users are generally left to do a good deal of the
work:

> bathe ... *v.* bathed, bathing, bathes. - *intr.* 1. To take a
>   bath; wash oneself. 2. To go swimming. 3. To become
>   immersed in or as if in liquid. -*tr.* 1. To immerse in
>   liquid. 2. To wash or wet. 3. To apply a liquid to for
>   soothing or healing purposes. 4. To suffuse....

In this entry from the *American Heritage Dictionary*, definition 4
equates *bathe* and *suffuse*, but it is probably a reasonable assumption that users will not fall into the trap of saying:

   * *I'm just off to suffuse the baby*

But a learners' dictionary cannot take this sort of liberty.   It
may sometimes be adequate, as an aid to decoding, to suggest that
"a" is substitutable for "b", as in the fourth sense from this
entry from the *Macmillan Learner's Dictionary* (1983):

determine ... *vti* 1 (cause to) decide firmly: *He determined to go abroad as soon as he'd finished his university course.* *vt* 2 find out (something) exactly: *Have we determined how long the journey will take?* 3 fix; decide: *The date for the meeting has now been determined.* 4 be the most important cause of.

In a sentence like *It is these factors which determine the level of interest rates,* the definition can be substituted for the definiendum with reasonable success. But if the user wishes to proceed from decoding to production, the definition as it stands is at best unhelpful, and at worst dangerously misleading:

Smoking is the most important cause of lung cancer

* *Smoking determines lung cancer*

So for encoding purposes the user needs to know not just that $a = b$ but that $a = b$ so long as conditions c, d, and e are met.[4]

Learners' dictionaries have a variety of ways of providing these extra layers of information. In the case of the rice cakes, for example (13 above), style labels would show that there is a register mismatch between *nice* and *moreover*; syntactic codes can show that *suggest* (12) is used neither ditransitively nor with an infinitive; and the case of the *impudent* prospective brother-in-law (11) could probably be resolved by means of a definition that said something about the typical status relationship between the speaker and the person so described.

The use of examples, moreover, offers a rich and flexible source of information to those students who know how to "read" them. It could well be argued that the provision of a series of carefully chosen examples is a particularly effective way of building up a complete picture of a word's salient features, because this to some extent replicates - however imperfectly - the process of repeated exposure by which native speakers achieve their competence.

3. Evidence of typical errors in relation to given words

So how, then, are lexicographers to make best use of all these available resources to get their message across to the learner?

---

4 For further discussion of these categories see Marilyn Martin (1984).

It would be all too convenient if we could make a neat rule about the distribution of information by saying, for instance, that the definition should take care of the semantic features leaving the examples to illustrate points of syntax, style, and collocation; or in other words, that the definition should tell you what it means and the examples should show you how it is used. This approach, however, would not address the real problem of the EFL dictionary entry. Here the challenge lies not in providing a uniform set of information types distributed evenly across the various available channels, but in knowing in the case of any particular word what information is most needed and getting this across in the most effective way possible. Any new word typically presents its own particular set of problems to the learner; the nature of these problems varies from word to word and in many cases is predictable. This fact emerged quite clearly from a recent experiment conducted by the Longman ELT Dictionaries and Reference Department in collaboration with the Applied Psychology Unit of the Medical Research Council in Cambridge.[5] The experiment set out to investigate the relative effectiveness for EFL students of different types of dictionary entries ("definition conditions"): definition only; examples only; and a combination of a short definition and a reduced number of examples. The students performed simple decoding and encoding tasks in varying definition conditions, including a "control condition" where they were given no dictionary information at all. For the decoding activity there were slightly more correct responses in the examples only condition and a reassuringly low score in the control condition, though these results remain suggestive and require further investigation.

The encoding activity, where students were asked to write sentences to illustrate the meaning and use of particular words, was inconclusive as to the effectiveness of particular entry types, neither confirming nor refuting our original hunches. What did emerge quite strikingly however, and is of considerable signifi-

---

5 A detailed account of the experiment is available in an unpublished paper by Alison Black (1985).

cance to ELT lexicographers, was the way that the errors produced in relation to a given word tended to be of the same type and that the pattern of their occurrence cut right across the different definition conditions. So for any given word students tended to produce the same type of error regardless of the type of dictionary entry they were using.

The examples below - a fairly representative selection - will help to illustrate this point. Note that in each case the *last* example shown is the odd one out because it represents an *atypical* source of error:

Target word: *reminisce*

(14) We stayed all morning *reminiscing* our childhood.

(15) The couple could *reminisce* the fun they had during the trip around the world.

(16) The grandmothers usually like to *reminisce* to their grandchildren their past life.

(17) It was the event of the year, one for *reminiscing*.

(18) My grandmother *reminisced* me about her childhood.

(19) I've told her several times not to *reminisce* about the accident to the child.

Target word: *debris*

(20) The street was full of *debris* so they decided to clean it.

(21) The garbage man forgot to collect the garbage so my dustbin was repleted with *debris*.

(22) He always gives the *debris* of the meal to the dog.

(23) I had to throw the *debris* away after clearing up my shelf.

(24) She kicked the vase from the table and it fell in many *debris*.

Target Word: *new-fangled*

(25) It's easier to do housework today than before. We have a lot of *new-fangled* machines.

(26) My brother is crazy about *new-fangled* machines.

(27) The *new-fangled* inventions of the computer are amazing.

(28) I worked at an office where they had *new-fangled* word-processors.

(29) A *new-fangled* vase hasn't got the same value as an antique one.

For *reminisce*, there were 10 "incorrect" responses, but only 2 of these could be attributed to semantic difficulty. In general, the meaning and flavour of the word (memory plus nostalgia) were well understood, but its syntactic behaviour posed considerable problems: the remaining 8 "errors" were all produced by a failure to appreciate that the verb was intransitive - and this despite fairly explicit marking in all definition conditions. The mis-apprehension may well arise because of the semantic closeness of *remember* and *recall* - both of which happen to be transitive. But whatever the reason, the students' responses demonstrate clearly that the greatest potential source of difficulty in the word *reminisce* is its syntactic properties.

A very different picture emerged in the case of *debris*, with 10 out of 14 errors clearly attributable to semantic failure. A few of the students were caught out by the slightly tricky "plural" ending (see 24 above) but for most of them syntax was not a problem. As the examples show (20 - 23 above) many of the students were unable to distinguish *debris* from near-synonyms in the same semantic field (*rubbish, garbage, refuse,* etc.). The chief source of error, then, was their failure to grasp the notion of destruction, usually on a large scale, as an important component of the word's meaning.

The great majority of students correctly applied *new-fangled* to the products of modern technology, with only 2 out of a total of 14 "incorrect" responses arising from failure to grasp this semantic feature (see 29 above for an example). In every other case of error, the students had misread the connotations of the word and assumed that it indicated a positive and appreciative (or at least, neutral) value.

With hindsight, it is easy enough to suggest remedies in these particular instances. Moreover, for nearly all our target words the dictionary entries did include information which - if properly understood - should have enabled the users to avoid precisely those traps into which many of them fell. But once a specific aspect of a word's meaning or use has been identified as a pri-mary source of error, the dictionary writer can target the problem and deal with it by "overkill": so for instance, *new-fangled* would

not only have a *derog* label, but also an example sentence that
showed quite unequivocally a disparaging attitude; while at *debris*,
both definition and example would focus on those features that
disambiguate it from similar words in the same semantic field.
The question that must be asked, however, is to what extent the
pattern of errors actually produced could have been predicted at
the outset: should we, in other words, have been able to anticipate that for word A the main problem would be syntax, for word B
it would be register, and so on?

4. The need for lexical analysis

There is of course no cut-and-dried answer to this question.
In the long run, perhaps, only a comprehensive analysis of learners errors can adequately perform the task of alerting dictionary writers to those features of a word that require particular
attention and emphasis. Allowance must be made, too, for the
possibility that the salience of certain problem features is linked to language background or level of attainment rather than the
character of individual items. Obviously, also, no dictionary
can ever hope to preclude all student error - and this is not in
any case a pedagogically desirable aim. But we would nevertheless
argue that many of the pitfalls are in fact highly predictable
and to some extent preventable, and that some progress can be
made towards dealing with them if the defining process is informed
by an analysis of each headword on the basis of its semantic,
stylistic, syntactic, and collocational features. Using this
sort of analysis, principled decisions can be made about the most
effective ways of presenting all the information relevant to a
given headword. This in turn argues for considerable flexibility
and diversity, both in the way the various features of a word are
distributed throughout the entry, and in the degree to which individual features may be singled out for special emphasis. The
precise structure of an entry should be determined by the particular character of the headword being defined, and it is probably
better to think of the entry as a closely interconnected whole
rather than as a series of discrete chunks. The process of
"defining", in fact, in the sense of narrowing down and pinpointing a word precisely, with all its individual features, is a pro-
gressive one that often only begins with the definition.

Jerzy Tomaszczyk

FL LEARNERS' COMMUNICATION FAILURE:
IMPLICATIONS FOR PEDAGOGICAL LEXICOGRAPHY

1. Introduction

'The study reported in this contribution draws on the author's
experience of 15 years as a freelance language editor for Polish
Scientific Publishers, Exports Division, and 8 years as a teacher
of translation at two Polish universities, both jobs involving extensive reading of texts on various topics written in English by
non-native speakers of the language. The aim of the study was to
examine a number of such texts for instances of deviation from target language (TL) norms in terms of the information provided by
dictionaries and thus to see what proportion of the mistakes made
might not have occurred if dictionaries had been consulted (cf.
Tomaszczyk 1979:112).

The usefulness of translated texts for this kind of study might
be questioned on the grounds that translation is bound to induce
interference phenomena to an extent that is not usual in other
types of performance in the L2.[1] One could argue, however, that
translation is likely to require greater reliance on reference books
than any other FL skill and is thus bound to produce more instances
of dictionary use and misuse. Furthermore, although translation
involves a complex process of interpretation on the part of the
translator, the reader of a translated text - provided that he has
access to the original - may be better able to know what meanings
the translator intended to convey. Finally, free composition -
a possible alternative as a source of relevant language data -
would be unlikely to yield as wide a range of phenomena of interest
as is possible with translated texts.

Much of the evidence for this study came from science texts.
Again, while certainly not typical of FL use, such texts are ordinarily quite unambiguous, which makes it relatively easy to establish the extent of the fit between the content of a message and

---

1 Robert Lado (1979) has found regular translation to cause greater interference than delayed interpretation across languages.

its form.   Moreover, in almost all cases the translators, and with science texts also the original authors, were available for consultation.

Evidence concerning dictionary use was obtained in two ways:

(1) A large number of texts produced by science translators and by students of translation[2] were examined for language errors which were then checked against dictionaries known to be available to the writers.

(2) Student behaviour in translation classes was observed to see how language problems are typically dealt with.   Additional samples of written language, including free compositions, essays and test and term papers were also examined for comparison.

2. Findings

A straightforward analysis of the errors discovered in the texts in terms of the information available in dictionaries showed that the vast majority of the errors would not have occurred if dictionaries had been used with skill.   More often than not, they seemed not to have been consulted at all.   This finding is confirmed by student behaviour in class.

When language problems arise, students first ask somebody for help - a class-mate, another class-mate, the teacher - and only if this does not produce an acceptable result will they consult a dictionary.[3]   For lexical items, it is almost invariably a bilingual one, with *OALDCE* or *LDOCE* being used primarily for grammar and rather infrequently at that.   If in L2 - L1 translation the item sought is not listed in any of the above works, students turn to the *Shorter Oxford Dictionary* or the *American Heritage Dictionary*.   Only very seldom do they question the information found and check it

---

2   4th year university English department students one year away from graduation to become English teachers, etc.   All have had 8-9 years of English and would be rated "advanced" or "advanced plus" according to the task-oriented oral proficiency guidelines developed by ACTFL/ETS (cf. Omaggio 1983:Appendix). Their writing skills are comparatively well developed.   The two-semester course in translation is merely an introduction to the complexities and special demands of this advanced skill.
3   The aim of the course being, among others, for the students to learn to solve problems themselves, I ordinarily refuse to help until after they have explored other possibilities.

against another source.   Interestingly, problems are chiefly associated with lexical items, mostly content words, and among those
chiefly nouns.

Some information about dictionary behaviour can also be obtained
by comparing fair copies with the rough drafts and notes which students also often hand in, and which bear witness to the details of
the process by which the final version has been arrived at.   The
number of language problems which students actually meet, judging
from the number of mistakes they make, turns out to be far greater
than the number of problems they identify as such.

Instances of incompetent dictionary use are relatively few:

(1) The *principal role* in X-ray detection *is starred* by photoelectric
absorption ... for *główną rolę odgrywa,* which the standard P-E dictionary defines as *to star (in a film);*

(2) ... by accepting eqn. 1.20 we *taciturnly* assume ... for *milczaco,*
which is correctly qualified in dictionaries as to context.

In a few cases dictionaries fail to supply the information
sought:

(3) It can be exploited as a means *to satisfy* some well-known needs
... *OALDCE* suggests *of+ing* as a complement after *means,* but does
not explicitly rule out *to+inf;*

(4) ... a thin anode which is transparent *for* its own radiation ...
for P *dla.*

A large proportion of the mistakes found in the material examined are word-for-word or morpheme-for-morpheme translations, clear
instances of interlingual transfer:

(5) ... do not let *anybody alien* into the house ... lit.for *nikogo*
obcego;

(6) A filter may be placed *on* the way of the emerging beam ...
for *na;*

(7) The binding energies are called edges of photoelectric absorption, or *shortly* - absorption edges ... for *krótko;*

(8) It can be shown that it is *purposive* to introduce the normalized
power ... for *celowe* (the original Polish sentence is as awkward

as its English rendering);

(9) minimalization, maximalization, optimalization, polarizator
P minimalizacja, maksymalizacja, optymalizacja, polaryzator
E minimization, maximization, optimization, polarizer

Much of the L1 lexical interference is in reality induced by transference of syntactic patterns or discourse organization patterns:[4]

(10) The number of nuclei ... increases not only with increasing EPM content in the blend but also with increasing *folds* of mixing.

The original Polish sentence, of which the above is an exact· replica, has *wielokrotność* in the place of *increasing folds,* which was derived by analogy:

If *dwukrotny, trzykrotny,* etc., are translated by *twofold, threefold,* etc., then the P compound noun *wielokrotność* must have the E phrase *increasing folds* corresponding to it. The plural marker on the E word may be related semantically to either of the two components *wielo* and *krotność,* i.e. "many" and "number of times", respectively. Interestingly, the P word is singular. The word *folds* was obviously created to fill a slot. Syntactic transference of this type is also evident in examples (1), (7) and (8) above.

Transfer going in the other direction is illustrated by

(11) *wicekanclerz,* for (university) *Vice-Chancellor* (P *rektor*);

(12) *sklep stolarski,* lit. for *carpenter's shop* (P *warsztat*).

Both of the above renderings are interpretable, but while (11) does not say much in the context, (12) is simply misleading (*sklep* is where one buys things, *warsztat* is where things are made or repaired).

Instances of less straightforward transfer-related processes include:

(13) ... the excess electrons may *diffund* into a p-type semiconductor. (P n. *dyfuzja* = E *diffusion;* P vb. *dyfundować,* cf. L

---

4 For instance, much awkwardness in translation between English and Polish results from differences in the use of passive and related constructions. In English passivization is the main thematization technique, its function being rendered in Polish by topic shift (cf. Grzegorek 1984:139).

diffundere, suggests E* *diffund.)*

(14) *several ten watts,* for *kilkadziesiąt,* i.e. *several dozen;* it is interesting that *ten* is not pluralized, just as *dozen* would not be (*dziesiąt* is plural).

Most of the mistakes listed above would not have occurred had any dictionary been consulted. It thus appears that the main source of mistakes is not so much lack of reference skills or the use of inadequate dictionaries as an unwillingness to consult reference books at all.

A comparison with similar data from texts not involving translation shows that the extent of formal accuracy correlates positively with the importance perceived by the students to be attached to correctness by their teachers. This suggests that the students, unlike so many teachers, are more concerned with the content of the message than with its form, at least to the extent to which they think they can get away with relative neglect of the latter (cf. Herbst and Stein, this volume). Nevertheless, even where formal accuracy is an obvious requirement, as in diploma theses or professional translation, there is enough evidence to show that the opening statement of this section is basically correct.

3. Discussion

On the face of it, this is a paradoxical situation. On the one hand, we have increasingly better dictionaries, especially of the monolingual EFL type, which meet the various needs of the user more and more satisfactorily, while on the other we have the FL learners for whom these works are specifically intended, and whose needs they are designed to serve, who nevertheless do not choose to take advantage of these remarkable resources.[5] The whole problem could be dismissed as a pseudo-problem on the grounds that reference books are for those who wish to use them. Were one to make some such assertion, however, one would, at the same time, have to question the case for pedagogical lexicography and other new devel-

---

5 When developing the questionnaire for the 1979 study I spoke to many successful language learners, from various language backgrounds, who insisted they had never used any dictionaries.

opments in teaching and learning aids, arguing that people learned
languages successfully long before such aids were even thought of.
Dictionaries are provided, however, not just to make learning possible, but to make it more effective, less time-consuming, less cost-
ly, indeed more enjoyable.

It can hardly be said that my students are exceptionally lazy;
the concept of fossilization was not invented with them specifically in mind. It would likewise be difficult to maintain that
they refuse to consult dictionaries because the books fail them on
too many occasions; in most instances this is simply not the case.

It seems that the state of affairs described above can be explained at least in part, in terms of the concept of competence.

Whatever definition of competence we adopt, it is obvious that
the FL learner starts out with a more or less complete mastery of
his native tongue and nothing in the way of L2 competence. If we
accept that competence, be it grammatical, sociolinguistic, discourse, or strategic, is - in each case - a set of relevant abilities enabling the speaker to perform in his language, i.e. produce
well-formed and acceptable pieces of communicative behaviour, as
well as a set of intuitions enabling him to judge the well-formedness and acceptability of his own as well as other people's behaviour, then it is clear that an FL learner will be able to perform those tasks only to the extent that he has acquired those
abilities and intuitions. The tasks include, among others, moni-
toring one's own behaviour, spotting errors in it, and correcting
them. Now it has been reasonably well established that the competence of adult learners (at least) never really reaches the
target level in every respect, however close to it some learners
may come in some skills or at some language levels. Thus, if an
FL learner or speaker cannot, by definition, be aware of all the
language problems he has, it is not surprising that it may often
not occur to him to try to deal with them. An important aspect
of the problem is that dictionaries, being alphabetized lists of
words, tend to promote or confirm the naive view of interlanguage
relations as involving word-for-word correspondences throughout
(cf. Snell-Hornby, this volume). Consider how frequently the
question "How do you say so-and-so in the other language?" can
only be answered by "Well, in point of fact you do not put it that

way at all". In other words, one - possibly the basic - reason why adult language learners are reluctant to consult dictionaries is that if the point of reference for judging the well-formedness of one's FL production is one's own (interlanguage) competence, reference books are redundant except for browsing or when dealing with the straightforward cases where an L2 word, phrase, etc., is not known.

Another relevant consideration is that for most FL learners the content of a message takes precedence over its form, a questionable but nonetheless widespread attitude.

Furthermore, dictionary consultation being as time-consuming as it is, one usually prefers to rely on what is more readily available (one's own competence), even if this involves resorting to avoidance strategies, often at the expense of accuracy.

Finally, in my experience adult learners invariably start out well equipped with reference books of all kinds which, being impatient to progress as fast as possible, they tend to consult rather more extensively than is good for them. Incidentally, about the only book they can reasonably well understand from the very start is the bilingual dictionary. In the initial stages of the learning process, however, this practice is particularly time-consuming and becomes increasingly more dissatisfying as reference needs grow and reference skills lag behind. The initial wholesale confidence in reference books is gradually replaced by dissatisfaction or even condemnation.

The four factors enumerated above are obviously interrelated and strengthen one another.

That interlingual transfer should play the role it does in FL production is not, perhaps, surprising. Research on the acquisition of native language vocabulary shows it to be a highly complex process, with different areas of vocabulary and kinds of semantic classifications being acquired in different ways. It is a process which also raises complex questions of storing, indexing (tagging), and accessibility, involving interrelations among forms and concepts and between forms and concepts, or between mental lexicons and mental encyclopedias - all of this being virtually inseparable from cognitive development (cf. McDonough 1981:71-73,

106, and Grosjean 1982:244-248).   There is little doubt that
learning the words of a second language takes place against the
background of the first, and involves fitting new words into a
conceptual system that is already there.   In the process, some
of the previously established distinctions of meaning may become
blurred or redrawn.   Relevant research has not yet produced a
clear picture of the situation, and most of it has been carried
out on first and second language acquirers anyway (cf. Meara 1980).
However, regardless of how many lexical stores bilinguals may have
and how well separated they can be, it is a generally recognized
fact that with adult FL learners the L1 never stops affecting the
L2.   The extent of the influence may be quite small with some
individuals, with the internal dictionary for the L2 not only ac-
quiring a measure of independence from that for the L1, but also
beginning to behave in ways similar to the latter (generative power,
some potential for creativity).   But unless FL speakers/writers
are thoroughly familiar with the conventions (rhetorical devices,
discourse rules) governing the production of a particular type of
text in the other language, they actually have no choice but to
reproduce native organizational patterns.   If the skeleton is L1,
it is no wonder that the words fall into place in accordance with
L1 usage conventions, and often also with L1 semantic and other
properties.   The result may then be a text which, at first sight,
looks L2 because it is made up of L2 lexical material, but where
the overall patterns used as well as the semantics are L1.[6]

Most of the errors found in this study can be treated as instances of communication failure only according to a broad interpretation of the term, perfect grammatical, lexical, etc., accuracy
being rarely required for successful communication between native
and non-native speakers.   Nevertheless, they have to be treated as
such if only because the erroneous form of the translated text
draws attention to itself in ways not intended by the original
author.

---

6   Deborah Tannen (1982) has found third generation Greek-Americans - no
    longer proficient in Greek - to follow Greek conversational strategies
    when talking English.

4. Implications for pedagogical lexicography

Implicit in the efforts to develop ever more adequate pedagogical dictionaries, together with users' manuals and training in reference skills, is not only a desire to help the learner towards native-like command of the language in question, but also a conviction that steady progress towards that goal and its eventual attainment are possible.   Such progress is said to be possible if the learner is provided with comprehensible input and if, at the same time, the affective filter is low (Krashen 1982).[7]   The affective filter is low when there is high motivation, self-confidence, good self-image, and low anxiety on the part of the learner.   Yet, whatever teachers may do in the way of creating conditions conducive to learning, there inevitably comes a point in interlanguage development where competence stops evolving and settles at a level usually well below native speaker proficiency.   The extent to which this is true seems to depend solely on which definition of competence one chooses to subscribe to.   Where native-like proficiency is insisted upon, as is generally the case with language teacher-trainees and intending translators, ensuring that some progress is made beyond the level at which fossilization would normally set in (under the given circumstances) requires removal of the factors that caused it in the first place, i.e. lowering the affective filter by creating an environment promoting further learning. With the type of adult FL learners who provided the language data for this study this is easier said than done.   In real life situations a wide variety of factors may combine to produce fossilization, with the teacher himself having little or no control over many of them.   After years of sustained and not entirely successful effort many a student comes to realize how far from the target he still is, and that the ultimate goal is in fact unattainable. And it would be unfair for the teacher to insist otherwise.   At the same time, constantly encouraging the students to put in more effort and insisting that they rely more on reference books may be

---

7 Krashen insists that his findings and hypotheses are for second language acquisition and not for FL learning.   Until convincing evidence to the contrary becomes available, it seems reasonable to assume a degree of basic similarity between SL acquisition and FL learning.

a way of undermining their confidence in their own ability. From
this point of view we are in a vicious circle. Instead of lowering the affective filter (by boosting self-confidence and lowering
anxiety) we may thus be raising it. On top of this, Krashen
(1982) reports on experiments which demonstrate that error correction inhibits rather than enhances acquisition. I would not like
to put undue emphasis on this aspect of the problem, but if this
is a relevant factor, as it seems to be, the situation calls for
great skill and tact on the part of the teacher.

The main findings of this study should not be taken to imply
that work in pedagogical lexicography, including training in reference skills, should be discontinued as valueless. It is clear
enough, however, that language learning involves much more than
the extensive use of reference books and that dictionaries are not
nearly as important to the average learner as some lexicographers
and most teachers consider them to be. Judging from what has been
said here so far, it seems reasonable to suggest that the whole
question of dictionary use and dictionary skills should be considered within the wider context of FL learning, of which it is an
integral part. Quite possibly, more effective pedagogical dictionaries and associated teaching strategies can be developed if
more attention is paid to relevant aspects of the language learning process. What seems to be needed is more research of the type
described by R.R.K. Hartmann (this volume) or that proposed by
Beryl Atkins and her colleagues (also in this volume).

Joseph A. Reif

THE DEVELOPMENT OF A DICTIONARY CONCEPT:
AN ENGLISH LEARNER'S DICTIONARY AND AN EXOTIC ALPHABET

1. Introduction

Learners' dictionaries have long since taken their place as one
of the basic tools of foreign language learning. The general
characteristics of such monolingual dictionaries are well-known
among lexicographers and language teachers, and for certain languages there are several to choose from.[1] This is especially true
of English, and publishers of these have a world-wide market for
their products. The Oxford series pioneered by A.S. Hornby, for
example, can be found in almost every non-English-speaking country.[2]
Recently other publishing houses have put out worthy competitors,
and sales representatives make regular visits to overseas markets
to introduce and lecture on the use of these dictionaries.[3]

However, successful as these dictionaries are, it would be too
much to expect that any particular one would be uniformly useful
everywhere. In all cases there are difficulties caused by linguistic differences between the local language and English, but in some
cases additional problems arise for the dictionary user. First
among these is the situation where the Latin alphabet is not the
basis for the writing system. From this point on, his difficulties
are added to by the abbreviations, codes, symbols, and style of
definition used. Often the user simply stops using a monolingual
dictionary altogether and turns to a more simply structured bilingual one with all the attendant deficiencies of this type.

This has been more or less the situation in Israel, where the

---

1 e.g. for learners of French and Russian as well as of English. The lack of
   such a dictionary for learners of German has been remarked on though Ilson
   (1985:2) reports seeing FL works for German, Spanish and Dutch.
2 This series ranges from the *Oxford Advanced Learner's Dictionary* through the
   intermediate *Oxford Student's Dictionary* to the *Oxford Elementary Learner's
   Dictionary*.
3 Notably, the *Longman Dictionary of Contemporary English* (1978) and the
   Chambers Universal Learner's Dictionary (1980).

Hebrew alphabet is not only very different from the Latin one, but is written and read in the opposite direction. There are many students for whom using a monolingual English dictionary is a daunting experience, especially under school pressures to obtain good marks. The following is a description of an attempt to deal with this problem and to persuade the Israeli student to feel that the learner's dictionary is an easily handled and helpful reference tool.

Traditionally, offerings, either to God or to the public good, are more acceptable if preceded by soul-searching and a critical examination of one's past deeds. This account of the development of a dictionary and its concept thus begins with the editor's personal experiences and his attempts to solve anologous problems. The final result was the *Oxford Student's Dictionary for Hebrew Speakers (OSDHS)*, which faithfully transmits its origins in the *Oxford Student's Dictionary of Current English (OSDCE)* - though in a form more accessible to Israeli users.[4]

2. The Situation in Israel

Instruction in English as a second or foreign language normally begins in the fifth grade of the Israeli school system. However, it is not until high school that it becomes necessary to invest in a dictionary. Until then, there is enough explanation and definition in the syllabus materials themselves, including bilingual glossaries, and there is little pressure to read texts not in the curriculum (cf. Snell-Hornby, this volume). With high school come preparations for the matriculation examinations, and consequently the need and motivation to acquire a learner's dictionary.

At this point it will be helpful to explain the special difficulties faced by students who do not have a "native" familiarity with the Latin alphabet. In order to appreciate the problem from the Israeli user's point of view, it is instructive to look at the behaviour of those native speakers of English who are thoroughly

---

4 Another "glossed" monolingual dictionary with similar teaching aims is the *Oxford Engelsk-Norsk Ordbok* (1983), also an adaptation of *OSDCE*, in which headwords, derivatives and compounds are translated, but not the example sentences.

fluent in both Hebrew and English. When presented with a bi-alphabetic text such as a road sign with a Latin alphabet transcription, the eye of such bilinguals goes to the transcription, even when the Hebrew is a well-known name like Tel Aviv, and even when the combination of Latin letters is highly unusual, such as PETAH TIQWA or ZIYYON. Now Israeli law requires that food products, to give a further example, have the names of the ingredients printed in Hebrew on the package. Other languages are permitted, but the Hebrew must be the more prominent. Even so, and even when the Hebrew names of the ingredients are simple words like *sugar* or *salt*, those bilinguals seek out the list in Latin letters. This is speaking of those who are completely fluent in Hebrew. How much greater is the feeling of alienation from the strange alphabet on the part of not-so-fluent speakers and readers!

The personal experience of the author may provide further enlightenment. Several years ago, after ten years of living in Israel and lecturing in Hebrew at university level, I took stock of myself and found that I did not regularly read a Hebrew publication directed to my intellectual level, something comparable to *The Times* or the *Scientific American*. So I subscribed to the morning newspaper *Haaretz*, which is generally considered the most literate general publication in Israel. I was surprised at the initial struggle that I had. I had not realized how, unconsciously, I had been avoiding confrontation with the writing system, and I have been reading Hebrew texts since childhood. I pushed on, but it was two or three years before I felt comfortable getting information on a wide range of intellectual subjects from a Hebrew source. I also found that there were idioms common to intellectual discussion which were not described anywhere and that certain styles were quite different from the normative standards of formal language. Once over this psychological barrier I found that my ability to scan such written material as official forms, product labels, and even handwriting increased.

This experience gave me considerable empathy for students following courses in which I lectured in English and for which the textbook and bibliography were also in English. This led to changes in my style of lecturing and in the way I prepared materials for the courses.

I began including Hebrew "glosses" in the lectures in addition
to the English explanations and paraphrases, and found that the
students became more alert, grasped the *English* meanings more
quickly, and followed the English presentation more easily.   In
the material that I prepared I reduced the number of abbreviations
and symbols and was generally more explicit.   I found that students
preferred to hear a word read aloud and not to be given a phonetic
transcription, unless, of course, the subject was phonetics.

In general, I reduced the amount of technical paraphrasing that
the students had to contend with, though it meant spending time
trying to find a Hebrew word or phrase to capture the fleeting
thought without giving a consecutive translation of the lecture.
These efforts helped to remove the foreignness barrier of the English
and helped also to gauge the degree of comprehension from the level
of attentiveness and other feedback.

The basic elements of this teaching approach may be listed as
follows:

(1) an intuitive appreciation of the strangeness of a foreign alphabet even to those who know the language fluently;

(2) the reassurance and motivation provided by glosses interspersed
throughout an English text;   and

(3) the reduction of codes, symbols, and abbreviations.

3.   Adapting a learner's dictionary

The most widely bought learner's dictionary at the high school
level in Israel has for some time been the *Oxford Student's Dictionary
of Current English (OSDCE)* by A.S. Hornby.   This is an adaptation for
those learning English up to the Intermediate level of the *Oxford
Advanced Learner's Dictionary,* and in turning our attention to the
problems of using a monolingual learner's dictionary this seemed
to provide a good starting point.   We found, not surprisingly,
that students approached the *OSDCE* with a great deal of initial
apprehension.   This was heightened by the daunting visual effect
of the various typefaces (bold roman, light roman, bold italic,
light italic) and the phonetic transcription.   To this could be
added the abbreviations for part-of-speech labels and symbols such

as "∿", which save space but none the less require a constant deciphering effort.

Incidentally, the abbreviations are in practice a greater obstacle than the phonetic transcription. The latter occurs within obliques immediately after the boldface headword and is followed by abbreviations in standard orthography and definitions. One of the first things the Israeli user learns is to skip over and ignore the transcription. In all my years of contact with these users I have not met a single one who referred to the transcription except when required to do so in the context of a specific lesson. Even linguistics majors prefer to take their chances with the standard orthography.

Other features, though intended to save space and expense, tend to accentuate the arcaneness of the dictionary for the Israeli user. For example, the boldface numbers which introduce separate definitions, and which are clear visual clues to those at home with the Latin alphabet, are often seen as an insertion or obstruction in a continuous line of print rather than as a signal for a new set of definitions - much as a footnote number must appear to a reader of an English text.

To gain further insight into the nature of the problem, we can consider the market in Israel for instruction books and materials on how to use learners' dictionaries. The most popular of these has been *Use Your Dictionary* by Menachem Bloch (1971; cf. Underhill 1980). This guide was tailored specifically to the second edition of the *Advanced Learner's Dictionary of Current English* (1963), which was the learner's dictionary in general use in Israel at the time. Since then other learners' dictionaries have appeared on the market, and Bloch has prepared a revised edition, *Use Your Dictionary as a Learning Tool* (1985), which covers Longman and Collins learners' dictionaries as well as the two Oxford titles. This is a textbook on the structure of learners' dictionaries and has sections on practising alphabetical order, decoding symbols and abbreviations, and increasing familiarity with the internal arrangement of entries. It also includes guidance on the ways English grammar is presented in dictionaries.

Such guides represent one response to the problems that our users

face, which is to accept the content and arrangement of these
foreign-produced dictionaries as they are. Our approach has been
the reverse: to restyle the dictionary to solve some of those user
problems, or, in other words, to make it user-friendly. To be sure,
the content of the dictionary has been retained. That is, we have
preserved *OSDCE* as a basically monolingual reference work for the
learning of English, one through which the user will learn to appreciate the value of paraphrase in the L2.

However, there were initial problems of a more practical nature.
First of all, the size of the *OSDCE* was considered a little too
small for the Israeli user. It suggested a technical manual for
a complex piece of machinery rather than a book to be leafed through.
There was no formal market research or psychological testing: the
decision to change the size was based simply on general experience.
The enlarged size is the same as that of the *Oxford Advanced Learner's
Dictionary of Current English*. Users of the new dictionary have reported less of a feeling of having to peer at the text for information. Yet it is still smaller than the average desk dictionary,
and thus still feels like a schoolbook that can be carried about.

Next we tackled the format of the entry itself. Our task was
to lessen the strangeness of its appearance. As suggested above,
the phonetic transcription was one feature to be discarded.
Firstly, the transcription is just too formidable for most people
to learn. And secondly, almost all testing in schools in Israel
is done in the written medium. Spelling is more important than
pronunciation. Israeli schoolchildren (and their parents when
helping them with their homework) syllabify aloud "Wed-nes-day"
and even "pah-lem" (for *palm*) so as to memorize the spelling.
In fact, the transcription often misleads them.

In place of the transcription we have prepared a diskette (floppy
disk) for use with personal computers equipped with sound capabil-
ity. The user will simply enter the headword and then be able to
listen to the pronunciation. In subentries for compounds and in
some examples *OSDCE* indicates main and secondary stresses (thus:
con'sulting room, *ˌback'pedal*). These have been retained in the text
of *OSDHS* because the diskettes do not have the capacity to include
more than the 20,000 main entries. As the technology improves

it will be possible to eliminate even these diacritical marks.

The next change in format was to start each numbered definition on a new line, though still headed by the boldface number. This arrangement makes the separate meanings easier to perceive and remember and facilitates the search for an appropriate sense when reading a text. Since a gloss is supplied for each sense at the end of and to the right of the numbered section, the formatting enables the user to scan the Hebrew at the same time.

Some increase in space was one of the disadvantages we had foreseen. We calculated that the Hebrew glosses would in most cases fill the space opened up by starting each sense on a new line. The glosses of course start at the right-hand margin of the column, and the marked difference in the visual appearance of the two alphabets obviates the need for indentation. The estimate turned out to be correct, and with the removal of the phonetic transcription the final expansion turned out to be less than ten per cent - 824 pages instead of the 755 pages of the *OSDCE*.

Other steps aimed at helping the user (though at a cost in space) were the following:

(a) Spelling out verb forms which require consonant-doubling. Thus, instead of (- *tt*-) after *abet* we supply the full form of the past tense *(abetted)*. Irregular forms of the past tense and past particple are given in full as in the *OSDCE*.

(b) Giving with adjectives such as *happy* the full comparative and superlative forms.

(c) Spelling out *sb* and *sth* as *somebody* and *something*

(d) Giving full forms in examples instead of "~".

As an example of the concern for detail that is part of the practice of lexicography, we considered replacing the symbol => with *see*, but using a regular typefont for it would risk confusion with the word to which the user cross-referred, while italics would lead to confusion with the end of an immediately preceding example. In any case, the arrow is an obvious symbol, and Israeli users are not puzzled by it.

Another symbol which we considered eliminating was the small

square ☐ which indicates a change in part of speech (e.g. from *n*
to *vt* in the entry for *contact*). Since the new use would in any
case be started on a new line all that would be necessary would be
to indicate what part of speech it was. However, on further consideration we took the opposite view and changed the symbol to a
boldface filled-in square in order to alert the user more emphati-
cally to the change in word-class.

Abbreviations of part-of-speech labels such as *n*, *adj*, *pl*, etc.,
were left as they were. At one point we considered scrapping them
because the Hebrew gloss usually gives this information unambigu-
ously. Hebrew morphology clearly distinguishes transitive from
intransitive verbs, for example. However, we wanted to preserve
the dictionary primarily as a monolingual reference work, and such
labels are important for English, in which word-class membership
is not consistently marked. Also, we were aware that students
use the book for answers to specifically grammatical questions, and
that they are often called on to identify parts of speech and other
grammatical categories. Despite reservations which some may have
concerning this method of teaching, it is still practised by many
teachers, and the student will tend to look for help on this point
in the dictionary. (Indeed, many of the teachers, perhaps most,
are not native speakers of English, and they too will want to have
this grammatical information in an accessible place.)

Except for grammatical labels, as already indicated, and for *eg*,
etc, and *ie*, which occur in ordinary English texts, all abbreviations
in *OSDCE* are spelt out in full in the new dictionary.

The most obvious new feature in this dictionary is the supplying
of Hebrew glosses for the various senses of a word and its subentries. We use the term "gloss" because we were not intent on
producing a bilingual dictionary which the student could use for
translating English texts into Hebrew; rather, we aimed to encourage him to understand English by providing limited help in the
mother tongue. Our guideline was "to whisper in the ear of the
user".

The translations are thus keys for the English definitions, and
the main differences between a bilingual dictionary and *OSDHS* are
as follows:

(1) A regular bilingual dictionary often gives a set of synonyms as possible translations of the headword.   We have given further translation possibilities only when necessary to avoid inaccuracies or to capture the particular meaning of a word in the English examples provided.   For example, the normal Hebrew expression translating *to contract out of something* also means "to be released from a contract" and does not necessarily convey the connotation that the initiative is taken by the person contracting out.   On the other hand, an alternative Hebrew expression which means basically "to cancel a contract" is much too emphatic for this entry. We therefore translated the English as "to cancel an obligation (in a contract)" and then added the more common "to be released" in order to convey the particular range in Hebrew of the English expression.

When the full set of glosses for a particular entry in all its senses is taken together, the result is often that more information is provided than in an ordinary bilingual dictionary of comparable size.

(2) In Hebrew dictionaries, verbs are cited in the 3rd person masculine singular past tense form.   This is the accepted lexicographic convention for Semitic languages.   Such a form usually indicates the root and conjugation most economically and clearly.

However, in Modern Hebrew, verbs in colloquial use are cited in the infinitive form with the preposition *le-* (="to").   Thus, English *speak* is translated as *ledaber* "to speak" and not as *diber* "he spoke".   This is the natural way in which a native Hebrew speaker would respond to the question "How do you say *speak* in Hebrew?" and it is the approach we have adopted for our dictionary.

(3) Figurative, highly colloquial, and slang terms are translated as far as possible by stylistically equivalent Hebrew terms.   If the Hebrew translation equivalent in such cases is the same as that of the literal English sense, we set it off in double quotes, according to Hebrew practice, in order to convey the relationship. Thus, *rosy* in the sense of "of the colour of red roses" is translated as *varod* and *rosy* in the sense of "good, bright, cheerful" is translated as *"varod"*.

We permitted ourselves considerable liberty at times in order

to maintain our policy of "whispering in the ear of the user".
However, there are limits to what people will accept as an innovation and still maintain respect for the innovator.   In Israel
there is an Academy of the Hebrew Language, whose function is to
preserve the character of the language from such onslaughts as
loanwords, slang, and other non-normative intrusions.   Though
people may tolerate these changes in everyday usage, they still
feel that certain kinds of "official" works should exercise a
normative function.   Dictionaries fall into this category.

The Academy busies itself, among other activities, with approv-
ing new Hebrew words denoting objects and concepts for which foreign
and otherwise non-normative items already exist in the language.
The problem is that even when the Academy approves a new word it
takes time for it to become current in usage.   Our solution to the
dilemma of what Hebrew equivalent to provide for the user in doubtful cases was to give the official word, but to follow it with the
better-known word in parentheses.   Thus, the gloss for English
anchovy is given as *afyan (anshovi)*.   As the approved Hebrew word
comes into more general use the loanword can be ignored or deleted
in later editions.   Not to include the officially sanctioned
Hebrew word at this stage would have damaged the reputation of the
dictionary even though it would have been reflecting actual usage.

(4) A modified vowel pointing system is used in which all full
vowels are indicated, but "shwa" only at the beginning of a word.
A text fully pointed according to traditional rules looks like a
Biblical passage, poetry, or something written for small children.
All other types of texts in Modern Hebrew are unpointed, and by the
fifth or sixth grade children have little difficulty with them,
including the fast-moving subtitles on foreign films and television
programmes.   However, wholly unpointed translations in a dictionary would be almost worthless because, except in the case of longer
translated examples, there is little supporting context and ambiguities would frequently occur.

(5) Grammatical terminology is not included anywhere in the Hebrew.
As mentioned above, Hebrew morphology is often an unambiguous
indicator of word class, and burdening the user with grammatical
terminology would defeat the object of our enterprise.

4. A comparison of *OSDCE* and *OSDHS*

In order to make the above descriptions clearer we shall now compare several entries from the original *OSDCE* and the restyling with Hebrew of the *OSDHS*.

con·struc·tion /kənˈstrʌkʃən/ *n* **1** [U] act or manner of constructing; being constructed: *The new railway is still under ~*, being built. **2** [C] structure; building. **3** [C] meaning; sense in which words, statements, acts, etc are taken: *Please do not put a wrong ~ on his action*, misunderstand its purpose. **4** [C] arrangement and relationships of words in a sentence: *This dictionary gives the meanings of words and also gives examples to illustrate their ~s.*
con·struc·tion·al *adj* of, involving, construction: *~al toys.*
con·struc·tive /kənˈstrʌktɪv/ *adj* helping to construct; giving helpful suggestions: *~ criticism/proposals.*
con·struc·tive·ly *adv*

OSDCE

con·struc·tion *n* **1** [U] act or manner of constructing; being constructed: *The new railway is still under construction*, being built. בנייה
2 [C] structure; building. מבנה; בניין
3 [C] meaning; sense in which words, statements, acts, etc are taken: *Please do not put a wrong construction on his action*, misunderstand its purpose. פירוש
4 [C] arrangement and relationships of words in a sentence: *This dictionary gives the meanings of words and also gives examples to illustrate their constructions.* מבנה
con·struc·tion·al *adj* of, involving, construction: *constructional toys.* של בנייה; מבני
con·struc·tive *adj* helping to construct; giving helpful suggestions: *constructive criticism/proposals.* בונה, קונסטרוקטיבי
con·struc·tive·ly *adv* באופן קונסטרוקטיבי

OSDHS

Fig. 1. Note that in the *OSDCE* the bold 2 appears on a separate line from its definition; and in the example for *constructional* the word is represented as "~*al*". In the *OSDHS* the arrangement is clearer, and *constructional* is spelled out. Note also that a translation is given for *constructively* even though there is no English definition.

con·tem·por·ary /kənˈtempərɪ *US:* -pəreri/ *adj* **1** of the time or period to which reference is being made; belonging to the same time: *Dickens was ~ with Thackeray.* **2** of the present time. **3** (*informal*) in the most modern style: *~ music.* □ *n* [C] (*pl* -ies) person of the same age, belonging to the same period, etc as another: *Jack and I were contemporaries at college.*

con·tem·por·ary *adj* **1** of the time or period to which reference is being made; belonging to the same time: *Dickens was contemporary with Thackeray.* בן-זמנו, בן-דורו
2 of the present time. בן-זמננו
3 (*informal*) in the most modern style: *contemporary music.* מודרני
■ *n* [C] (*pl* contemporaries) person of the same age, belonging to the same period, etc as another: *Jack and I were contemporaries at college.* בן אותו דור

Fig. 2. Note that the plural *contemporaries* is spelt out in full.

con·tent[1] /kən'tent/ adj **1** not wanting more; satisfied with what one has: *Are you ~ with your present salary?* **2** willing or ready (to do something): *I am ~ to remain where I am now.* □ n [U] the condition of being satisfied: *to one's heart's ~*, to the extent that brings as much satisfaction or happiness as one wants. □ vt satisfy: *As there's no milk we must ~ ourselves (= be satisfied) with black coffee.*
con·tented adj satisfied; showing or feeling satisfaction, happiness: *with a ~ed look/smile.*
con·tent·ed·ly adv

con·tent[1] adj **1** not wanting more; satisfied with what one has: *Are you content with your present salary?* מְרוּצֶה; מִסְתַּפֵּק **2** willing or ready (to do something): *I am content to remain where I am now.* מוּכָן ■ n [U] the condition of being satisfied: *to one's heart's content*, to the extent that brings as much satisfaction or happiness as one wants. שְׂבִיעוּת־רָצוֹן ■ vt satisfy: *As there's no milk we must content ourselves (= be satisfied) with black coffee.* לְהַשְׂבִּיעַ רָצוֹן; לְהִסְתַּפֵּק
con·tented adj satisfied; showing or feeling satisfaction, happiness: *with a contented look/smile.* מְרוּצֶה; שֶׁל שְׂבִיעוּת־רָצוֹן
con·tent·ed·ly adv בְּסִיפּוּק
con·tent·ment n [U] state of being content. שְׂבִיעוּת־רָצוֹן

Fig. 3. Note the clearer indication of a change of part of speech with the filled-in square of the *OSDHS*. The absence of a phonetic transcription contributes to the openness of the format.

5. *OSDHS* and the learner of Hebrew

The *OSDHS* was intended for the native Hebrew speaker learning English, and the changes and innovations in format and content were designed with his or her needs in mind. However, the dictionary also provides a partial solution to the encoding problems of an English speaker learning Hebrew.

All the existing bilingual English-Hebrew dictionaries give a list of translation equivalents of a headword with almost no further information on how to choose the appropriate Hebrew equivalent for a particular meaning of that headword or its use in a specific context. This is a problem when the synonyms are of different registers, but even more so when the senses of the English item are semantically far-ranging. Consider, for example, *to apply for a visa, to apply a plaster, to apply sanctions, to apply one's energies, to apply research,* and *to apply* in the sense of "have a bearing on": all these have different Hebrew translations. How can the user of an ordinary bilingual dictionary (i.e. one with few differentiating examples) make the right choice?

A dedicated student might check each one in a parallel Hebrew-English dictionary and thereby eliminate some of the possibilities. But such diligence usually palls quickly, and the user ends up taking chances. In the *OSDHS* this problem is neatly solved. The English speaker is given the appropriate Hebrew immediately after each separate sense, collocation, and idiom. This is

especially helpful in the case of adverbs, which are translated
into Hebrew even when there is no English definition in the *OSDCE*.
Hebrew does not have a grammatical formative comparable to the
English - *ly* for deriving adverbs, but rather forms adverbial expressions in a variety of ways beyond the guessing talents of most
students of the language.

6. Conclusion

   A frequent complaint from dictionary editors is that users ignore
the instructions carefully provided in the introductory matter.
The *OSDHS* was edited with this constantly in mind.   The user should
be able to go straight to the entry and get full benefit from the
dictionary.   To smooth his path even further we took the step of
not including *any* explanatory material apart from the short list of
abbreviations of English grammatical labels.   It is our hope that
the experience of future users will prove this to be not a rash
omission but a commonsense service to the user.

Mary Snell-Hornby

TOWARDS A LEARNER'S BILINGUAL DICTIONARY

1. Introduction

In a market saturated with language teaching material, there is
still one item conspicuously absent: a bilingual dictionary designed to meet the specific needs of the learner.[1] The result is
that foreign language students fall back on the traditional general-
purpose concise or pocket dictionary, which is ironically the type
of reference book least suitable as an aid to language learning.
Recent studies show a growing awareness of the situation, and in
view of the expanding dictionary market and the current interest in
users' needs, the time may have come to fill the gap. I would
therefore like to present, from the viewpoint of the language teacher, some concrete proposals for a pedagogically designed learner's
bilingual dictionary (LBD), as distinct from the general user's
pocket bilingual dictionary, although within the limited scope of
this paper there is little I can do beyond clearing the ground and
presenting some broad basic principles. The aim is to stimulate
discussion between teachers and lexicographers on what is academi-
cally desirable and what is feasible in practice.

As there has always been a human need to communicate, even beyond language barriers, it is not surprising that foreign language
learning, and with it translation and bilingual lexicography, have
a very long history. Maybe that is the reason why this is an area
of knowledge not only bound by tradition, but often even paralyzed
by unquestioned fixed ideas and prejudices. One such fixed idea
is epitomized in that naive question "What's x in English?", suggesting that a word "is" another word in the foreign language.
This is the principle of elementary approximation underlying the

---

[1] The situation described in this paper is essentially that of Western Europe,
focussing on the learning of English as a foreign language, and with special
reference to the language-pair German/English. While the argumentation may
apply to some extent to other language types and culture groups, no claim is
made to universal validity.

vocabulary lists generations of schoolchildren are compelled to
learn by heart, a principle which is unfortunately consolidated in
the traditional small-size dictionaries such learners buy, use and
stick to - thus perpetuating a practice that has in essence prog-
ressed no further than the ancient bilingual word lists on the clay
tablets of Old Babylonia.   Such an approach to language comparison
presupposes the existence of some static and absolute tertium comparationis, in relation to which universal concepts are simply given
differing labels in various languages.   For the language learner
this illusion comes dangerously close to reality, because usually
he does indeed approach the foreign language from the firm ground
of what he instinctively accepts as being absolute - although this
is in fact not a universally valid tertium comparationis, but simply the system of his own native language.[2]

Such illusions have no place in the pedagogical bilingual dictionary.   On the one hand it must do justice to the immensely
complex web of relationships which in fact exists between the vo-
cabularies of any two languages, and on the other it must anticipate the learner's problems, which are conditioned not only by the
formal difficulties of the foreign language but also by L1 interference.   For this reason the LBD should not be designed as an
isolated reference book of vocabulary items, but should be inte-.
grated both into an overall concept of grammar, pragmatics and
semantics, and into a basic concept of language learning.

2.   The LBD and the language learning process

In the concept I am putting forward here, the learning process
is viewed in three basic stages.   During the first stage, and
particularly in the case of a first foreign language, the dictionary plays no part, neither should the learner be confronted with
isolated vocabulary lists, from which items are memorized and mentally ticked off once and for all in terms of the suggested native
language equivalents.   We should rather envisage a modern language
course based firmly on texts and typical situations, the vocabulary

---

2   It is particularly revealing that a number of "universals" postulated by
    transformational grammar are not only based on English, but even help to
    show up specifically English idiosyncrasies (cf. Snell-Hornby 1983).

being presented as items in context. In the accompanying glossary, lexical items, phrases and even whole sentences may be translated for reference, but the learner should understand that basically the glossary applies only to the text concerned.[3] The learning process thus encourages from the outset a growing awareness of the foreign language as an independent system of communication seen against a sociocultural background that differs from the learner's own. The deepening insight into the foreign language system naturally entails a gradual weaning away from the text as a necessary basis for vocabulary learning, and - in the second stage of the learning process - the lexical items are hypostatized in relation to the language system. This is the stage when independent reference works may be introduced. As however the grammatical system is in principle easier to internalize than the infinitely complex lexical system of any language, the preliminary reference work should rather be a *learner's grammar* in simple language and with a rich fund of examples (with translations) implicitly contrasting the foreign grammar with the learner's own.[4] The third stage of the learning process is reached when the student has sufficient command of the foreign language system to compare its lexical structure with his own; it is at this stage that the learner's dictionary - both bilingual and monolingual - is most necessary and most valuable, and it is also the earliest stage of the learning process at which translation exercises have any point at all.

---

3   This is already a feature of recent language courses, particularly those designed for adult education; information from Germany and Switzerland indicates that schools are more conservative and tend to perpetuate the use of traditional vocabulary lists. See Hartmann 1985 for the role of vocabulary in foreign language teaching and learning.

4   It is clear that syntactic pattern codes as now used in learners' dictionaries can hardly benefit a student who has not grasped the underlying grammatical principles, such as those of complementation, concord, etc. As examples of the contrastive approach in learners' grammars, see the adaptations of Luscher's German grammar (1975) for speakers of various languages, also the English grammar by Ungerer et al (1984).

Stage in learning process	Language base	Grammatical system	Lexical system
1	Text ⟷	Related Grammar ⟷	Glossary
2	L2 system	Learner's grammar	
3	L1 – L2 systems		LBD

Fig. 1: Language learning and the LBD

3. Active and passive dictionaries

It has already been convincingly argued (e.g. Hausmann 1977; Kromann et al. 1984a) that bilingual dictionaries should be differentiated into "active" and "passive" types. This goes back to an idea originally put forward by Ščerba (1935), who drew "a rigorous distinction between dictionaries aiming to facilitate translation from the native to the foreign language and those conceived as an aid to decoding foreign-language texts" (Kromann et al. 1984a:208).[5] If we take the active dictionary as working from L^1 to L^2, we can compile four different bilingual dictionaries per language pair (cf. Al-Kasimi 1983:157), which for German and English would be as follows:

User L1	Active (L1-L2)	Passive (L2-L1)
English	E – G	G – E
German	G – E	E – G

Fig. 2: Types of bilingual dictionary

This distinction has vital implications for the learner: while the passive dictionary helps him to *understand* the foreign language (as in reading comprehension and L2-L1 translation), the active diction-

---

5 In lexicography focussing on Russian as a foreign language, the concept of active and passive dictionaries has been successfully put into practice, as in Bielfeldt's Russian-German dictionary (1982) and German-Russian dictionary (1983), which are however not specifically pedagogical dictionaries.

ary helps him to *use* it (as in essay-writing and Ll-L2 translation). This leads us on to the vexed question of translation and the bilingual dictionary. As a relic from the heyday of Latin, Ll-L2 translation is unfortunately still used in schools as a mechanical exercise for learners whose language proficiency is inadequate for the task, and who develop the fatal belief that a translation is simply a string of dictionary equivalents for the words in the source text. Hausmann comments as follows:

> "Generationen von Schülern basteln sich mit sträflich fehlkonzipierten Wörterbüchern Hinübersetzungen übelster Art zusammen und wähnen sich auch noch in dem für das Behalten und die Fixierung verheerenden Glauben, das Ergebnis sei Französisch, eine Situation, die sich auf der Universität leider allzu oft fortsetzt." (Hausmann 1977:58)

I can fully endorse his remarks for university students of English. The state of affairs he describes is not due solely to inadequate dictionaries, but also to the abuse of translation as an exercise at too early a stage, when a dictionary with an adequate amount of microstructural information would only confuse the learner.

At the other end of the scale it is illusory to believe that the general bilingual dictionary is sophisticated enough to be an ideal tool for the professional translator. There is however a stage in language learning when both the activity of translation and a specifically designed bilingual dictionary are both necessary and valuable: at the third stage of the learning process depicted above, when lexical structures can be compared and differentiated as an aid to active mastery of the foreign language (cf. Snell-Hornby 1985b).

Differentiation between an active and a passive LBD would have radical consequences for dictionary design, and the varying merits and drawbacks are still open to debate. Whereas the active dictionary focusses on information within the article (including grammatical data and meaning discrimination), the passive dictionary (as described in Kromann et al. 1984a and 1984b) focusses on the *headword*, while an undefined list of suggested equivalents would suffice for the article.[6] In the latter case the learner would

---

6 This is however not the principle followed in Bielfeldt's dictionary, which concentrates on explanation and illustrative examples, and frequently provides encyclopaedic information.

surely be better served by an L2 monolingual dictionary such as
ALD or LDOCE, supplemented by a full-size bilingual dictionary:
experience in advanced language teaching and in translation teaching shows that the learner can understand a foreign language text
better if unknown words are explained in terms of their own language system and against their own sociocultural background without
being rendered as foreign language equivalents which are often inadequate and contrived.   The LBD envisaged here is therefore of
the active type, addressed to the advanced or professional learner
to further proficiency in *using* the language (cf. Tomaszczyk 1983),
and permitting coordination with a monolingual learner's dictionary.

4.   Grammar, semantics and pragmatics in the LBD

I have already expressed the conviction that the LBD should not
be simply a glorified word-list, but should be integrated into an
overall concept of grammar, semantics and pragmatics.   At the same
time, all information given in a dictionary must of necessity be
as compact as possible.   So it stands to reason that full use
should be made of abbreviation systems and pattern codes.   Studies
have however shown (Béjoint 1981 and Heath 1982) that in monolingual English dictionaries such codes are usually ignored by the
user.   Heath even concludes:

> "If syntactic pattern codes are used, they should be able to be understood
> without the need for constant reference to an introduction or a back-cover.
> The usefulness of codes, which are after all only a grammatical shorthand, is
> impaired by overcomplexity and a striving for perfection." (Heath 1982:106)

A better solution would surely be guidance from the teacher on how
to use the dictionary, assuming the student's willingness to read
the introduction and to use the cross-references.   I agree however
that pattern codes cannot be expected to do justice to the complexities of grammatical usage in the living language, and students
often cannot make sense of the patterns because they do not know
what terms like "adjunct" and "anomalous finite" mean.   So I propose that the learner's grammar mentioned earlier should be used
both as a preliminary introduction to the LBD and as a companion
reference volume.

Far more daunting than grammatical codings however are the lexical problems of semantic structure and interlingual relationships.

From the outset the learner should be sensitized to the *varying complexity* of these relationships and not be presented with an over-simplified system of equivalences which he later has to unlearn as his command of the language develops - a situation which the university language teacher is continually faced with. Until now contrastive semantics has provided no overall concept for classifying interlingual relationships (most existing studies are either too abstract or limit themselves to too few items), and I can do no more than point out the problems and offer a very general and tentative outline by way of solution.

As a basic principle we may say that the simplest interlingual relationship - i.e. the closest "equivalence" - exists at the level of *terminology* and *nomenclature* (though even here reservations are called for, cf. Arntz and Schmitt, both in press); that the most complex relationships are found when items express perception and subjective evaluation, especially when conditioned by *sociocultural norms;*[7] and that little or no relationship (usually called "nil-equivalence") exists at the level of *culture-bound elements* (cf. Tomaszczyk 1983 and 1984) - with varying stages of gradation in between. We can distinguish five basic groups of prototypes:[8]

(1) Terminology/Nomenclature

e.g. *oxygen:* Sauerstoff

(2) Internationally known items and sets

e.g. *Saturday:* Sonnabend/Sonntag

    typewriter: Schreibmaschine

    but: *to type:* mit der Maschine schreiben, tippen

(3) Concrete objects, basic activities, stative adjectives

e.g. *chair:* Stuhl, Sessel

    cook, boil: kochen

    technical: technisch, fachlich, Fach-

---

7 This problem of "dynamics in meaning" has been further investigated in Snell-Hornby 1985a.

8 The concept of the prototype and its importance in linguistic categorization is discussed in Vannerem and Snell-Hornby (in press).

(4) Words expressing perception and evaluation, often linked to sociocultural norms

e.g. *clout, thrill, bustle, bleak*
     keifen, kitschig, gemütlich

(5) Culture-bound elements

e.g. *haggis, wicket, drugstore*
     Pumpernickel, Privatdozent, Sechseläuten.

It is not possible here to enlarge on or refine this outline, but even so I would venture some tentative conclusions: firstly, the degree of semantic overlap is determined as much by *sociocultural* as by purely linguistic factors, and the more idiosyncratic a lexical item is to the specific culture of a language community, the more difficulty it causes for the foreign learner. Secondly, from the contrastive viewpoint the so-called Hard Words turn out to be the easiest, while everyday words can be the hardest (cf. Cowie 1983). Thirdly, the degree of difficulty increases according to the *perspectivity* of the lexical item, concrete, static objects being easier than words dependent on perception or evaluation. Finally, the methodological problems of the LBD cluster round Groups 2-4; terminology is a separate issue for which specialized dictionaries are required (cf. Moulin 1983); while culture-bound elements are best explained by definition as in monolingual dictionaries.[9]

A differentiated approach to interlingual relationships would of course lead to differentiated structuring of the dictionary article. Until now theoretical work on bilingual lexicography has been based on the assumption that the article must necessarily consist of foreign language equivalents which are "immediately insertable" (Kromann et al. 1984a) in the TL text. In our view however, equivalence of this type is basically restricted to items of Groups 1 and 2 listed above, and possibly, with considerable meaning discrimination, to some of Group 3. Our list shows a gradual transition from "equivalence" via "equivalence with discrimination" (Group

---

9 In an active learner's dictionary as envisaged here, culture-bound items already lexicalized in the TL (e.g. *pumpernickel, Drugstore*) should of course be differentiated from those which have not and which need explanation or paraphrase (*Privatdozent, haggis*), the latter being rather a matter of encyclopaedic information than of interlingual relationships.

3) to "partial over-lapping" (Group 4) and definition (Group 5).
This transition should be reflected in the basic design of the LBD
articles.   Thus in the case of the more complex lexemes (Group 4)
the traditional alphabetical arrangement might well be supplemented
by a presentation in contrastive semantic fields, to which the main
body of the dictionary would act as index (cf. Snell-Hornby 1983).

A final word concerns *examples*, which, as has already been emphasized (e.g. Hausmann 1977 and 1981), are of supreme importance for
the learner, in enabling him both to recognize grammatical usage
and to situate items in context.   They should include common idioms and fixed phrases, and highlight problems of grammatical structure (e.g. complementation), collocation and pragmatic effect.[10]
In the LBD the examples would be presented in both languages, and
they should above all be prototypes of *current* language usage.

5.   The German-speaking student as dictionary user

Prompted by Hartmann's survey of the use of dictionaries by
learners of German in Southwest England (Hartmann 1982 and 1983b),
I handed round a similar questionnaire to 35 students of English at
the Universities of Zürich and the Saarland.   The groups were too
small to provide more than an indication, but the user profile that
emerged suggests that a large-scale survey of dictionary usage at
German universities is long overdue.   Three main points should be
stressed: firstly, nearly all the students use dictionaries practically every day, both monolingual (English) and bilingual, but
with only a very hazy idea of their identity (a dictionary referred
to as "pond's" - for PONS - was frequently cited, along with
"Longman's ALD"), and dictionaries available at home were inadequate
and outdated ("An old Langenscheidt - about 1930").   Secondly, by
far the most common motive for using a dictionary was to check *meaning*; next came *correct usage* and *translation*, with *grammar* and *pronunciation* last.   Thirdly, the dictionary was expected to be an inex-

---

10   The realization of speech acts is closely bound to culture and specific
      language structure (cf. Snell-Hornby 1984), and is not adequately explain-
      ed through lexical confrontation such as occurs in the bilingual diction-
      ary.   The examples thus provide an essential link to an important aspect
      of language learning to which a conventional dictionary cannot do justice.

haustible fund of information requiring the minimum in cost and effort from the user. Most students thought a dictionary should include modern technical terms, AE and BE variants, slang, dialect, phrases and idioms, synonyms and antonyms, as well as encyclopaedic information; it should also make use of colour and at the same time be small and cheap.

It is not irrelevant here that in the German-speaking countries dictionaries traditionally play a different role than in England. For the average German native speaker, including even teachers of German (cf. Kühn and Püschel 1982), the dictionary prototype is the one-volume *Duden 1 (Rechtschreibung)*, which has a minimum of microstructural information and is referred to as a final authority in formal matters such as spelling and hyphenation, but it is hardly used to gain insight into the creative genius of the language. The compiler of a dictionary for the German learner might take this into consideration and expect a user with somewhat authoritarian expectations and a limited knowledge of the dictionaries available. An extreme but by no means exceptional case was the university student who, when asked in an examination to describe a thesaurus, replied: "Isn't it a kind of prehistoric animal?"

6. The bilingual dictionary and words in context

Finally, I should like to illustrate some of the problems outlined above by drawing on concrete examples from a class in German-English translation. My starting-point is an observation by Fritz Güttinger, himself a professional translator: "Ein zweisprachiges Wörterbuch Kann einem ein Wort erklären, aber es liefert kaum je die passende Übersetzung dafür." (Güttinger 1963:90)

This remark, which runs contrary to much theoretical work on bilingual dictionaries,[11] can be confirmed again and again in translation. One example is the simple word *Wiedersehen*, as in the newspaper headline "Wiedersehen mit Belfast" *(NZZ, 7.4.78)*, introducing an account of a visit to Belfast after an absence of some

---

11   Cf. Zgusta 1984 and Kromann et al. 1984b.

years.   Having once learnt that *wiedersehen* "is" *to meet again*, students promptly translated the headline as "Meeting Belfast Again" or
"Reunion with Belfast", without being aware that a reunion or meeting
is limited to human participants.   The title "Belfast Revisited" is
therefore a more suitable translation.[12]   A similar example, discussed by Honig and Kußmaul (1982:9), is the message televised to the
world at the end of the Olympic Games in Innsbruck in 1976:   "Auf
Wiedersehen in Lake Placid".   The translator had obviously learnt
that *Goodbye* is the English equivalent of *Auf Wiedersehen*, but was not
aware of differences in function, namely that when time or place of
reunion are named *Goodbye* cannot be used, so that an expression such
as "See you again in Lake Placid" would have been more appropriate.
Part of the aim of the LBD must be to sensitize the learner to such
differences and to provide *guidance on usage* in the form of well-chosen
examples.

In the text on Belfast already referred to, the town is described
as follows:

"Ganze Straßen, die einstmals von regem *Geschäftstreiben erfüllt* waren,
stehen ausgebrannt und mit vermauerten Schaufenstern da."

The problem lies in the phrase *von regem Geschäftstreiben erfüllt*, rendered literally by students with expressions like "filled with busy
life" or "full of lively business".   However, what in German is expressed in a nominal or adverbial phrase is in English often rendered
more naturally in a verb phrase, and English abounds with semantically "loaded" verbs such as *bustle*, which by a process of *redistribution of components* serves admirably as an English translation:

Fig. 3:   Redistribution of components

---

12 This again shows the limitations of the conventional bilingual dictionary:
    this use of *revisited* is not so much lexicalized in the language system as
    anchored in the English cultural heritage.   In translation classes
    encyclopaedic information and cultural knowledge - such as reference to
    Wordsworth's poem *Yarrow Revisited*, Evelyn Waugh's novel *Brideshead*

The sentence would then run: "Entire streets, once *bustling with activity and business,* are now burnt out, the shop windows walled in." Traditional bilingual dictionaries provide little help here, and I have found the problem is best solved with the help of the system of contrastive semantic fields mentioned earlier (cf. Snell-Hornby 1983:95-6, 239).

This last example is a convincing illustration of the much-cited anisomorphism of language, precisely the problem that a suitably designed bilingual dictionary could help the learner recognize and overcome, given an adequate amount of condensed, well-selected and clearly presented information about the foreign lexical items, in relation both to each other and to the lexical system of the learner's native language. Such a dictionary would however be a highly sophisticated reference tool, and it would presuppose the learner's willingness to make full use of the information it provided. Certainly, there is no substitute for language competence, and a dictionary is not the language.[13] But it should be more than a mere collection of words, and for the learner an active bilingual dictionary could be an indispensable guide to the wealth inherent in words. There are however two basic requirements: firstly, the principle of elementary approximation must be replaced by the principle of differentiation, and secondly, the dictionary must take its proper place in an integrated, holistic concept of language learning.

Revisited and the title of its German translation *Wiedersehen mit Brideshead* - often feature as prominently as purely linguistic explanation.

13 Cf. Widdowson (1979:248): "... communicative competence is not a compilation of items in memory, but a set of strategies or creative procedures for realizing the value of linguistic elements in contexts of use, an ability to *make* sense as a participant in discourse, whether spoken or written, by the skilful deployment of shared knowledge of code resources and rules of language use." As a reference book of lexical items, the dictionary offers a language potential which is then realized in language use. There are of course stable and formulaic aspects of vocabulary, such as stable collocations, phraseologisms, conversational formulae, etc. (cf. Cowie, in press), but the real problems for the language learner lie in the dynamic element in lexical meaning referred to here (cf. Snell-Hornby 1985a).

PART III

PROGRESS IN DICTIONARY

DESIGN

Rosamund Moon

MONOSEMOUS WORDS AND THE DICTIONARY

1. Introduction

   Traditionally, dictionaries divide words into "senses" on syntactic and/or semantic grounds, and this very tradition sets up the ex-
pectation that when information about a word is presented in a dictionary entry as a series of (usually numbered) sense-divisions,
there will be syntactic and/or semantic differences between those
divisions.[1]   The term "sense" itself as used in dictionary metalanguage implies semantic difference.   Bilingual dictionaries have
their own reasons for establishing sense-divisions and I do not propose to discuss them here.   I want to consider instead monolingual
dictionaries and their practice of dividing up into senses not only
words that are clearly polysemous, but also, using much the same conventions, those that have a very narrow range of meanings, sometimes
only a single one.   That is, I want to raise the issue of whether
all words that are treated as polysemous in dictionaries are actually
polysemous.   I should perhaps emphasize here that I am limiting my
discussion to monolingual dictionaries of English, and that I am not
considering issues of homography as opposed to polysemy.

Monosemous, monosemy and *monoseme* are perhaps all misnomers as I use
them in this paper.   These terms should strictly be reserved for
words with a single meaning, a single referent, and a single grammatical function.   Random checks in the *Collins English Dictionary* and
the *Concise Oxford Dictionary* suggest that many of these words are technical terms, such as the names of animals or plants, etc., or rare
register-specific words;   they represent no real problem for lexicographers and dictionary-users (Sweet:1899/1964).   The words that
interest me would more accurately be termed "quasi-monosemous":[2]

---

1 I am indebted to colleagues at Birmingham who have read this paper and discussed
   it with me.
2. Terminology is a problem.   I continue to use *monosemy* or *quasi-monosemy*, for
   want of better terms.   Catford discusses various terms such as *oligosemy*,
   eurysemy, and *stenosemy* (1983:24): of these, *stenosemy* ("for words having a
   restricted or narrow-ranging meaning") is most appropriate for the words that
   I am discussing.

they have a single meaning or semantic core underlying their various uses, and yet they are difficult to explain in a single dictionary sense and definition. The interpretation of these words tends to be heavily context-dependent. Lexicographers carve up the word in order to explain it in relation to its various contexts - the larger the dictionary, the more the word is carved up - and as a result the single core meaning is dissipated. A related category consists of words with some clearly distinguishable senses, but also a number of "senses" that are in fact linked by a single underlying concept or different aspects of a single concept (Stock 1984, Sinclair 1985). Many of these quasi-monosemous words are non-register-specific, core vocabulary items, although they occur throughout the lexicon, and include grammatical as well as lexical items. How helpful is it for the user of an EFL dictionary if lexicographers dissipate the single central meaning that the native speaker perceives? How helpful is it for the user of a native-speaker dictionary if lexicographers misrepresent the nature of such words?

I shall be discussing some individual lexical items later in order to develop the notion of "quasi-monosemous" more fully; for the present, I shall exemplify it by reference to *mouth*, which is a polysemous word. Most dictionaries would pick out senses that have to do with the opening of a cave, the open end of a bottle or jar, etc., and the point where a river joins the sea, in addition to the "oral" sense. However, a larger dictionary might also divide the "oral" sense into:

(1) the opening: *He took the cigarette out of his mouth*

(2) the lips: *She had a wide and smiling mouth*

(3) the cavity: *He put the meat into his mouth*

These three sub-senses have different referents, synonyms, and superordinates. Yet such fine splitting is surely false on common-sense grounds. How far do we ever think of the three referents as separate or indeed separable? It seems rather that they are merely separate aspects of the same entity. Consider the following examples, taken from the Birmingham Corpus:

(a) He lay against a log, his mouth gaping.
(b) ... moustache that drooped down at the corners of his mouth.

(c) She had a thin mouth.

(d) He put a hand to his mouth.

(e) I sat with a pipe in my mouth.

(f) I'd hold it in my mouth and not swallow.

(g) ... with blood spilling from his mouth.

(h) ... took my chances of getting hit in the mouth.

(i) ... the huge red mouth opening wider and wider.

In some of these examples, there is no clear signalling of any particular aspect of the mouth: in others, one aspect is signalled more
clearly than another. In each case, this is because of context or
real-world knowledge. For example, (c) picks up on aspect (2),
but this is because the adjective *thin* predicts the aspect where shape
is likely to be a relevant variable. Real-world knowledge makes
clear the difference between (e) and (f) even though in (f) we do
not know what *it* refers to. In the bizarre circumstances of someone putting a cigarette *inside* their mouth, the surrounding text would
disambiguate by reference to eating, swallowing, chewing, perhaps
choking, etc., or else a different form of words would be chosen, for
example, *He put the cigarette right into his mouth.* I would suggest that
none of the examples listed above is ambiguous.

Of course, many dictionaries do not split so finely, and others
give a single definition which refers explicitly to the various
aspects I have mentioned. My point is that only lexicographers
would ever think of regarding or analysing the "oral" sense of *mouth*
in this way in the first place.

There is an argument that such fine categorization is needed in
an EFL dictionary, as other languages may have separate words for
these "senses": English itself has a different word *lips* for
"sense" (2), although *lips* and *mouth* are not exact synonyms. This
is an interesting argument, but it seems to me to contain two flaws.
Firstly, most people would regard a mouth as a single entity, not
three, and to sub-divide its sense would destroy any hope of conveying native-speaker intuitions of what *mouth* means. Secondly, it
would be unrealistic for a monolingual EFL dictionary designed for
a global market to attempt to account for the vocabulary structure
of all other languages - or even of the major ones.

A related problem occurs when words - or senses of words - have a specialist meaning for one group of people as well as a general meaning.   To an astrophysicist *space* is a continuum, and the nearest synonym I can think of is *everything;* to most people, *space* is what lies outside the earth's atmosphere.   To the former, this planet is part of space: to the latter, it is not.   Two senses, or two aspects or conceptions of the same sense?   Catford (1983:13-14) makes a similar point when he talks of how the word *insect* has a much narrower reference for a zoologist than for people in general, to whom spiders (and indeed a variety of other creatures) may be insects. Should we recognize a separate sense of *insect?*

   The polysemy - or monosemy - of an individual word is not an absolute.   The number of senses that a dictionary ascribes to a word may reflect the nature of that dictionary and its publisher's house style: large dictionaries contain more senses as well as more headwords.   There is no space here to explore the criteria that lexicographers use to establish discrete senses of a word.   Stock (1984) has written about some of these, and Cowie (1982) and Cruse (1982) both discuss grammatical and semantic criteria in relation to the problems of identifying cases of polysemy.   I will only comment that most of the criteria employed break down at times;   that, as Cowie (1982:53) and Cruse (1982:68) both suggest, more than one criterion is usually needed;   and that there seem to be few hard-and-fast rules, over and above the working practices of individual dictionary houses.

2.   Delexical verbs

   "Delexical" verbs are an obvious example of the kind of monosemy that interests me.[3]   They are high-frequency words, basic to English, which have a wide range of contexts and collocates, but only a slim core of meaning.   They also reflect the tradition in monolingual lexicography of splitting finely the most frequent words and treating them in great detail.   Cockeram's dictionary of 1623 did not include the verb *take*, Bailey in 1721 gave it 18 senses, Johnson in 1755 gave it 134, and Murray et al (1933) gave it 341:   the practice

---

3 In the second edition of the *Advanced Learner's Dictionary* (1963) Hornby uses
   the term "heavy-duty verb" - ed.

proliferates. *OED* sets out to provide a detailed historical analysis of word use. Is there any purpose, other than the historical one, in providing such a detailed treatment of the word? How many native-speakers ever have any difficulty in using or understanding *take*, apart from technical (or obsolete) senses, or a few idioms in restricted currency? We manipulate dozens or even hundreds of senses of the word with ease. This to me is the crux of the matter. Are these "basic" words in English as complicated as lexicographers make them appear?

Ruhl (1979:93) says:

"Common verbs such as *take, give, come, go, break* and *hit* are monosemic and are judged as polysemic by dictionaries and linguists because their essential general meanings are confused with contextual, inferential meanings."

and in an earlier paper (1975:441) he complains:

"A generalization that can not be grasped consciously - such as a single meaning for *take* - is simply denied."

Lexicographers are forced into denying this too, because we have not yet solved the problem of how to convey such a single meaning within the traditional framework of a dictionary. Murray, the arch-splitter (341 senses of *take!*), nonetheless recognized the problem. In the introductory matter to the article for *take*, he refers to three broad groups of meanings: (1) "seize, grip", hence "appropriate"; (2) "receive or accept what is handed to one" and (3) "assume, adopt, ... comprehend, ... contain". He goes on to say:

"For the common element of all these notions *take* is the simple and proper term for which no simpler can be substituted. It is one of the elemental words of the language, of which the only direct explanation is to show the *thing* or *action* to which they are applied."

Murray here advocates categorization according to context and collocation, and he also shows his awareness of the delexical nature of the verb.

The verb *keep* is one of the least complex of those with delexical senses. In analysing the data for it in the Birmingham Corpus, I originally carved out 30 senses for the simple verb (together with about sixty for idiomatic phrasal verbs) by grouping together object-collocates. For example, the group of collocates denoting promises, agreements, appointments provided evidence of one sense, while that suggesting laws and rules provided evidence of another. This approach is easy: it is much harder to try to work out what "meaning" accrues to *keep* in each set of contexts than it is to separate out and define those contexts, but how true a representation of the word does this provide? And if the "context" approach is used, should a dictionary entry not warn the reader that this is the case, as indeed Murray did for *take?*

I later reorganized my thirty senses for *keep* according to my conception of the meaning and function of the verb itself, and developed six broad groupings, as shown below. I would not argue that these groupings are polished or perfect, only that they are an alternative way of looking at the meaning of a word - from the inside of the word out, rather than from the surroundings of the word in. Of these six general groupings, it is significant that the distinctions in the sixth are mostly marked by the particles used - *away, out, from,* etc. - or by the semantic force of the object-complement. In the end, even these six groupings overlap or shade into one another.

keep

(1) to (cause something/somebody) to stay in the specified state, condition, place, etc.; to continue to go in the same direction; to do something (in various idioms)

> *keep warm*
> *keep somebody awake*
> *keep somebody in hospital*
> *keep to the left*
> *keep right on till the end of the road*
> *keep an eye open*
> *keep guard/the peace/ silence/order*

(2) to repeatedly do something; to persist in something

> *keep thinking about it*
> *keep coughing*

(3) to last, continue (in good condition)

> *the butter won't keep*
> *your news can keep*
> *I hope you're keeping well*

(4) to have/possess/store/stock/retain possession of something; to reserve something for somebody; to be in charge of/run; to look after somebody/something

> *keep something for your private use*
> *keep a job*
> *keep the tickets until Monday*
> *keep booze in the house*
> *keep your card in a safe place*
> *keep a fine range of wines*
> *keep pets/chickens*
> *keep servants/a boat*

keep a shop/a hotel
keep you in the luxury ...
may the Lord bless you and
   keep you.
keep house
keep a diary

(5) to adhere to;   *keep promises/agreements*
    to observe   *keep laws/rules*
                         keep the Sabbath

(6) to avoid something, restrict   *keep away from the edge*
    somebody/something, prevent   *keep out intruders*
    something   *keep information from somebody*
                                     keep somebody too long
                                     sorry to keep you waiting

3. Adjectives

Adjectives are notoriously hard to divide lexicographically into senses.   They are often heavily context-dependent and flexible, taking on as many meanings as you like or have space for.   One example is the adjective *light*.   I am not trying to suggest that *light* is monosemous, but it seems to have only two main strands of meaning: "not heavy in weight" and "not intense or great in amount, degree, etc."   These intertwine. Further variations in the meaning of *light* depend as much on its noun-collocates as on anything intrinsic to the adjective itself.

Here are ten context or collocate groupings.   (I am ignoring etymology: (2) would often be treated by dictionaries as a homograph related to or derived from the noun *light*.)

(1) not very great in amount,   *a light rain was falling*
    degree or intensity   *a light crop of tomatoes*

(2) weak in colour, not dark   *a light blue shirt*

(3) blowing gently   *in the light breeze*

(4) easily woken or disturbed   *a light sleep*
                                  a light sleeper

(5) not strong or deep in sound   *her light voice*

(6) small in quantity and easily *a light lunch*
    digested

(7) containing only a small amount   *a light white wine*
    of alcohol

(8)	causing relatively little damage, suffering, hardship	*light injuries*
(9)	easy and not onerous	*light housework*
(10)	graceful and gentle	*her light graceful step*

To explain the meaning of *light* in each context requires a different form of words, hence a different "sense", and certainly there are different synonyms, near-synonyms, antonyms, and superordinates for each.   However, to treat each context as separate would be to define the context of the adjective within the nominal group rather than the adjective itself.   *Light* in all these contexts has the notion of "not great in intensity or depth, to only a small degree", and the variety of noun-collocates reflects the ubiquity of *light* and the flexibility of its use against the background of its essential polysemy.

4.   The noun *top*

Finally, I want to consider the noun *top*.   Leaving aside the name for the child's toy - which many dictionaries would treat as a homograph - *top* occurs in a large number of contexts but really has one basic meaning: the highest point or the highest, higher, or uppermost part of something.   An analysis of the data in the Birmingham Corpus shows clearly that, in most uses of the word, the noun is not used in isolation but requires some elucidating support in the linguistic or situational context.   We say *the top of the hill* or *the hill-top:* if we say *when we reached the top*, the existence of the hill or mountain is clear either from the preceding text or the situation.   This is a fact of the world as well as of language - *top* is a word used to specify position or place in relation to something. Perhaps it is also a fact of the world that *sitting on the top of a Liverpool bus* must refer to the upper deck rather than to the roof: if we meant the latter, we would choose a different form of words. It is not necessary to set up a sense of *top* to mean "top deck". Other contexts in which *top* is found use a concept of hierarchy or scale *(at the top of her profession, at the top of the class, the top of the unemployment league)* or a concept of directionality in which something is considered as having one end higher than the opposite one *(the top of the page, the top of the street, at the top of the garden)*.   In the last two of these, *top* and *bottom* appear synonymous, but the top of the garden is the end that you walk *up* to.

Top is also used to mean a cap, covering, or lid, but support is still usually found in its linguistic environment in references to the object that the top belongs to. Only the sense of *top* to mean a piece of women's clothing seems to exist in comparative contextual isolation. Most dictionaries would treat these two uses as separate senses. The difference between these and other uses of *top* lies primarily in the fact that they have to do with separable, concrete objects: in other contexts *top* is used to refer to position with reference to a whole that it cannot be separated from.

I am not saying that any dictionary entry for *top* should have only one sense, apart from the ones just mentioned: I *am* saying that it is misleading to imply that *top* has a large number of discrete meanings. In most cases there are only discrete contexts: discreteness is ensured by the context, not by *top* itself.

Top is perhaps a special sort of noun, but there are many more of a similar type. I mentioned *mouth* above: others, in particular *book* and *door*, are discussed by Cruse (1982:74ff). The problem is widespread.

Conclusion

It is easy for lexicographers to recognize quasi-monosemous words such as those I have discussed above, since they will inevitably present categorization difficulties. Solutions to the problems of handling them are less obvious. Traditionally, two main approaches have been used: (1) the use of definitions containing hedges or consisting of several parts, typically separated by semi-colons, which cover different "aspects" - an approach that works better for some words than for others - and (2) fine, rather than broad, categorization. This, I maintain, may misrepresent the nature of the word and destroy its semantic integrity. Definitions become too narrow, overspecific, and context-bound. Ruhl (1975:438-9) discusses how such definitions force polysemy onto words that are barely polysemous by overspecifying and undergeneralizing their meanings. Although a definition may be accurate in an individual context, this is because the context itself has allowed the word to take on a more specific meaning *in that context;* in other contexts, that definition will be inappropriate.

Are the definition problems insurmountable?   Is it possible to write definitions that are neither context-bound and overspecific, nor so vague that they are meaningless?   Niedzielski (1984) addresses the problem of an entry for *set* in an English-French bilingual dictionary, and develops a paradigm to show its essential and basic meanings.   This may be one solution.   Another would be to abandon the notion that definitions must substitute syntactically for the word or sense defined, and instead to write short accounts of meaning and function: this is, in any case, what entries for grammatical items such as *the*, *and*, and *be* generally do.

The conventional dictionary format is in itself another problem. The standard linear presentation of senses forces a notion of hierarchy onto the senses explained, whether that hierarchy is determined by history, frequency, or semantics.   Yet links between senses and gaps between senses are rarely linear or constant, and certainly not with the words that I have been discussing.

Lexicographers are caught in a trap: the nature of our work is that it is word-based, but words do not exist in isolation, and their contexts cannot be ignored.   Context shows up meaning in a polysemous word: in the quasi-monosemous words that I have been discussing, the context focuses or colours the meaning to a varying degree.   We cannot separate a word from its context, nor would it be desirable to do so.   At the same time, I suggest that too often we define and analyse the context, and look for diversity rather than unity.   We look too hard around the word we are working on, and not hard enough at what it means in itself, or what it adds to its context.

A.P. Cowie

SYNTAX, THE DICTIONARY AND THE LEARNER'S COMMUNICATIVE NEEDS

Few developments in monolingual EFL lexicography in recent years
have aroused as much critical and speculative comment as the grammatical treatment of entry-words.   The period since 1974 has seen
an extension of the dictionary coverage of particular syntactic
features, and a growth in the use and sophistication of coding
systems.   Feedback from the classroom is now accumulating in the
form of a vigorous and well-documented literature with a number of
characteristic perspectives, some mainly linguistic, others more
directly concerned with practical issues of interpretability and
usefulness.   The analytic strand is well represented by Herbst
(1984a,b), whose research has revealed serious flaws in the treatment of adjective and verb complementation in the *Oxford Advanced
Learner's Dictionary of Current English (OALDCE)* and the *Longman Dictionary
of Contemporary English (LDOCE)*.   His colleague Heath (1982, 1985) has
published valuable comparative surveys of selected grammatical features in these dictionaries and the *Chambers Universal Learners' Dictionary (CULD)*, pinpointing omissions of codes and supporting examples.
Heath lays great emphasis on simplicity and directness of presentation, and like Braecke (1981) argues for the adoption of symbols
which have a mnemonic value and are thus easily remembered (cf.
Cowie 1984).   Others again, and most notably Jain (1978, 1981),
have assessed the effectiveness of particular dictionary treatments
in enabling the learner to avoid or correct performance errors.

In all this critical work, the predominantly syntactic emphasis
of recent developments has not been seriously challenged, though
Stein (1979) has argued strongly that more attention should be given
to word formation.   Nor has the lexicographers' point of focus
(sentence structure) been called in question.   The issues, rather,
have been the adequacy of particular sentence-based descriptions
(Herbst 1984c, Lemmens and Wekker, forthcoming) and the extent to
which their presentation can be understood and applied by the
foreign learner.   The search for improvements within tried and
familiar limits is understandable at the end of a decade which has

seen much innovation and in which research, or hard experience, has brought home to lexicographers the gap which still exists between descriptive sophistication and the reference skills of many ordinary users (Béjoint 1981, Cowie 1981). At the same time, at least at the level of reflection and debate, lexicographers cannot afford to disregard signs of gaps opening up in another direction: between current working assumptions on the one hand and developments in linguistic and language-teaching theory on the other.

Precisely this may have happened through our continuing preoccupation with the kind of grammatical knowledge needed to use entry-words correctly in decontextualized sentences and phrases. We have, I believe, largely failed to recognize the importance for EFL lexicography of grammar above the sentence, as reflected for instance in Halliday's work on the information structure of the clause (Halliday 1967-1968), and in Widdowson's influential publications on communicative language teaching, in which the central role of textual cohesion in our production and understanding of normal discourse is constantly stressed (Widdowson 1978, 1979). The result of this unconscious neglect is not that we have ignored altogether the part which certain words and constructions play in producing or understanding connected discourse. In fact, as I have remarked elsewhere, the second edition of *OALDCE* (1963) contained helpful treatments of the 'backward-referring' uses of some determiners (Cowie 1984), and the same is true of more recently published dictionaries. The effect rather is that for want of an appropriate theoretical perspective, our treatment of relevant items has been patchy and unsystematic.

Words and constructions with "discourse potential" make up an area where the domains of the grammar and the dictionary overlap in varying degrees - a point I illustrate below with reference to the passive construction. Successful language learning means recognizing the complementary roles of the two aids (Snell-Hornby, this volume). For much of the rest of this paper I shall develop this theme, taking as examples certain syntactic properties of verbs, and also various "grammatical" parts of speech, including pronouns, determiners and conjuncts (e.g. *furthermore, in any case, at all events*). My aim will be to examine the principles that determine which items and grammatical properties are to be included in the dictionary, as likely to contribute to discourse, and how those items and properties are to be treated.

The passive construction well illustrates the point that normal communication calls for the ability to adapt simple, declarative, active sentences to fit a variety of contexts. The advanced student should be able, for example, to recognize that B1 (rather than B2) is an appropriate response to A:

(A and B are discussing a break-in at B's flat)

A: What happened to your new watch?
B1: It was stolen.
B2: A thief stole the watch.

The knowledge called for here has several interrelated aspects. It clearly includes the ability to transform an active sentence into a passive one. But it also involves being able to recognize that B1 is a more appropriate response to a question which seeks information about an event ("What happened?") rather than its causer or the object affected - these two having already been established in the preceding context (linguistic or situational).

Where can the learner expect to be told about this? Most of the details he needs to consider are for the grammar rather than the dictionary. These are: the rules governing the passive transformation; the principles which state that, in a one-clause sentence, the neutral position of the nucleus is (generally speaking) the last open-class word in the clause, and that this indicates where the "new" information lies (Quirk et al 1972:938-942); and the possibility of replacing, as "given" information, *your new watch* by the pronoun *it*.[1] All these are principles which apply in very many individual cases. So for the necessary guidance the learner turns to a pedagogical grammar; and a number are now on the market which deal with the formal means by which "new" and "given" information are conveyed (Quirk and Greenbaum 1973, Leech and Svartvik 1975).

However, whether the passive transformation is possible at all depends first on a verb's class, and within certain classes on the

---

1 The reply *The thief 'stole it* is also possible. Here, *the thief* may refer back to an earlier mention of *a thief* (Susan Ramsaran, personal communication).

individual verb.   Here the necessary guidance must be provided by
the dictionary.   Consider:

(1) He was *reinstated* by the tribunal.

(2) They are *put off* by his manner.

(3) It will all be *gone into* by our committee.

In all these examples, the passive construction allows the agent/
cause to be given end-focus, where it will be interpreted as new
information.   But the learner must first know if the change is
permissible.   Most transitive one-word verbs (including *reinstate*
and *interpret*) have passives, as do the majority of transitive phrasal
verbs (*put off*, *take down*, etc.).   No labelling to this effect is
thus necessary in a general EFL dictionary, where many competing
demands for space have to be met, though it is helpful to identify
verbs in which the passive is usually or often preferred to the
active (Stein 1979).   The "prepositional" verb (*go into* in (3),
above) is quite different: by no means all members of the class
allow the passive transformation (Cowie and Mackin 1975: xxxviii),
and there is a good case for marking in general EFL dictionaries
those prepositional verbs which *do* permit it.

The division of labour between grammar and dictionary which is
needed to account for the syntax and discourse functions of the
passive on the one hand, and the peculiarities of individual verbs
on the other, is in keeping with Sweet's view of the dictionary as
"a collection of isolated phenomena of the language" (Sweet 1899/
1964: 139).   What Sweet did not foresee, of course, was that the
practical dictionary might incorporate its own grammar, either in
the form of a tabular presentation of "basic" clause patterns (*OALDCE*,
ODCIE) or as a matrix plotting the intersection of various functional
slots (thus "intransitive *v*", "linking *v*") and constituent classes
(*to*-infinitive, *-ing* form, etc.), as in *LDOCE*.   What we must now
ask is whether this grammar should also deal with the mechanics of
passivization and other transforms.   Such guidance is already a
feature of both volumes of *ODCIE*, where the special grammatical
problems associated with idioms argue for its inclusion.   The case
for providing such help in the introductions to general EFL works
is less clear-cut.   A simple description, with examples, of only
one or two transformations per verb pattern can occupy much space;

and it seems sensible to encourage learners to look outside the dictionary for general guidance, especially as a complementary approach to the use of dictionary and grammar in language teaching can be defended on broader pedagogical grounds. It is worth noting that examples of the passive were provided in the second edition of *OALDCE* below several verb tables, thus:

Verb Pattern 6

1   He kept me waiting.
4   I heard him giving orders.
Note the passive construction:
1   I was kept waiting.
4   He was heard giving orders.   (1963:xviii)

However, this simple treatment of the transform was not kept up throughout the scheme - there are no indications of what happens in indirect object patterns, for example - and probably on the grounds that what could not be done fully should not be done at all, the feature was dropped from the third edition (1974).

Let me return now to individual dictionary entries and to the question of how transforms, and their discourse functions, are handled there. Sometimes the reasons for backing up an explanatory label or code with related example sentences are particularly compelling. A case in point is a clause pattern in which the direct object is followed by a prepositional phrase denoting a starting-point (or "source"), and in which the position of the nucleus is the final noun:

(4) We stripped the bark off a 'tree.

This is of course transformationally linked to a sentence in which *bark* and *tree* are transposed, with "source" becoming the direct object:

(5) We stripped the tree of 'bark.

Here the structural shifts, and the association of the nucleus first with *tree*, then with *bark* have produced not a change of meaning but a possible alteration in what we perceive as given and new information: *the bark*, which may be "given" or "new" in (4), contrasts with *bark* ("new" in (5)); *a tree*, which is "new" in (4), contrasts with *the tree* ("given" in (5)).

How are these facts to be presented? In *OALDCE* 2, sentences illustrating the patterns shown at (4) and (5) were not as a rule given the same content words. Nor were they always juxtaposed. Consider, from that edition:

> strip ... ∿ *the bark off a tree*
> *(wallpaper from a wall); ...*
> *They ∿ped the house of all its furnishings.*

The relatedness of the patterns was thus not made apparent to the learner. The corresponding *OALDCE* 3 entry, however, reflects a change of policy. It was decided to illustrate the structural relationship by devising pairs of sentences containing the same nouns and separated by an oblique stroke:

> strip ... ∿ *paint from a surface/*
> ∿ *a surface of paint,* ... ∿ *the bark off a tree/*
> ∿ *a tree of its bark.*

These conventions were supported by indicating in a more abstract form, and in bold print, the underlying variant patterns:

> ∿ sth (from/off sth), ∿ sth/sb (of sth)

As a comparison of the *OALDCE* 3 examples and those at (4) and (5) will show, however, the new style of exemplification did not always succeed in conveying the different discourse functions of the related patterns. Some improvement could be achieved by adjusting determiners in such a way that non-final noun phrases were always definite, and final ones indefinite:

(6) strip *the* paint from *a* surface/
    strip *the* surface of paint

But for various reasons this is a far from ideal solution. One problem is that *the* has various referential uses. In a sentence such as

(7) The Council are clearing the streets
    (sc. of snow, leaves, rubbish)

the streets will not necessarily, or even usually, refer to a specific network of streets mentioned in the preceding context ("these streets around here"). The reference is non-specific ("streets in general") and the phrase signals new information – a point which is underlined by its position. Now since many nouns behave in a similar way to *street* with respect to article usage *(the front door, the garden wall, the radio)*, it is only to be expected that a proportion of dictionary examples will show the definite article in a position commonly associated with new information.[2]

A further difficulty in the way of illustrating discourse patterns by means of examples has to do with contextual deletion of objects and other sentence constituents (Cowie 1984). Consider these examples:

(8) Don't answer the phone.

(9) Don't answer it.

(10) Don't answer.

Example (9) is a possible reply to a question such as *What happens if the phone rings?* and shows the use of a pronoun object when what it refers to has already been given (as here by *the phone*). But (10) is also an acceptable reply; it illustrates the point that after certain verbs *(answer, reply, notice,* etc.) a direct object can be removed altogether, provided that an antecedent phrase is present - or at least strongly suggested. ((10) could therefore also be a reply to the question *What shall I do if someone rings?).* If (9) or (10) were chosen as example sentences, their incomplete nature would need to be shown, perhaps by supplying the questions to which they are answers. This approach must be seriously considered, especially as object deletion is a property of particular sub-classes of verbs. But followed consistently it could lead to an unacceptable enlargement of entries.

So far in this paper I have discussed some possible consequences for dictionary design of explaining and illustrating those syntactic properties of verbs which have "discourse potential". Much the same could be said of nouns and adjectives, since many of these have "complements" - collocated phrases or clauses - some of which are deletable in the circumstances just outlined for verbs. Compare (11) and (12) (and their lengths as possible examples):

---

2 The non-specific use of *the* in *the bark* (example 4) helps to make possible its interpretation as new information.

(11) Can you give me a description of the thief?

(12) You must have seen the thief. Can you give me a description?

But cohesion in discourse calls for more than knowledge of the relevant syntactic behaviour of major-class words. Of crucial importance also is the ability to handle pronouns, determiners and conjuncts (i.e. connecting items with discourse functions). The part played by personal pronouns and the definite and indefinite article in helping to distinguish new from given information has already been briefly noted. How are these uses to be treated in entries for the grammatical items concerned?

We should recognize that entries for the third-person pronouns *he, she* and *they, him, her* and *them*, can contain only the briefest of information. Their anaphoric (or "referring-back") function - the one discussed earlier in relation to the passive - is the chief one, and this is repeatedly illustrated throughout the dictionary in entries for other words.[3] The anaphoric use of these words will have been learnt long before the advanced level is reached, and it is almost inconceivable that any user should refer to the relevant entries for purposes of revision.

Entries for the definite article and such other determiners as *many, much, few* and *little* - all of which can be used anaphorically - are a different case. They are more complex grammatically, as witness the pronominal and adverbial uses of *much* and *little*, and though all will be taught at some stage as topics in grammar, there is much to be said for concentrating all the information about a particular pronoun or determiner at a single point, as the dictionary is designed to do. Within such a presentation the anaphoric use of each item should be distinguished and briefly contextualized, as in the following examples of pronoun anaphora from *OALDCE, LDOCE* and *CULD* respectively:

---

3 Note, for example, at *issue* in *OALDCE*, ∿ *warm clothing to the troops;* ∿ *them with warm clothing.* It must be recognized, however, that while many entries containing the subject and object pronouns (in *OALDCE, LDOCE* and *CULD)* imply the previous occurrence of a noun, relatively few entries actually *show* that noun.

such ... *He is a brilliant scholar and is everywhere recognized as such,* as a brilliant scholar.

much ... *When you've cooked meat, there's never as much as when you bought it.*

many· ... *'Were there a lot of people there?'* *'Not very many.'*

Let us turn finally to adverbs and prepositional phrases used to indicate how one sentence relates to another in continuous discourse. This syntactic category, called conjuncts by Quirk et al (1972:520), is divided into a number of functional subclasses (thus, "reinforcing", "equative", "result"). To the "transitional" subclass belong *by the way* and *incidentally,* which can be used to change the topic of conversation:

(13) By the way, what time does the bar open?

As in the case of determiners, there is little likelihood of conjuncts being acquired by reference to a dictionary. In fact, their role in structuring discourse has prompted some materials designers to make their uses a feature of advanced writing and reading programmes (Allen and Widdowson 1974:xvi-xvii). There are, however, stronger reasons than in the case of determiners for providing the additional support of reliable reference tools. A particular difficulty is that many conjuncts are stereotyped phrases or clauses with idiosyncracies of grammar and collocation. Compare

(14a) To start with/*To end with

(14b) For a start/*For an ending

(15a) First of all/Last of all

(15b) In the first place/*In the last place

These restrictions suggest that though "grammatical" in function, conjuncts can pose the same kinds of learning difficulty as idiomatic phrases which more closely resemble nouns or adjectives - *one's first impression,* say, or *first past the post* - and that they need careful treatment in general as well as specialized learners' dictionaries (cf. Cowie et al 1983:xvii).

In EFL lexicography we still for the most part operate with a set of grammatical assumptions which make the word the central point of focus and the sentence its outer defining frame. These

limitations are reflected both in our inadequate treatment of well-
understood, and in grammars well-described, discourse functions of
quite common words and constructions, and in the predominantly
sentence-based character of dictionary examples.   There is, I
believe, a pressing need for lexicographers to enlarge their perception of the kinds of grammatical understanding which the learner
requires in order to communicate naturally in English.   This paper
is offered as a contribution to that process and as a stimulus to a
debate which is now overdue.

Robert Ilson

ILLUSTRATIONS IN DICTIONARIES

1. Introduction

Illustration is one of the five basic explanatory techniques in
dictionaries, the other four being exemplification, discussion,
definition, and translation (see, for all but translation, Ilson,
forthcoming).   I understand illustration broadly, so as to include
tables and diagrams as well as pictures - indeed all forms of "non-
linear presentation" (M.N. Lamy, personal communication) in which
the display is in some sense iconic; that is, in which the form
of the display represents the items displayed or their relations
to one another.   Illustrations are signs as well as symbols.

It has been argued that illustration is an "onomasiological"
technique (going from concept to name) in contrast to the other
four techniques, which are "semasiological" (going from name to
concept).   However, in real dictionaries illustrations are generally accessed semasiologically; that is, by looking up the
lexical unit that is illustrated.   Nevertheless, group and composite illustrations (see section 3) may also be used onomasio-
logically: users who look up a particular illustrated item may
come away having learnt the names of several other illustrated
items as well.

As suggested by A.P. Cowie (whose many helpful comments I gratefully acknowledge), I should like to present a "catalogue raisonée"
of the types of illustration at present available in dictionaries.
But I shall also consider some types of illustration potentially
available *to* dictionaries if their makers extend the notion of
illustration further.   For my convenience if not my readers', I
shall use a "double macrostructure": first discussion, then, in
an appendix, the specific illustrations discussed.

2. The Single Noun

The typical dictionary illustration is of a single noun, as in
the *Oxford Advanced Learner's Dictionary (OALDCE)* picture at *spiral*

(Plate 1a). The visual complement represented by a picture is especially appropriate at a headword like *spiral*, and the actual picture portrays a range of spirals that the verbal definition and examples can hardly suggest.

The desirability of illustrating more than one token of a given type is implied by the next illustration, that of the motorway *cloverleaf* in the eighth edition of *Webster's New Collegiate Dictionary (W8)* (Plate 1b). It will be obvious that this picture of a cloverleaf is valid only for those countries that drive on the right. Lefthand drivers may make the necessary adjustments mentally, but at least two other solutions are possible. One is to provide a more schematic picture without details of the flow of traffic. The other is to provide two pictures, one for right-hand drivers and one for left-hand drivers. In other words, one should provide either *less* detail or *more* (Ilson 1986).

3. Several Nouns

It is often convenient to illustrate several nouns together. There are both *group* illustrations (of related nouns) and *composite* illustrations (of a whole with labelled parts). In this area the Duden Bildwörterbücher have been pioneers. Collective illustration not only saves space, but allows the referents of the nouns to be contrasted explicitly. Collective illustration does, however, raise the problem of where to put the illustration and how (or whether) to cross-refer to it from the dictionary entries of the individual items illustrated.

The "raison" of this part of my "catalogue raisonée" is provided by Fillmore's classification of "word-fields or semantic domains" (Fillmore 1978:162-165). There is no reason to suppose that Fillmore's categories are meant to be mutually exclusive: thus, for example, the pair *girl/woman*, one of Fillmore's "Contrast Sets", may also be said to exhibit the characteristics of a two-member Fillmore "Paradigm".

Fillmore's "simplest kind of domain structure" is the "Contrast Set", such that "to know the meaning of one member ... is to understand the whole set". Fillmore's examples include *tall/short*, *dead/alive*, and even *girl/woman;* thus, the category includes adjectives as well as nouns. Fillmore points out that the members of these Contrast Sets may exhibit "the various forms of semantic oppositeness", and these are discussed by Lyons and other semanticists (see Palmer 1981: section 5.4); thus, *tall* and *short* are gradable antonyms (contraries), whereas *dead* and *alive* are typically non-gradable antonyms (contradictories or complementaries); arguably, *girl* and *woman* belong to this latter category, too. Perhaps the so-called "relational opposites" (converses) - like *parent/child* - would also fit among Fillmore's Contrast Sets (Palmer 1981: section 5.5). I have found no Contrast Sets of nouns illustrated in dictionaries, and I doubt whether the illustration of noun Contrast Sets on their own is either feasible or worthwhile.

Second comes Fillmore's "Taxonomy": "a set of words linked to each other through the relation of superordination". An imperfect example is *OALDCE's* illustration of *quadrilaterals* (Plate 2a). Although all the figures illustrated are hyponymic to *quadrilateral*, Bas Aarts has pointed out to me that the illustration is not a true taxonomy because the figures are all presented only as co-hyponyms. A more revealing display would have made explicit the taxonomic hierarchy *square* → *rectangle* → *parallelogram* → *quadrilateral*. Here is a case where semantic theory might improve the lexico-graphic treatment of terminology. But the problem is that *rectangle* (say) is *both* a co-hyponym of *square* (in ordinary language) *and* a superordinate of *square* (in the terminology of geometry). One possible solution would be to illustrate a *square* inside a *rectangle* inside a *parallelogram*, so that their shapes would suggest their status as co-hyponyms while their placement (and relative sizes) would suggest their places in the terminological hierarchy; *quadrilateral* would not be illustrated at all, but would be the headword at which the group illustration is located. Thus in the true Taxonomy the relation "superordinate to" is logically "transitive": "x superordinate to y superordinate to z" implies "x superordinate to z". However, for a practical classification of dictionary illustrations it is better not to make logical transitivity a necessary condition for a Taxonomy: without this requirement the Taxonomy becomes a category in which most group illustrations fit naturally.

Third is Fillmore's "Partonomy": "a collection of words linked by a part-while relationship". The most "obviously structured" Partonomies also exhibit their constitutive relation, "part of", in a logically transitive series, as in *fingernail → finger → hand*. However, here too it is practical to abandon the requirement of such transitivity: then the Partonomy becomes the natural home of composite illustrations, like that at *bicycle* in the *Longman Dictionary of Contemporary English (LDOCE)*, where *handlebars* and a *saddle* are both parts of a *bicycle*, but neither is part of the other (Plate 2b). But even without obligatory transitivity, "parts of" is a problematic relation; for example, it is questionable whether *pannier* and *saddlebag*, say, are parts of a *bicycle* in the same criterial way as *handlebars* and *saddle* are. Yet that is hardly a reason for not illustrating them at *bicycle!*

Fourth is the "best known and most discussed kind of semantic domain structure", the "Paradigm": "a group of words having one feature in common and distinguished from each other by features that each discriminate more than one pair of words". A standard example is "the livestock paradigm, in which words having to do with farm animals are arrayed according to such features as 'male'/ 'female'/neutered', 'adult'/'young'/'infant' ... and so on". The *LDOCE* Animal Table (placed in an *LDOCE* appendix and partially reproduced as Plate 3) shows a Paradigm.

A fifth, "minor", domain structure is the "Cycle", exemplified by *morning/afternoon/evening/night*. "Some cycles represent natural phenomena, others, such as the weekday names, stand for artificial cyclic systems." The short extract from the *Dictionnaire du Français Langue Etrangère (DFLE*, Level 1) may be said to illustrate the weekday cycle in a passage of continuous prose whose linearity happens to be appropriately iconic to the set of words it displays, though failing to show the "eternal return" of the cycle: that might have been handled by arranging the words in a circle (Plate 4). Note that the week here begins with Monday ("lundi") rather than with Sunday ("dimanche").

A sixth structure, also "minor", is the "Chain": "a set of words linked by some sort of rank ordering relation and differing from a partonomy or a taxonomy in not allowing the possibility of two terms at the same level" (as *handlebars* and *saddle* are with respect to *bicycle*).   "Military titles provide an example", as shown by part of the table of military ranks at *rank* in the *Longman New Universal Dictionary (LNUD)* (Plate 5).   Note that the higher the rank, the nearer the top of the table.   Tabular presentation is perhaps the only effective way of conveying such information. A.P. Cowie points out that military ranks allow more delicate sub-divisions, like that between *commissioned* and *non-commissioned* offi-cers or that based on grouping under the superordinates *general officer*, *field officer*, and *company* (or *junior*) *officer*.

The seventh type Fillmore calls the "Network, illustrated by systems of kinship terminology.   A network is constructed by a small number of primitive relations (rather than by a single rela-tion, as with a partonomy).   In the case of kinship terminology these are most typically 'married to' and 'parent of' ..."   Of course within kinship systems sub-systems exist exhibiting such phenomena as converseness *(parent/child)* and complementary *(brother/sister)*.   There are many kinship diagrams in dictionaries: the one in the *Longman Active Study Dictionary of English (LASDE)* uses pictures to reinforce the differences of generation and sex, even though (as Michael Rundell pointed out to me) the pictures of *father-in-law* and *mother-in-law* have been transposed (Plate 6).   Kinship diagrams in dictionaries tend to have a single point of orientation *(Helen* for *LASDE)*; a partial exception is to be found in the illustration at *parenté* "kinship" in the *Dictionnaire du Français Contemporain (DFC)* (not reproduced here).   It would be interesting to consider whether one could construct a kinship diagram in which the relationship between any two of the people shown was visible at a glance.

The eighth type, which Fillmore thinks is "the most central and powerful of them all", is what he calls, for want of a better term, a "Frame": "a lexical set whose members index portions or aspects of some conceptual or actional whole".   He offers by way of example the "commercial event schema": *buy, sell, pay, spend ... price, money, change ...* etc.   It is hard to find dictionary illustrations that constitute true Frames, but perhaps the *street* scene at the back of *Collins English Learner's Dictionary (CELD)* might be classified here (Plate 7), as could, conceivably, the *LDOCE* illustration of *bicycle* and other Partonomies.   My unease at classifying even the *street* illustration here corresponds to the unease of many language-teaching methodologists at syllabuses organized round "situations", and comes precisely from their lack of a real "conceptual or actional" underlying unity. Nevertheless there is a recent recognition that the mental representation of such "situations" is part of the pragmatic knowledge that native speakers of a language use to anticipate what people are likely to say about them and to organise their own responses (Widdowson 1983; and see the entry *script* (also called *frame)* in the *Longman Dictionary of Applied Linguistics).*

4. Other Parts of Speech

Kipfer (1984:48) says "... of course, pictures can only help one understand NOUNS." But Kipfer is wrong. That illustrations of other parts of speech can benefit dictionary users I hope to show with the following examples, some from dictionaries, some from other language books. Note that all illustrate groups of words rather than single ones (and are, indeed, group rather than composite illustrations): this may be a necessary condition for illustrating other parts of speech. Furthermore, it can be argued that the illustrations shown are not of words, but of simple sentences: "Linus is *short*"; "The snail is *on* the wall"; "She is *throw*ing the ball".

4.1. Adjectives

Tall and *short* are illustrated at the "unmarked" form *tall* in a children's dictionary, the American *Charlie Brown Dictionary (CBD)* (Plate 8a). Here, at last, is an illustration of one of Fillmore's Contrast Sets. However, the verbal explanation is a necessary complement to the picture. Note that dictionaries often give "Antonyms" of the lexical units they explain: the lexical units are typically adjectives, and the Antonyms are undifferentiated by semantic type.

4.2. Prepositions

Basic spatial uses of prepositions (many of which are also adverbs) are illustrated in Richards (1943:31) (Plate 8b). A better-known illustration is that in *A Comprehensive Grammar of the English*

Language (Quirk et al 1985:674, not reproduced here).

4.3. Verbs

Verbs of motion are illustrated effectively in *LASDE* (Plate 9), where motion verbs of related meaning are illustrated close together (see also Fillmore 1978:162). Earlier still, some of the verbal "Operators" of Basic English had been illustrated (Ogden 1944:167), not reproduced here).

5. Sense Development and Polysemy

Illustrations can attempt to show the relation between different senses of polysemous words, such as those of *arm* (Ogden 1944:91) and *ala* (a *Planeta* dictionary, in Werner: 1982:86), a Spanish word one of whose senses corresponds to a sense of English *wing* (Plates 10a and b). Ogden has also done something similar for the English modal *may* (1944:173, not reproduced here). Note that I am using "polysemy" as lexicographers do, not as most linguists do (compare Kempson 1977: section 6.1).

6. Metaphor

One may even consider the possibility of using tables to attempt to account for institutionalised systems of linguistic metaphors. A suggestive example is provided in Lakoff and Johnson (1980:4) for the analogies drawn in English between *argument* and *war* (Plate 11). If used in a dictionary, such a table might be sited at *argument* and be considered a development of the "exemplification" of its collocational possibilities. Note that the items thus exemplified are of different parts of speech, a characteristic that may relate this sort of table to Fillmore's "Frames".

7. Comparison

The explicit comparison of polysemous items may be effected best by tabular means, as in the *LDOCE* treatment at *must* of *must*, *have to*, *needn't*, and *can't* (Plate 12). French dictionaries (such as the *DFC* and the *Trésor de la Langue Française (TLF)*) are far in advance of English ones here (Plate 13). *DFC* restricts these comparisons to "function words", calling its tables TABLEAUX DE GRAMMAIRE (p. vi). However, there is no reason to conclude that only such lexical units may be compared in this way.   It could be argued that in contrast to the devices discussed up to now, "Comparison" is a category of presentation rather than of linguistic analysis.   But to argue thus is to ignore that the dictionary is . a dialectical unity of form and content: a lexicographic "convention of order and arrangement" (in the sense of Ilson 1984) is itself a statement about the content of what is ordered and arranged.

8. Componential Analysis, Selectional Restrictions, Collocations

These may be displayed advantageously in tables, as in the displays of verbs of "damaging" from *The Words You Need* (Rudzka, Channell, *et al* . 1981: 24-25).   Note the suggestive similarity in form between the display of Components (Plate 14a) and that of Selectional Restrictions/Collocations (Plate 14b).

9. Bilingual Applications

All the preceding illustrations have been monolingual.   But similar techniques can be applied in bilingual dictionaries, as suggested by the example from Hartmann (1976:190), in which Lehrer's work on cooking terms in various languages (1969, 1974) is applied creatively by Heger (1969) and Poten (1975) to contrast English and German componentially (Plate 15).   More prosaically, though still usefully, there are various bilingual and multilingual picture dictionaries of the Duden type (like the *Diccionario Ideográfico Polígloto:* Spanish plus English, French, and German).

10. Pedagogical Applications

Dictionary illustrations can encourage not only language comprehension, but also language production.   Here, the French are again in the lead, as is shown in the discussion of the *DFLE* treatment of *conduire* "to drive (a car)" by Lamy (1985:32) (Plate 16).

11. Conclusion

Throughout this presentation I have assumed but not defended the proposition that dictionary illustrations are a Good Thing rather than a Bad Thing.   Not everyone would agree (though even dictionaries without pictures often have appendices illustrating symbols and displaying the principal parts of irregular verbs in tabular form). However, I believe that *illustration* is one of the most exciting "growth areas" in all of lexicography, and I look forward to the emergence of a new profession: that of dictionary illustrator.

12. Appendix: Illustrations

spirals

Plate 1a: Single noun:
spirals (OALDCE 3).

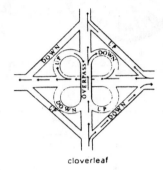

cloverleaf

Plate 1b: Single noun:
cloverleaf (W8).

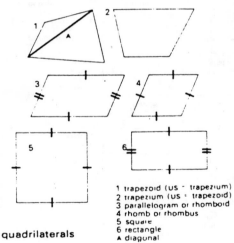

1 trapezoid (US = trapezium)
2 trapezium (US = trapezoid)
3 parallelogram or rhomboid
4 rhomb or rhombus
5 square
6 rectangle
▲ diagonal

quadrilaterals

Plate 2a: Taxonomy:
quadrilaterals (OALDCE 3).

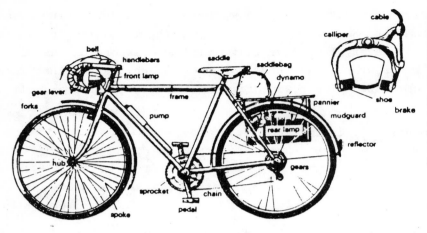

Plate 2b: Partonomy: *bicycle (LDOCE)*.

ANIMAL	MALE	FEMALE	YOUNG	GROUP NOUN	NOISE—all are verb and noun: some are also interjections
cat	tom(cat)	queen	kitten		purr miaow *interj*
cattle (*pl.*)	bull	cow	calf	herd	bellow (of bull) moo (of cow) *interj*
chicken	cock	hen	chick	brood (of young)	crow (of cock) cockadoodledoo (of cock) *interj* cluck (of hen) *interj* cackle (of hen) cheep (of chicks) *interj*
dog	dog	bitch	pup(py)		bark whine growl bowwow *interj*
dolphin, porpoise, whale	bull	cow	calf	school	
donkey					heehaw *interj* bray
duck	drake	duck	duckling		quack *interj*

Plate 3:   Paradigm: *animal table (LDOCE)*.

S. 1. La *semaine* comporte sept JOURS : LUNDI, MARDI, MERCREDI, JEUDI, VENDREDI, SAMEDI, DIMANCHE. Le mot s'emploie aussi (phrase 3) pour désigner la semaine de travail (en général cinq jours en France, du lundi au vendredi). — **2.** On emploie couramment DANS HUIT JOURS, DANS QUINZE JOURS comme syn. de *dans une semaine, dans deux semaines.* — **3.** En semaine désigne la semaine de travail par oppos. au WEEK-END, au DIMANCHE. — **4.** Un journal, une revue qui paraissent chaque semaine sont des HEBDOMADAIRES.

Plate 4:   Cycle:
semaine (DFLE 1).

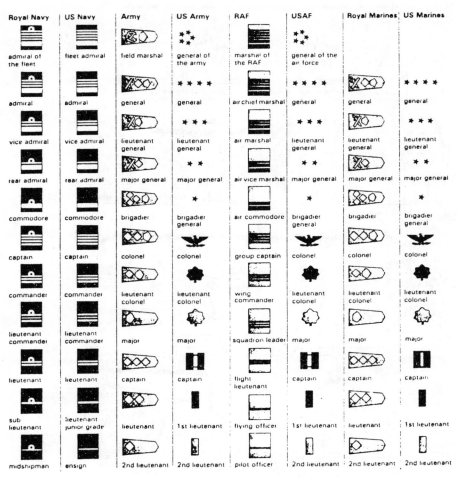

Royal Navy	US Navy	Army	US Army	RAF	USAF	Royal Marines	US Marines
admiral of the fleet	fleet admiral	field marshal	general of the army	marshal of the RAF	general of the air force		
admiral	admiral	general	general	air chief marshal	general	general	general
vice admiral	vice admiral	lieutenant general	lieutenant general	air marshal	lieutenant general	lieutenant general	lieutenant general
rear admiral	rear admiral	major general	major general	air vice marshal	major general	major general	major general
commodore	commodore	brigadier	brigadier general	air commodore	brigadier general	brigadier	brigadier general
captain	captain	colonel	colonel	group captain	colonel	colonel	colonel
commander	commander	lieutenant colonel	lieutenant colonel	wing commander	lieutenant colonel	lieutenant colonel	lieutenant colonel
lieutenant commander	lieutenant commander	major	major	squadron leader	major	major	major
lieutenant	lieutenant	captain	captain	flight lieutenant	captain	captain	captain
sub lieutenant	lieutenant junior grade	lieutenant	1st lieutenant	flying officer	1st lieutenant	lieutenant	1st lieutenant
midshipman	ensign	2nd lieutenant	2nd lieutenant	pilot officer	2nd lieutenant	2nd lieutenant	2nd lieutenant

Plate 5:   Chain: *rank (LNUD)*.

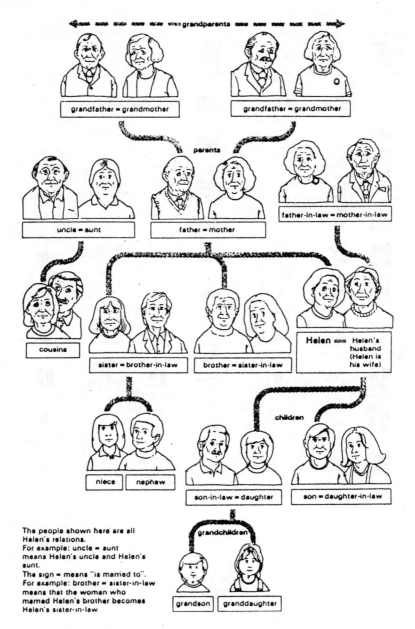

The people shown here are all
Helen's relations.
For example: uncle = aunt
means Helen's uncle and Helen's
aunt.
The sign = means "is married to".
For example: brother = sister-in-law
means that the woman who
married Helen's brother becomes
Helen's sister-in-law.

Plate 6:   Network: *family tree (LASDE)*.

Street

	4. signposts	8. letter/pillar	13. van	curb
1. street light	5. traffic lights/ signals	box	14. pram, (*US*)	18. pavement, (*US*) side-
2. lamp post/ standard	6. motorbike/ cycle	9. litter bin	baby carriage	walk
3. office block	7. (traffic) policeman	10. motor scooter	15. pedestrian/	19. shop window
		11. bus	zebra crossing	20. railings
		12. car, (*US*) automobile	16. Belisha beacon	21. steps
			17. kerb, (*US*)	

Plate 7: Frame: *street scene (CELD)*.

tall   Linus is **not** very **tall**.   He is **short**.

Violet is **taller** than he is.
Her head is above his.

Violet is **taller** than the
   snowman.   She is the
   tallest of them all.

Plate 8a: Contrast set: *tall (CBD)*.

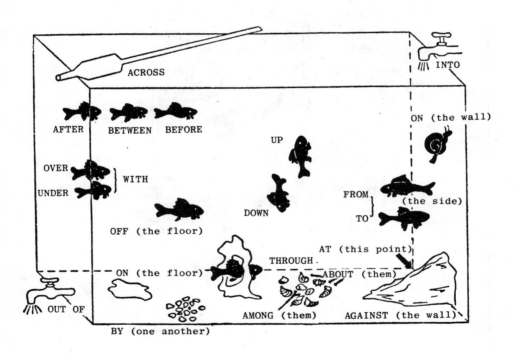

Plate 8b: Prepositions (Richards 1943:   31).

Plate 9:   Verbs: *verbs of movement (LASDE).*

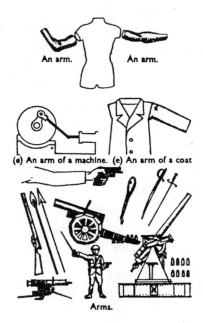

Plate 10a: Polysemy:
arm (Ogden 1944: 91).

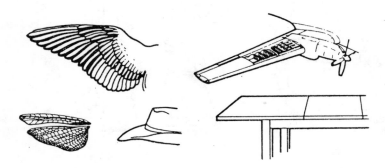

Plate 10b: Polysemy: *ala* (Werner 1982: 86).

ARGUMENT IS WAR

> Your claims are *indefensible*.
> He *attacked every weak point* in my argument.
> His criticisms were *right on target*.
> I *demolished* his argument.
> I've never *won* an argument with him.
> You disagree? Okay, *shoot!*
> If you use that *strategy*, he'll *wipe you out*.
> He *shot down* all of my arguments.

Plate 11:   Metaphor: *argument is war*   (Lakoff and Johnson 1980: 4).

must¹—USAGE

Must I means that I want you to, while **have to** means that it is necessary for some outside reason. Compare: **a** *You must stay for dinner* (= because I want you to) **b** *I'm sorry you have to stay for dinner* (= there's nowhere else to go). **Be to** is like **must I**, but would not be used in this way for an invitation. It is often used for official commands, instructions, and arrangements: *Officers* **must**/*are to wear their uniforms at all times* (military order); *We are to arrive at 6 o'clock* (arrangement). But as **must** has no past tense, we speak of necessity in the past with **have to** or **be to**, except in reported speech: *I said he* **must**/*was to go* is different from *I was sorry he had to go*, just as it would be in the present.

Some (*esp. AmE*) speakers also use **have to** for **must II**: *You have to be joking!* For the relation between **need** and **must**, see the table.

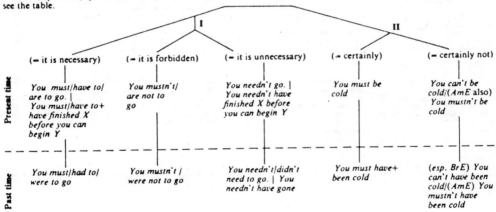

Plate 12:   Comparison: *must (LDOCE)*.

entre	**parmi** (toujours avec un nom pluriel ou un collectif)

1° Indique un intervalle défini par plusieurs points formant une limite :
a) **en parlant de choses :**
Les Andelys sont sur la Seine entre Paris et Rouen. Mettez cette phrase entre guillemets, entre crochets. Il hésite entre ces deux possibilités;
b) **en parlant d'êtres animés :**
Il s'est assis entre la maîtresse de maison et une invitée qu'il ne connaissait pas;
c) **dans des expressions :**
Entre deux, à moitié.
Entre les deux, moyennement. *Être entre ciel et terre,* haut en l'air. *Parler entre ses dents,* murmurer. *Nager entre deux eaux,* ménager deux partis. *Prendre entre deux feux,* attaquer de deux côtés à la fois. *Lire entre les lignes,* aller au-delà du texte pour en saisir le sens profond. *Entre quatre yeux* (fam. : *entre quatre-z-yeux*), en tête à tête (= dans un entretien qui doit aller au fond des choses).

2° Indique un intervalle de temps défini par plusieurs points formant une limite :
Téléphonez-moi entre midi et deux heures. Entre deux voyages à Paris, je pourrai vous recevoir. Entre les deux guerres, il se produisit une crise économique désastreuse.

3° Indique un ensemble dont fait partie un être ou une chose que l'on distingue :
a) **avec des noms de choses :**
Entre plusieurs solutions possibles, choisissez la plus simple. La plupart d'entre elles (de ces voitures) sont hors d'usage;
b) **avec des noms de personnes :**
Entre tous ceux qui se sont présentés, il est le seul à avoir fait une excellente impression. Quelques-uns d'entre eux ont souri à ce bon mot.

Entre autres, entre autres choses, d'une manière plus particulière : *Sur cette question, il y a, entre autres, un livre remarquable d'un savant italien.*

4° Indique un espace délimité par deux ensembles, et qui sert de cadre à l'action considérée :
L'allée menait droit au château, entre deux rangées de chênes. Les invités défilèrent entre deux rangées de valets. Il a grandi entre des parents désunis (syn. : AU MILIEU DE). *Il s'est échappé d'entre les mains de son gardien. Nous pourrons discuter librement toi et moi; nous serons entre nous* (= en tête à tête).

5° Indique une relation ou un rapport de réciprocité entre deux ou plusieurs groupes d'êtres vivants :
L'égalité entre les hommes. Il y a entre eux une vieille querelle. Entre nous, il est inutile de faire des manières. Qu'y a-t-il entre eux? Une amitié réelle existe entre eux.

6° Indique une comparaison entre des êtres ou des choses (souvent sous la forme *entre... et*) :
Il existe une dissymétrie entre les deux parties de l'ouvrage. Entre lui et son frère, il y a de nombreux points communs.

1° Indique un ensemble dont fait partie une chose ou un être que l'on distingue soit pour l'isoler, soit pour l'englober :
a) **avec des noms de choses :**
Parmi toutes les solutions possibles, il a choisi la plus simple (= de toutes les solutions). *Ranger le mot « loyal » parmi les adjectifs;*
b) **avec des noms de personnes :**
Parmi tous ceux qui se sont présentés, il est le seul à avoir réussi toutes les épreuves de ce jeu. Il n'est qu'un employé parmi d'autres.

2° Indique un ensemble qui sert de cadre à l'action considérée :
Il s'avance parmi les blés mûrs (syn. : AU MILIEU DE). *Venez vous asseoir parmi nous* (syn. : À CÔTÉ DE). *Allant à l'aventure parmi les rues obscures* (syn. : DANS).

3° Indique un groupe de personnes de qui relève telle ou telle chose abstraite :
On trouve rarement l'égalité parmi les hommes (syn. : CHEZ). *Ce geste provoqua l'étonnement parmi ceux qui l'avaient connu. Parmi les savants, son nom est respecté.*

Plate 13: Function words: *entre, parmi (DFC)*.

	partially destroy	cause loss of value	with inanimate objects	OR	with abstract objects	have a bad effect on	cause physical pain	OR	cause mental suffering	OR	cause wounds, bruises, broken limbs	make worse, less, weaker	in function or quality	make less than perfect	by doing or giving too much	OR	Completely ruin
damage	+	+	+		+												
harm						+											
hurt							+		+								
injure						+					+						
impair												+	+				
mar					+									+			
spoil						+									+		+

Plate 14a: Componential analysis: *damage*, etc. (based on a matrix in *The Words You Need*).

	sb's car	a painting	the environment	one's health	sb's reputation	children	one's legs	sb's feelings	sb's pride	sb's speech	sb's enjoyment	sb's happiness
damage	+	+	+	+	+							
harm		(+)	+	+	+	+						
impair				+	+					+	+	
hurt						+	+	+	+			
injure				+		+	+					
mar				(+)	+						+	+
spoil		(+)	+	(+)		+					+	

Plate 14b: Selectional restrictions, collocations: *damage*, etc. (based on a matrix in *The Words You Need*).

Lexeme$_{En}$	Definitionen	'with liquid' S$_5$	'with fat' S$_4$	'on open fire' S$_3$	'in oven' S$_2$	'gently' S$_1$	Begriffskern N$_1$	'mit Flüssigkeit' S$_1$	'mit Fett' S$_2$	'auf offenem Feuer' S$_3$	'im Ofen' S$_4$	'langsam' S$_5$	Definition	Lexeme$_{Dt}$
cook	N$_1$	0	0	0	0	0	+	0	0	0	0	0	N$_1$	kochen
boil	N$_1$S$_1$	-	0	0	-	+	+	+	-	0	0	0	N$_1$S$_1$	kochen
simmer	N$_1$S$_1$S$_5$	+	0	0	-	+	+							
fry	N$_1$S$_2$S$_3$	0	-	+	+	-	+	-	+	+	?	0	N$_1$S$_2$S$_3$	braten
								+	-	-	+	-	0	N$_1$S$_3$	rösten
bake	N$_1$S$_4$	0	+	-	0	0	+	0	0	-	+	0	N$_1$S$_4$	backen

Plate 15: Bilingual applications: *Cooking terms* (Hartmann 1976: 190).

conduire [kɔ̃dɥir] v. t.
I. (sujet qqn) **conduire qqn (quelque part)**
*Ça me rendrait service que tu me conduises
à la gare : c'est loin et j'ai mal aux pieds !*
● *Qui est-ce qui conduit Julien à l'école,
aujourd'hui ?*
II. (sujet qqn) **conduire (une voiture)** *Son
mari ne lui laisse jamais conduire la
voiture, il a peur quand ce n'est pas lui qui
tient le volant !* ● *Charlotte vient d'avoir
son permis de conduire, elle pourra aller à
son travail en voiture maintenant.*

G. 1. Conj. 51. — 2. Au sens II, le compl. est
le plus souvent sous-entendu.
S. 1. Au sens I, *conduire* a pour syn. ACCOMPA-
GNER, AMENER et EMMENER. RECONDUIRE, RACCOM-
PAGNER et RAMENER qqn sont également syn.,
mais impliquent en outre qu'on conduit qqn à
un endroit où il avait été auparavant. — 2. Au
sens II, *conduire* a pour syn. en langue
soutenue PILOTER, qui se dit aussi pour les
avions.
L. **conducteur, trice** (n.) [sens II] Celui qui
conduisait a perdu le contrôle du véhicule → *le
conducteur a perdu le contrôle du véhicule.*
◆ **conduite** (n. f.) [sens II] *Elle conduit
rapidement → elle a une conduite rapide.*

Plate 16: Pedagogical applications: *conduire (DFLE 1).*

P.D. Drysdale

THE ROLE OF EXAMPLES IN A LEARNER'S DICTIONARY

1. Introduction

Examples are often overlooked in the discussion of lexicography,
either because they are considered to be less important than definitions, which may be true, or because they are thought to involve
less of the lexicographer's skill, which is not true. A healthy
corrective is supplied by Landau (1984:166):

> "The illustrative quotations or invented phrases that exemplify meaning are
> a critical part of the dictionary definition and should not be regarded as
> mere appurtenances. Illustrative quotations can convey a great deal of
> information about collocation, variety of usage (degree of formality, humor-
> ous or sedate context), connotation (affective implications), grammatical
> context (if a verb, does it take an indirect object?), and, of course
> designative meaning."

When examples are mentioned, and Landau is no exception, it is
often to argue the pros and cons of using made-up examples rather
than quoted citations. This debate refers back, of course, to
the particular status of examples in historical dictionaries, in
which they are both content and authority. Aitken (1973:259)
makes the point forcefully:

> "Nevertheless, as I see it, these definitions remain subservient to the
> citations themselves, which I regard as the really important part of the
> contents of such a dictionary."

In a dictionary designed for students, whether they are learning
their own first language or a subsequent one, examples often have
to illustrate specific usages, contrasts, or collocations and have
to do so in styles and registers that are both idiomatic and intel-
ligible at the students' level of comprehension. It is often
difficult to find a citation that meets all these requirements
concisely, even with the aid of a computer searching a large linguistic data base. On the other hand, reliance on made-up
examples involves the risk of creating some sentences that are
forced and artificial, whether awkwardly stilted or inappropriately
colloquial. In practice most student dictionaries have confined
themselves to made-up examples, although a mixture of these and
citations, as in the *Oxford Dictionary of Current Idiomatic English*, would

seem the most effective way of both making pedagogical points and reflecting actual usage.

A plea for greater attention in learners' dictionaries to the "sphere of applicability" of words was made some years ago by the late Ladislas Orszagh (1969:219). He emphasized (1969:216) the need for "the setting out in dictionaries of the ecology of the words, of their contextual interrelations, of their habitual associations." Although he advocated the use of typographical signs to give some of the "ecological" information he had in mind, he certainly saw examples as providing part of the answer.

To build all this ecological information into a dictionary implies that the book is to be what Snell-Hornby (this volume) calls an "active" dictionary, that students are going to use it for productive as well as interpretative purposes. In other words, it is assumed that they will use it not only to find out what words mean - and what they mean in the particular contexts in which they are found - but also to discover (or confirm) how words are to be used, and whether a given word may or may not be used in a particular environment. To quote Orszagh (1969:219) again:

> "In many English dictionaries we look in vain for the notional, conceptual sphere in which an adjective or a verb tends to be used .... Is the word *gracile* used only of persons, or animals, or things, or concepts, or all four of them? Is *immobile* used in a literal sense only, or also figuratively? If so, with what kind of nouns? With what sort of words do *rampageous* and *immitigable* habitually associate? Why is it not indicated that *bracing* can refer not only to meteorological phenomena (such as air, climate, wind), but may be used in a figurative sense with abstract nouns as well?"

While accepting Orszagh's pleas, one has to admit that for many students much of the time - perhaps for most students most of the time - providing them with dictionaries for productive as well as interpretative purposes is wishful thinking. It is perhaps one of many things that lexicographers do as acts of faith; they provide material because they believe it should be there, but with no confidence at all that it will be used. As Cowie (1983:107) says:

> "However, there is considerable evidence that foreign learners use their EFL dictionaries for interpretative rather than productive purposes, and may in addition be disinclined to master the systems used to codify grammatical patterning. Much needs to be done to help foreign students use such information to fuller advantage."

One advantage of examples is that they bypass some of these problems by providing students with many varied and easily accessible models and demonstrations of words in actual use. For the lexicographer, however, the provision of effective examples is, as indicated above, not as simple as it looks, and the process is, as we shall see, full of traps.

Much of my experience has been with North American dictionaries of English for schools. Whereas British student dictionaries tend to give highly compressed information about many entry words, sets of graded dictionaries like the Dictionary of Canadian English series, the Thorndike-Barnhart (now called the Scott Foresman) series, on which the Canadian books originally were based, and the more recent Macmillan school dictionaries, prefer to give quite extensive information about a restricted list of entry words. Example sentences (almost always made-up examples) in these series have been given considerable importance, and they serve several discrete functions, classified here as follows:

(1) To supplement the information in a definition.

(2) To show the entry word in context.

(3) To distinguish one meaning from another.

(4) To illustrate grammatical patterns.

(5) To show other typical collocations.

(6) To indicate appropriate registers or stylistic levels.

I shall briefly discuss each of these types of example, illustrating their use from the *Canadian Junior Dictionary (CJD)* (1977/79), which is designed for children aged approximately 9-12, before going on to consider the same types as represented in three foreign learners' dictionaries.

2. Examples in school dictionaries

2.1. To supplement the information in a definition

At its simplest this involves giving instances - identifying a class by naming one or more of its members:

antiseptic ...: *Iodine is an antiseptic.*

> appliance ...: *Can openers, vacuum cleaners, washing machines, refrigerators, etc. are household appliances.*

In other types of entry more descriptive information is given, which may even become almost encyclopaedic in nature:

> archaeology ...: *Students of archaeology excavate the sites of ancient towns and then study the traces or samples they find of tools, pottery, jewellery, etc.*

2.2. To show the entry word in context

The basic purpose here is to aid interpretation and encourage imitation by placing the word in a typical and acceptable semantic environment:

> appearance 2 ...: *The singer made her first appearance in a concert in Montreal.*

With some care an example of this kind can often become what Clarence Barnhart used to call a "forcing illustration", one that can only be read with the correct interpretation of the entry word:

> apology 2 a poor substitute: *One piece of toast is only an apology for breakfast.*

> appease 1 satisfy: *A good dinner will appease your hunger.* 2 make calm; quiet: *The mayor appeased the angry crowd by promising to build more houses.*

Although this practice is admirable, the danger of trying to use too many forcing examples is that one ends up with sentences that are improbable or, worse still, artificial:

> apparent 3 seeming; that appears to be: *The apparent thief was innocent; we found the real thief later.*

2.3. To distinguish one meaning from another

This function is illustrated in the examples given above for *appease* as well as in the following pair:

> anxiety 1 uneasy thoughts or fears about what may happen; a troubled, worried, or uneasy feeling: *Mothers feel anxiety when their children are sick.* 2 eager desire: *Her anxiety to succeed led her to work hard.*

This practice is especially useful in the case of entries with many meanings, such as *call, hand, hold, set, take,* where it is much easier for a student to scan an entry looking for an example showing a context similar to the one he wants than it is for him to wade through a long sequence of abstract definitions.

2.4. To illustrate grammatical patterns

This function is often served incidentally, by examples introduced to meet other needs.   They can, however, be composed to show such grammatical possibilities as nouns that are both count and non-count (cf. *a dozen fine blooms* and *apple trees in bloom*), adjectives that are restricted to attributive or predicative position, or are followed by particular prepositions (*susceptible to flattery*), or verbs, especially auxiliaries, with irregular forms and special functions (*He will come, won't he?*).   Moreover, even in a dictionary where entries are not uniformly differentiated by means of word-class labels examples can be chosen, and occasionally labelled, to show a word in use as different parts of speech:

> another   1 one more: *Drink another glass of milk (adj.).   He ate a bar of candy and then asked for another (pron.).*   2 a different: *Show me another kind of hat.*   3 a different one;   someone or something else: *I don't like this book;   give me another.*

2.5. To show other typical collocations

The value of this function is immeasurable and can go a long way towards meeting the pleas of Orszagh.   Some of the possibilities can be seen from the following examples for three different adjectival meanings of *blind*:

> blind 3 hard to see;   hidden: *We were warned about the blind curve on the highway.*   6 without thought, judgement, or good sense: *blind fury, a blind guess.*   9 with only one opening: *The wild horses were driven into a blind canyon.*

These entries show typical collocations as integral parts of example phrases or sentences.   But where space allows, as in a specialized dictionary, such collocations can be treated separately from examples (Cowie 1978).

2.6. To indicate appropriate registers or stylistic labels

Within the limited vocabulary range of a junior dictionary there is little scope for using examples to illustrate slang or professional jargon, especially as there is often among editors a pedagogic tendency to exemplify only what will be accepted as good usage.   There are, however, cases in which examples are used to suggest limited fields of application.

3. Examples in foreign learners' dictionaries

When we come to consider how well examples in these six different functions are used in current foreign learners' dictionaries, we find that, while many sample phrases and sentences are given, and while their uses in recent years have been considerably extended, the space allotted to them could be used more effectively if the purposes served by examples were better understood. The examples in the following discussion are taken from three dictionaries: *Chambers Universal Learners' Dictionary (CULD)*, *Longman Dictionary of Contemporary English (LDOCE)*, and *Oxford Advanced Learner's Dictionary of Current English (OALDCE)*.

3.1. To supplement the information in a definition

On the whole, examples of this kind are less frequent in the learners' dictionaries than in the *CJD* . The teaching aims are different and there is arguably less need to give what might be called encyclopaedic information (Sweet 1899/1964). However, there are instances where exemplification and information go hand in hand, as in:

> dilate ... *The pupils of your eyes dilate when you enter a dark room.*
> *(OALDCE)*

With this compare a pure example, which is also briefer:

> *Her eyes dilated with terror.* *(LDOCE)*

In an entry for another scientific term, the attempt to combine illustration of meaning with information can prove clumsy as well as wordy:

> element ... *Both* HYDROGEN *and oxygen are elements, but water, which is formed when they combine, is not.* *(LDOCE)*

3.2. To show the entry word in context

The danger here is that one can use a great deal of space showing words in use without really adding much linguistic or ecological insight, as in the following example, which rather confusingly repeats a key word from the definition but does little else:

> diaphragm ... a thin layer of muscle separating the chest from the abdomen: *He has strained a muscle in his diaphragm.* (CULD)

A noteworthy feature of contextual examples in learners' dictionaries is the way in which several phrases or sentences are used to show the semantic scope of a definition, as in:

> develop ... l *Plants develop from seeds. A chicken develops in the egg. We must develop the natural resources of our country, ... The plot of the new novel developed gradually in the author's mind.* (OALDCE)

> develop ... l *The plan developed slowly in his mind; She has developed into a very beautiful girl; It has developed into a very large city.* (CULD)

It must be borne in mind that different dictionaries are likely to split the semantic range represented by such examples into separate meanings in different ways. So we find, for example, that the notion of ideas or plans maturing in the mind, which is treated as closely allied to the sense of physical growth in both the above entries, appears with a distinct, narrower definition in *LDOCE*, with an attempt at a forcing example:

> develop ... 2 [Tl] to study or think fully, or present fully: *I'd like to develop this idea a little more fully before I go on to my next point.* (LDOCE)

Of especial value to students of English both as a foreign and as a native language are examples that give clear contexts for the figurative uses of words:

> giant ... 3 *(fig)* ... *Einstein is one of the giants of twentieth-century science.* (CULD)

> giddy ... 2 ... *(fig) She was exhausted after her giddy round of parties and dances.* (CULD)

There are many good instances of such examples in all three dictionaries. But why do two of them give figurative definitions for *anchor* - "anything that gives stability or security" *(OALDCE)* and "a person or thing that provides strong support and a feeling of safety" *(LDOCE)* - without providing an example? And why does the third offer only the following?

> *He leaned over the cliff, using a bush as an anchor.* (CULD)

Surely the important feature to illustrate here is the use of the word to refer to a person or abstract quality, as in *His wife was*

his anchor or *Her love was the anchor that kept him sane*.   Why, too, do
none of the three dictionaries offer an example for the figurative
meaning of *pulse*, as in *the pulse of the nation*, or *the steady pulse of
her thoughts?*   (For further comment on poor coverage of figurative
senses in dictionaries, see Urdang 1979.)

As with figurative meanings, so with idioms: examples are of
particular value to the foreign learner, and they are commonly
given in the three dictionaries.   Sometimes, however, here as
elsewhere, an attempt at a forcing example can result in the
addition of words that are colourful but, in terms of the example's
function, unproductive:

> shoulder ... *shoulder to shoulder* ... *(fig) We'll fight this battle ·
> shoulder to shoulder, and we'll show the management that they can't
> treat their staff like slaves.   (CULD)*

3.3. To distinguish one meaning of a word from another

As noted in the discussion of *CJD*, this function is especially
important in entries having many distinct meanings, where the
regular provision of examples makes it easier for a student to find
the meaning he wants.   It is less easy, however, in those dictionaries where there are many special typographical conventions and
where, as in *OALDCE*, there is - to my eye at least - too little
distinction between the roman and italic fonts.   If examples are
to serve their various purposes, they must, particularly in long
entries, stand out clearly from the rest of the text.

3.4. To illustrate grammatical patterns

The importance given to this function could be shown from many
entries, but let us look simply at the range of grammatical information supplied by the examples in *LDOCE* for the different meanings
of the verb *argue*.   This includes information about transitive
and intransitive uses, about different classes of objects and
complements, and about acceptable prepositional choice:

1   *He argues well. | They argued the case for hours. | He argued that
     she should not go.*

2   *He is always ready to argue (about politics) (with George).*

3   *The way he spends money argues him to be rich/a rich man/that he is
     rich.*

4   *The scientist argued that his discovery had changed the course of
      history.*

5   *Do what you are told and don't argue (with me).*

6   *She argued him into/out of his decision. | to argue Jim out of
      leaving his job.*

Each of these subentries also carries, within square brackets, a
grammatical coding and indications of the appropriate prepositions,
but the examples are of more immediate value to the student.   The
distinctions between meanings are in this case as much grammatical
as semantic and, because they are difficult to explain except by
demonstration, examples are essential.

3.5.   To show other collocations

One device all three learners' dictionaries is the use of the
slash to separate alternative forms in examples.   It may be used,
as in the *LDOCE* example for *argue 3,* above, to show alternative
syntactic structures, but it is also frequently, and ably, used
to show alternative collocations:

archaeological ... *archaeological research/remains/findings.*   (CULD)

electric ... *an electric current/torch/iron/shock; electric light;
      electric flex/cord; ... (OALDCE)*

It is also important to show collocations of headwords used in
figurative senses, many of which develop into set phrases:

hive ... *What a hive of industry!*   (OALDCE)

hive ... *The shop was a hive of activity.*   (CULD)

It is worth noting here that there is a temptation, when preparing school or general dictionaries, to avoid the obvious examples, the set phrases and the cliches, and to stretch students'
minds and experience of the language by encouraging them to be
creative, so that one might give, for this meaning of *hive,* an
example like *The office was a hive of misdirected energy.*   But the
foreign learner needs the set phrases and the expected collocations, and the editor must judiciously restrain his creativity.

3.6.   To indicate appropriate registers or stylistic levels

Like those of school dictionaries, editors of learners' dictionaries exploit this function of examples less than one might suppose,

preferring to rely on labels such as *slang* or *informal* on the one hand and *legal* or *tech* on the other. *LDOCE* seems to make the most effort to provide colloquial examples where these are called for, as for instance to illustrate the informal idioms under *job:*

> *He's gone, and a good job too!*

4. Other devices

There are three further devices that add to the value and spatial economy of examples in learners' dictionaries: defining examples, naming examples, and examples that are themselves defined.

A 'defining' example combines the headword (or a compound or phrase containing it) and the defining words (the 'definiens') within the same sentence. The closeness between such an example and a normal definition is shown as follows:

> grand ^{1} ... 5 ... *The grand old man of British politics is old, experienced, important and probably popular.* (LDOCE)

> grand old man ... an old, experienced, important and probably popular politician.

A 'naming' definition also contains the headword (or a phrase of which it is an element), but in this case the order of definiendum and definiens is reversed, with the former coming last, often after the verb *call:*

> grade ^{1} ... 2 ... An elementary school in the US has eight grades and is called a 'grade school'. Its teachers are called 'grade teachers'. (OALDCE)

Examples that are themselves defined (or 'glossed') provide a way of explaining a specific figurative meaning of the headword, or of a compound or phrase incorporating it, without introducing a new numbered sense. The mechanics are handled in various ways:

> call 4 ... *He felt the call of the sea,* ie to be a sailor. (OALDCE)

> develop ... [within a series of unglossed examples] *We must develop the natural resources of our country,* make the minerals, forests, etc. available for use. (OALDCE)

> electric ... [following several unglossed examples] *the electric chair,* used for electrocuting criminals; *electric blue,* steely blue; *an electric guitar,* one that has amplifiers for the sound; *an electric eye,* a photo-electric cell. (OALDCE)

ovation ... *They gave the president a standing ovation*   (= They stood
and applauded him).   *(CULD)*

The ways in which learners' dictionaries have extended the uses
of examples are indeed admirable, but the impression remains that
examples are often used without due regard to their full range of
possible functions.   It is hoped that the discussion of the various functions listed here will help to bring examples under the
same degree of conscious editorial control as that which is normally applied to definitions.

Carla Marello

EXAMPLES IN CONTEMPORARY ITALIAN BILINGUAL DICTIONARIES

1. Introduction

Most Italian bilingual dictionaries printed in Italy are intended for Italian native speakers.   Those which are most frequently
purchased are in one volume, contain more than 100,000 entries and
aim to be useful tools for students from secondary school to university, for teachers, and indeed for anyone who has to work regularly in a foreign language.[1]

Abridged versions are also available,[2] although the large comprehensive dictionary in one volume is the most popular, reflecting consumer conviction that a dictionary should contain as much
information as possible and last for the whole of the user's lifetime.[3]

The bilingual dictionaries whose examples I have examined are
the following:

(1) Mario Hazon, *Grande dizionario inglese-italiano italiano-inglese*,
    Garzanti, Milano, 1st edition 1961.   30th reprint, December
    1982; 120,000 entries, 2110 pages.   In this paper I shall use
    the abbreviation "Hazon".

(2) Giuseppe Ragazzini, *Il nuovo Ragazzini. Dizionario inglese-italiano
    italiano-inglese*, Zanichelli, Bologna, 2nd edition 1984.   (Revis-
    ed version of the 1st edition, which appeared in 1967).
    128,000 entries, 2112 pages.   "Ragazzini".

---

1 I warmly thank Prof. Giuseppina Cortese and Mr. A.P. Cowie for reading and
   commenting on a previous version of this paper.   The Sansoni-Brandstetter
   dictionary of German and Italian in two volumes and the Sansoni-Harrap dictionary for English and Italian in four volumes are meant for both an
   Italian and a foreign readership.   Among the dictionaries considered in this
   paper only "Robert & Signorelli" claims to have been prepared for both French
   and Italian users.
2 Garzanti's smaller dictionaries for English and French have 67,000 and 66,000
   entries respectively; Zanichelli's *Boch minore* has 62,000 entries; Zanichelli & Longman's abridged edition of Ragazzini has 67,000 entries.
3 Advanced-level students begin to realize that dictionaries grow old rather
   fast.   However, they tend to buy an up-to-date monolingual dictionary of
   the L2 rather than a recent bilingual dictionary.

(3) Malcolm Skey, *Dizionario inglese-italiano italiano-inglese* (Adattamento e ristrutturazione dell'originale *Advanced Learner's Dictionary of Current English* della Oxford U.P.) Società Editrice Internazionale, Torino, 1977; about 50,000 entries, 1894 pages. "Skey".[4]

(4) *Dizionario Garzanti francese-italiano italiano-francese*, Garzanti, Milano, 1st edition 1966. 19th reprint, January 1983; 120,000 entries, 2029 pages. "Garzanti".

(5) Vincenzo Ferrante and Ernesto Cassiani, *Dizionario moderno italiano-francese francese-italiano*, Società Editrice Internazionale, Torino, 1973; 118,000 entries, 2238 pages. "Ferrante - Cassiani".

(6) Raoul Boch, *Dizionario francese-italiano italiano-francese*, Zanichelli, Bologna, 1978; 2nd revised edition 1985; 137,000 entries, 2175 pages. "Boch".

(7) Robert and Signorelli, *Dictionnaire français-italien italien-français. Dizionario francese-italiano italiano-francese*, Signorelli, Milano, 1981; "339 entries and translations", 3008 pages. "Robert & Signorelli".

I have chosen these dictionaries because:

(a) English and French are the foreign languages most commonly taught in Italy. Consequently, dictionaries of English and French are the ones which are most widely used;

(b) from questionnaires distributed in the last two years to teachers and students of foreign languages,[5] it appears that dictionaries (1) to (6) are the best known and the most frequently purchased. (7), though less well known than the others, deserves close examination.

In this paper I deal mainly with examples, i.e. with any phrase or sentence that *via mention* illustrates the sense and collocation of

---

4 While the numbers of entries quoted for the other six dictionaries were drawn from prefaces or flaps, I estimated, counting the average number of entries per page, that "Skey" has about 50,000 entries.

5 Questionnaires were distributed to 42 teachers in Turin: 11 teach in junior high schools and 31 in senior high schools of different kinds. 15 teach French, 23 English, 3 German and 1 Spanish. Different questionnaires were distributed to 58 university students of foreign languages. 25 were first-year students at the University of Turin and 14 at the same level at Padua University, while 19 were in the second and third years at the University of Turin. Although this is too small a population for a serious survey of dictionary use in Italy and although questionnaire techniques have been severely criticized by Hatherall (1984:184) and discussed by Hartmann (in this volume), I do believe that, with due caution, we can draw some useful conclusions from the answers collected.

the translation(s) of an entry in the L1-L2 section and the use and collocation of the entry in the L2-L1 section. I stress *via mention*, because bilingual dictionaries are full of metalinguistic phrases and sentences which illustrate uses and collocations as part of grammatical and/or encyclopaedic explanations.[6]

For instance in the following article, drawn from "Garzanti", *il méchoit, il mécherra* are not examples, but form part of the grammatical information:

> méchoir [meʃwaːr] (*usato talvolta al pres. e al fut. dell'indic.*: il méchoit, il mécherra), *v.i.impers.* (*arc.*) male incogliere.

In this other article, also drawn from "Garzanti", *(essenza)* at 2 is not a mention of the Italian word, but a metalinguistic use of it, serving as a short definition of the sense of *bergamotto* which can be translated into French by *(essence de) bergamote*.

> bergamòtto, *s.m.* 1. (*varietà di agrume*) (*albero*) bergamotier, bigardier; (*frutto*) bergamote (*f.*) 2. (*essenza*) (essence de) bergamote (*f.*) 3. (*pero*) (*albero*) poirier à bergamotes; (*frutto*) poire bergamote.

Finally, in the article *colazione* (see below), drawn from "Ragazzini", *(del mattino)* and *(la prima)* are co-occurrence restrictions of the headword in a given sense and as such they are different from phrases such as *la colazione del mattino* and *la prima colazione*, which might very well appear as examples in a differently shaped article.

> colazióne, *f.* 1 (*del mattino*) breakfast: una c. all'italiana e una all'inglese, a continental breakfast and an English one 2 (*di mezzogiorno*) lunch; luncheon: Vieni a c. domani, come to lunch tomorrow; la c. offerta dall'ambasciatore, the luncheon offered by the ambassador. ● c. affrettata, quick lunch □ c. alla forchetta, (stand-up) buffet lunch ⊔ c. di lavoro, working luncheon □ c. sull'erba, picnic □ fare c., (*la prima*) to have breakfast, to breakfast; (*a mezzogiorno*) to have lunch, to lunch.

A good balance between exemplification, metalinguistic labelling and explanation is more helpful than anything else for production and comprehension. Enlarging editorial explanations is dangerous.[7]

---

6 For a detailed discussion of the difference between the autonymic (='mention') and metalinguistic function of each component in a dictionary entry, see Rey-Debove 1971: 28-29, 258 et seq. In Marello (forthcoming) I discuss Rey-Debove's approach in relation to bilingual dictionary entries.

7 When usage or grammatical notes are very long and detailed they become clumsy and even superfluous, because Italian students do not read them or do not know how to use them.

Examples remain chiefly responsible for the achievement of a good translation.

2. Graphic representation of examples

Italic is in our seven dictionaries the typeface of metalanguage: as will be noticed also in the quoted instances of articles, usage levels and register labels, qualifications of the translation of the headword (i.e. *(varietà di agrume)*, *(di mezzogiorno)*, etc.) and co-occurrence restrictions are generally in italic.

"Boch" is an exception, giving qualifications of the translation of the headword, or defining glosses as others call them, in round-bracketed roman:

> fumetto s.m. 1 (riquadro a forma di nuvoletta che racchiude le parole nei fumetti) bulle (*f.*), ballon 2 bande (*f.*) dessinée

In our seven dictionaries italic and bold roman alternate as typefaces for examples in the language of the headword; roman and bold roman for translating items and for the examples translated in the target language.[8]

The best results for the eye are obtained by using bold roman for examples in the language of the headword (as we find in "Ferrante - Cassiani" and "Ragazzini"): examples printed in such a typeface catch the eye of the reader much more than those printed in italic.

The worst results are to be found in "Robert & Signorelli", which adopts an overcrowded 3 column per page arrangement. In addition, it is rather difficult to distinguish between short but complete definitions (italic within square brackets) and other metalinguistic features and truncated definitions (italic within round brackets). See for instance:

> **encenser** |ãsãse| *v.tr.* **1** [*honorer en agitant l'encensoir*] incensare: *encenser l'autel, un cercueil* incensare l'altare, un feretro ◊ (*par anal.*) (*se dit du cheval qui remue sa tête de bas en haut*) incensare *intr.* **2** (*fig.*) [*flatter, louer outre mesure*] incensare, sviolinare (*fam.*): *encenser un personnage influent* incensare, adulare un personaggio influente.

> **monologue** |monolog| *s.m.* **1** monologo*: *monologue comique à dire en société* monologo comico da recitare in società **2** [*discours d'une personne qui ne laisse pas parler ses interlocuteurs*] monologo **3** [*discours d'une personne seule qui parle, pense tout haut*] monologo → **soliloque** ◊ (*dans un roman*) *monologue intérieur* monologo interiore.

---

8 Ilson (1984:81) gives a survey of types of graphic representation in English dictionaries which shows many similarities with mine.

Finally, it may be worthwhile to notice that when there is no translation for the headword, but only a partial translation followed by an explanation, some of our seven dictionaries ("Ragazzini", "Hazon", "Garzanti") maintain for such "pseudotranslations" the same typeface adopted for true translations.   Compare

Cheddar ... *n.* formaggio compatto, di colore bianco o giallo
  "Ragazzini"

Cheddar ... *s.* varietà di formaggio dolce "Hazon"

brie ... *s.m.* "brie" (formaggio fermentato tipico della Brie)
  "Garzanti"

with these other articles

Cheddar ... *s.* formaggio 'cheddar' *(dalla pasta compatta e liscia)*
  "Skey"

brie ... *s.m. fromage fermenté à pâte molle et croûte moisie* ⊠
  "Robert & Signorelli"

"Robert & Signorelli" is the dictionary which best stresses the impossibility of translating this kind of word: the sign ⊠ is used to mark "le manque de traduction", as clearly stated in the introduction (p. 17).

Co-occurrence restrictions of the headword in a given sense are printed either in roman (like the translation, see "Hazon") or in italic (like usage levels and register labels, see "Ragazzini" and "Skey").

to address ... *vt* 1 indirizzare *(una lettera, ecc.).*   "Skey"

to address ... *v.t.* 1 indirizzare *(una lettera, un pacco, ecc.).*
  "Ragazzini"

to address *v.t.i.* 1. ... 2. metter l'indirizzo su (una
  lettera, ecc.) "Hazon"

Actually, the linguistic status of co-occurrence restrictions in lexicographical articles is not very clear: they do not appear to be as metalinguistic as usage levels, register labels or grammatical information, but they are also different from phrases given as examples.   Different typefaces might reflect this unclear status.

3.   Examples, idioms, compound nouns, proverbs: where and when

In the dictionaries examined the following categories of words are generally left without examples:[9]

(a) special (i.e. technical or scientific) senses of polysemous entries, or entries belonging to languages for special purposes (specialist registers);

(b) derivatives given as entries or subentries;

(c) nouns (more than any other part of speech). This may be connected with the fact that nouns are also the most numerous class of entries.

Whilst the absence of examplification from the L2-L1 (i.e. English-Italian or French-Italian) section may not be particularly harmful, in the production (encoding) section some examples would be welcome, even in entries belonging to specialist fields.[10]

Typically, items from specialist fields are not in urgent need of exemplification, because they are often monosemous and do not pose problems of collocation, but whenever the bilingual lexicographer is aware that such items receive different treatment in the two languages, he should give either useful examples or draw attention to any discrepancy in a usage note, a metalinguistic comment.

Derivatives very often pose problems of collocation because they can select prepositions which are different from the ones required by the words from which they derive. Italian is very rich in derivatives and recent written use of nominalized derivatives such as *funzionamento, detrazione* and of adjectival derivatives such as

---

9 To deal with the most important aspects of exemplification in bilingual dictionaries Al-Kasimi (1983:111) can serve as an analytic grid. Steiner (1984) presents interesting guidelines for reviewers of bilingual dictionaries. In Bartholomew - Schoenhals (1983:59-69) there is much practical advice for obtaining good illustrative examples from native speakers; such suggestions can also be used as criteria for evaluating the effectiveness of examples in dictionaries which have already appeared.

10 For instance *bronchite* in Italian can be used in the plural *Ho avuto due bronchiti quest'anno,* while in English we translate *I have had bronchitis twice, this year.* "Hazon", "Skey" and "Ragazzini" do not record this difference. See also Cousin (1982:271) for discussion of the same problem in French-English dictionaries.

funzionale, sostitutivo, is giving rise to more.

The three Italian-English dictionaries considered give no (or little) help to the Italian user translating *funzionamento a gas, detrazione per familiari a carico, funzionale per l'uso che se ne vuol fare, sostitutivo del modulo A;* the four Italian-French dictionaries are more helpful, above all for *sostitutivo* and *detrazione.* It is surprising that bilingual lexicographers comparing two languages such as Italian and French, which are not structurally dissimilar, should give more attention to these details than editors of Italian and English dictionaries. Yet the English translations of the above-mentioned phrases are farther from the Italian structure than the French are.

Idioms, compound nouns and proverbs are often, in bilingual lexicographic articles, mixed up with examples. An idiom is a peculiar exemplification of the use of the headword and for this reason, perhaps, is not always distinguished from other examples. Compound nouns in Italian are often formed by lexicalised phrases such as *giacca a vento* (anorak), *guardia del corpo* (body-guard), *pista di rullaggio* (taxiway), and Italian traditional bilingual lexicography has never dealt with them in a separate section. In the English-Italian section or in the French-Italian part each dictionary is guided by different criteria. "Ragazzini" and "Skey" list in a special section at the bottom of the entry idioms, compound nouns, proverbs, indeed everything that can not be placed within one of the numbered sense-divisions. "Skey" fills this section in a more sensible way: consider, for instance, the "Ragazzini" entry for *sympathy* and compare it with "Skey".[11]

"Hazon" and "Garzanti" have the same structure. Examples of all sorts are untidily listed within very large sense-divisions. Entries such as *to be, to have, by, to, as; avoir, être, faire; avere, essere, fare, da, dare, conto* also have a special section called "Fraseologia". This section is not mentioned in the preface, and there are many long entries without "Fraseologia". In the Italian-

---

11 In "Ragazzini", *letter of sympathy,* placed in the special section, is far from the appropriate meaning of *sympathy* ("condoglianze"). In "Skey" it follows immediately the list of possible translations in an entry without numbered meanings or special sections.

French section of "Garzanti" *da* is without "Fraseologia", although
it is as long as the *da* entry of the Italian-English section of
"Hazon". However, if we compare the entry *prendere* in the two dictionaries, we will notice that the French one, which is more recent,
has a more sensibly subdivided arrangement of senses.

"Boch" lists proverbs separately in two appendices and places
idioms within sense-divisions. In the longest entries like *prendere*,
"Boch" even creates absurd senses in order to distribute every idiom
which has that verb as a constituent.[12]

In "Ferrante - Cassiani", idioms and proverbs are at the bottom
of the entry. There is a tendency, which is not explicitly stated
in the preface, to gather roughly similar idioms under *ad hoc* numbered senses, so that the special "phraseological" section is never
very long. Sometimes, however, an idiom treated as a numbered
meaning of the headword would have been better placed in the phraseology section and viceversa. See, for instance, examples for
accidente in the Italian-French part of "Ferrante - Cassiani".

"Robert & Signorelli" follows the organization of the mono-lin-
gual *Petit Robert* for the French-Italian section and tries to imitate
it in the Italian-French one. Idioms ("locutions") are "reparties
au voisinage du sens du mot auquel elles se réfèrent" (Introduction,
p. 9). When it is impossible to follow such an arrangement waste
baskets are created: see, for instance, section III under the
entry *prendere*, whose metalinguistic explanation says "the meaning
of the following expressions is determined by the direct object".
It is a cleaner solution than the one adopted by "Boch" with its
subdivision into expressions with "things for subjects" and expressions with "animals or persons for subjects".

With regard to idioms, we have not yet addressed a complex problem which generally bilingual dictionaries do not face: the question
of distinguishing between idioms and fixed or stable collocations.

---

12 *Prendere una brutta piega* "to take a turn for the worse", a typical idiom,
   is listed by "Boch" under sense 29 of *prendere*, and metalinguistically defined as "occurrence in sentence indicating change of state, with a thing
   as grammatical subject". Under 29 also appear *prendere fuoco* "to take
   fire" and *prendere il largo* "to make oneself scarce", which also occur with
   animate subjects. The new edition (1985) has not changed in this respect.

With Cowie (1986) we can distinguish:

(a) pure idioms, such as *blow the gaff, easy on the eye,* etc., which
are opaque and typically resist lexical substitution, passivization,
nominalization and pronominalization;

(b) figurative idioms, such as *catch fire, do a U-turn* etc., which are
partially motivated and sometimes admit minimal lexical variations;

(c) restricted collocations, such as *a blind alley* or *break one's
journey,* in which one element has a figurative sense determined by
the other or by a small set of substitutable elements, as in *raise
a siege/blockade* and *a cardinal error/sin/virtue;*

(d) routine formulae, such as *I see what you mean* or *I couldn't agree
more,* which are relatively fixed expressions used to perform speech-
act functions or to organize discourse interaction.

An examination of Italian bilingual dictionaries brings one to
the same conclusion as that reached by Cowie (1986:19):

> "The continuing use, in the bilingual dictionaries, of a single typeface for
> composites [i.e. types (a), (b), (c)] and illustrative examples, often makes
> retrieval of the former arduous and time-consuming for the native speaker
> and well-nigh impossible for the foreign user."

The two main strategies adopted in Italian bilingual dictionaries
in order to arrange phraseology both have their drawbacks. In my
opinion, large phraseology waste baskets are worse than the distribution of idioms under the sense divisions of one or more components: type (b) and (c) composites, above all, can be consistently grouped. Pure idioms (type (a)) are more difficult to arrange.

The distribution of examples and idioms is indeed an indirect
way of testing whether one particular subdivision of meanings is
more satisfactory than another. It is not surprising, therefore,
that, among the seven dictionaries examined, "Robert & Signorelli"
and "Skey" are the most consistent in their distribution procedure;
they derive from monolingual dictionaries (the *Petit Robert* and the
2nd edition of *OALDCE,* respectively) which devote great attention to
the subdivision of meanings in their entries.

No Italian dictionary, monolingual or bilingual, has ever attempted a radical decision such as the one adopted by van Dale diction-

ary series.   Van Dale dictionaries adopt an arrangement of examples, composites and routine formulae based first of all on the notion of co-occurrence of the headword with the other part of speech and then on meaning.   The sign ¶| shows composites or routine formulae where the headword has a peculiar meaning, and cannot be distributed under the numbered sense-divisions.   To enter into further detail about the van Dale arrangement would take us too far: I have examined the question in detail in Marello (forthcoming) from which I draw the following sample of re-elaboration, according to van Dale criteria, of the "Ragazzini" entry to answer.

to answer ['a:nsɔ*], *v. t.* e *i.* **1** rispondere (*in quasi tutti i sensi*): **to a. a letter (the phone, the door, the bell),** rispondere a una lettera (al telefono, alla porta, al campanello); **This instrument does not a. my purpose,** questo strumento non risponde al mio scopo; **The ship wouldn't a. her rudder,** la nave non rispondeva al timone **2** pagare lo scotto; pagare di persona: **The guilt was mine and I answered for it,** la colpa fu mia e pagai lo scotto **3** (*anche* to a. a purpose) rispondere a uno scopo; esser utile; servire: **That won't a. at all,** ciò non servirà affatto. ● (*fam.*) **to a. back,** rispondere (*in modo impertinente e sgarbato*); ribattere; rimbeccare ⊔ **to a. blow with blow,** ribattere colpo su colpo ◻ **to a. for,** rispondere di; essere responsabile di; farsi garante di ◻ (*naut.*) **to a. (to) the helm,** ubbidire al timone; sentire il timone ◻ **to a. to,** rispondere a; reagire a (*una sollecitazione*) ◻ **to a. to the name of,** rispondere al nome di; chiamarsi ⚊ **to a. (to) one's hopes (a description, etc.),** rispondere (o corrispondere) alle proprie speranze (a una descrizione, ecc.) ⊔ (*tel.*) **answering machine,** segreteria telefonica.

Ragazzini 1984

Re-elaboration according to van Dale criteria (from Marello (forthcoming))

(to) <u>answer</u> ['a:nsə*] < v.> <u>0.1</u> *rispondere* ⇒ *ribattere* <u>0.2</u> *pagare lo scotto* ⇒ *pagare di persona* <u>0.3</u> *rispondere a uno scopo* ⇒ *esser utile, servire* ◆ <u>1.1</u> to ∿ the bell, the door, a letter, the phone *rispondere al campanello, alla porta, a una lettera, al telefono;* to ∿ a blow with a blow *ribattere colpo su colpo;* to ∿ (to) the helm *ubbidire al timone, sentire il timone;* this ship wouldn't ∿ her rudder *la nave non rispondeva al timone;* answering machine *segreteria telefonica* <u>1.3</u> to ∿ a purpose *rispondere a uno scopo;* this instrument does not ∿ my purpose *questo strumento non risponde al mio scopo* <u>1.¶|</u> to ∿ (to) one's hopes, a description *rispondere, corrispondere alle proprie speranze, a una descrizione* <u>5.1</u> to ∿ back *rispondere (in modo impertinente e sgarbato), ribattere, rimbeccare* <u>5.3</u> that won't ∿ at all *cio non servira affatto* <u>6.1</u> to ∿ <u>to</u> *rispondere a, reagire a;* to ∿<u>to</u> the name of

rispondere al nome di, chiamarsi; <u>6.2</u> to ~ <u>for</u> *rispondere di,*
essere responsabile di, farsi garante di; the guilt was mine and
I answered <u>for</u> it *la colpa fu mia e pagai lo scotto*

Note: the conventions used in <u>answer</u> and *<u>rispondere</u>* represent
bold roman and bold italic respectively.[13]

4. Translating from and into Italian

According to the results of the small survey I conducted among
Italian teachers and students, of the 42 teachers who were inter-
viewed, 20 answered that they used bilingual dictionaries mainly
for production and 15 that they used them mainly for comprehension.
7 did not answer.

Of the 58 multiple-answer questionnaires returned by students,
49 indicated (very) frequent use of bilingual dictionaries to read
L2 texts; 41 (very) frequent use to translate from L2 to L1; 43
(very) frequent use to write L2 compositions. If we regard reading in L2 and translating from L2 as decoding activities, it appears
that students use bilingual dictionaries slightly more often for
comprehension (cf. Béjoint 1981). It is therefore important that
examples in the L2-L1 section of the various dictionaries reflect
the foreign culture adequately.

But is there any need for examples to represent the foreign
culture in the L1-L2 section? Such a need, implied in Al-Kasimi's
test question "Do quotations represent the culture of the speakers
of the target language?" (1983:111), is not so pressing in my opinion, because in production users are more likely to need examples
which translate their culture into the L2 culture and language.
An Italian user does not look for examples, in the Italian-English
part, which represent English culture; he is more likely to use
examples which help him in expressing Italian culture in English.

Current Italian bilingual dictionaries devote almost the same
amount of space to both sections (L1-L2 and L2-L1): among our

---

13 I thank Prof. B. Al for his checking of my re-elaboration and I refer to
his paper, Al (1983), and to the introductions of van Dale dictionaries
for fuller information about criteria followed in this new arrangement
procedure.

seven dictionaries only "Robert & Signorelli" has a noticeably larger Italian-French section (1658 pages against the 1282 of the French-Italian part).   Even "Skey", whose preface states that the English-Italian section is the more important, devotes almost the same number of pages to both.   "Skey" aims at a higher quality of examples rather than at a larger quantity of entries.

I do not think there is any need to enlarge the L2-L1 section, eating up some of the space now devoted to the L1-L2 part, solely on the ground that productive activities are slightly less practised than a decade ago.   Productive activities are the most difficult to cope with and dictionaries must have a well-developed L1-L2 section to meet their users' needs.   Besides, while in comprehension the users questioned also consult monolingual dictionaries of the foreign language, in production they mainly draw on the L1-L2 section of the bilingual dictionary.[14]

In the seven dictionaries considered, true examples are always translated into the target language.   Compound words are sometimes only partially (and very differently) translated.   See, for instance, how "Ragazzini" and "Skey" translate *fine-drawn* and *fine-spun*.   Pure idioms and proverbs are, if possible, translated: of course, sometimes there is no corresponding expression in the target language and the lexicographer is obliged to give simply poor "explaining" translations.   For instance, "Boch" explains more than it translates the French proverb *Qui ne peut galoper, qu'il trotte*, with the Italian *Bisogna regolare la propria andatura sulle proprie possibilità*.

5.   Do examples illustrate the usage of the word?

When asked which kind of discrepancy between the mother tongue

---

14 Such results are confirmed by the study of Sora (1984).   Besides distributing questionnaires, she gave 39 Italian students - in their second year of university studies - a language exercise and allowed them to use dictionaries.   In the reading comprehension, students used mainly monolingual English dictionaries, while in the composition half the subjects preferred bilingual dictionaries.   Despite these findings, however, it should be noted that the information provided for encoding in monolingual EFL dictionaries is fuller and more varied than in the bilingual works discussed here.

and the foreign language (syntactic, semantic or stylistic dis-
crepancies) was dealt with least satisfactorily in bilingual dictionaries, the 58 university students answered as follows: 12
indicated syntactic differences as the least well handled, 29
semantic differences and 27 differences in language register.
The total of distinct replies was 68: this was due to the fact
that many indicated both semantic differences and differences of
language register.

Only 17 students out of 58 declared that they were totally satisfied with their bilingual dictionaries. The others could choose
from among four reasons for dissatisfaction ("I can't find the
word"; "I can't find the translation which fits my context"; "I
don't get sufficient help in choosing the appropriate translation";
"I don't get enough grammatical information"). Of these, a majority complained that (very) often they did not find a matching
translation or help in discriminating among the various translations
which were offered. Furthermore, 41 declared that they usually
checked in the L2-L1 section the translation suggested in the L1-L2
section. They explained their behaviour by saying that in this
way they find the best translation "with more precision". "Skey"
openly advises its users to follow such a practice (p. xxiv), but
this is an isolated case (cf. Moulin, this volume).

On the whole, the results of the questionnaires show that examples are not sufficiently informative.[15] Of course, if students
were better trained to use bilingual dictionaries, they would possibly find more information than they do at present. This is probably true for examples illustrating syntactic and semantic differences between the languages. On the other hand, differences of
stylistic level or of register remain problems still to be solved
by the lexicographers, not by the users. One of the most recent
of our seven dictionaries, "Ragazzini", translates the Italian
vulgar expression *Non fare cazzate!* by the relatively inoffensive

---

15 I have had to omit any reference to the problem of balance between brevity,
    informativeness and readability in examples. Nuccorini (1984) deals with
    this topic from the particular perspective of 'standards of textuality',
    as defined in de Beaugrande and Dressler (1981).

Don't do anything stupid! But even considering vulgar speech as an area where dictionary compilers might prefer (here in relation to the L2) to be prescriptive rather than descriptive, mistakes in language register correspondences can be found everywhere. From Italian bilingual dictionaries of the future, we expect above all substantial improvements in the correct translation and labelling of stylistically marked entries and uses.

Thomas Creamer

BEYOND THE DEFINITION:
SOME PROBLEMS WITH EXAMPLES IN RECENT
CHINESE-ENGLISH AND ENGLISH-CHINESE BILINGUAL DICTIONARIES

1. Introduction

The inclusion of examples of usage in any general language bilingual dictionary is essential. The user of bilingual dictionaries, whether a beginning or advanced student, is a language learner. As such, he or she requires more from a dictionary than pronunciations, definitions and parts of speech. Often the information the learner is seeking, such as usage, collocations and points of grammar, can be effectively and efficiently demonstrated by the inclusion of carefully chosen examples. (See also Drysdale, this volume).

The purpose of this paper is to examine the use of examples in recent Chinese-English and English-Chinese bilingual dictionaries. To use examples successfully, the lexicographer has to overcome four main problems. The first problem concerns the definition. Is the definition too narrow or too broad for the examples given? The second problem has to do with the example itself. Does the example exemplify the use of the entry? The third problem concerns the placement of the example. Is the example in its optimum place in the dictionary or should it be placed elsewhere? A possible final problem is the absence of examples. Would an example help to clarify the definition and the use of the entry?

The three dictionaries selected for this discussion are *A Chinese-English Dictionary*, *A New English - Chinese Dictionary* and *A Large English-Chinese Dictionary*. *A Chinese - English Dictionary* (汉英词典 *Hàn Yīng Cídiǎn*, hereafter *Chinese - English*) was compiled under the direction of Professor Wu Jingrong 吴景荣 at the Beijing Institute of Foreign Languages and published by the Commercial Press (商务印书馆), Beijing, in 1978. It contains over 6,000 head characters and more than 50,000 character combinations. According to its preface, the dictionary is "a medium-sized language reference work, especially

for translators, English teachers and students of English." Because of its overall excellence and the lack of any other reliable
and up-to-date Chinese - English dictionary, *Chinese-English* is generally the first choice of translators from Chinese to English.

A New English-Chinese Dictionary (新英汉词典 *Xīn Yīng Hàn Cídiǎn*, hereafter *New English-Chinese)* was published in 1975 by the Shanghai
People's Publishing House (上海人民出版社). It was compiled by a
team of more than seventy language specialists from the Shanghai
area headed by Professors Ge Chuangui 葛传椝 , Lu Gusun 陆谷孙
and Xue Shiqi 薛诗绮 ; all three from the English Department of
Fudan University. The dictionary contains more than 50,000 headwords, and another 30,000 compound entries and expressions. *New
English-Chinese* was the first English-Chinese dictionary compiled
after the establishment of the People's Republic of China (1949)
and has received international acclaim for its coverage of modern
English, detailed definitions, excellent translations and numerous
examples of usage.

New English-Chinese is currently being revised and enlarged in
Shanghai by Translation Press (译文出版社). Under the direction
of Lu Xiu 路修 and Gu Jun 顾浚 , a staff of approximately fifty
language specialists hope to publish a new edition in the early
1990s, tentatively titled *A Large English-Chinese Dictionary* (英汉大
词典 *Yīng Hàn Dà Cídiǎn*, hereafter *Large English-Chinese)*, of 150,000
entries. I spent six months in China in 1982 under the auspices
of the CETA (Chinese-English Translation Assistance) Group working
on the *Large English-Chinese*. In addition to general work on the
dictionary, I spent a great deal of time reviewing examples.
Comments on *Large English-Chinese* are based on the manuscript from
letter A to M. Because the dictionary was in draft form, the
examples cited here may not appear in the published version of the
dictionary. Nonetheless, the examples noted do give some insight
into the approach and methods of the compilers.

2. Problems with definitions

The first problem with the use of examples concerns the relationship of the definition to the example. Although a definition cannot be expected to encompass all possible meanings of a word, it

should be written broadly enough to include occurrences which are related in meaning and to exclude others which are not. If a definition is written too narrowly, accompanying examples may confuse rather than clarify the meaning. Confusion may also result if a definition is written too broadly.

Two instances in *Chinese-English* illustrate the difficulty of a narrow definition. The head character 畅 *chàng* is defined as follows:

> 畅 *chàng* 1. smooth; unimpeded: 畅行无阻 pass unimpeded/流畅 easy and smooth; fluent 2. free; uninhibited: 畅饮 drink one's fill.

The first definition is precise and the examples are apt. However, the example in the second definition is beyond the scope of the definition. The definition should be divided into two separate glosses. The meaning of "free; uninhibited" is apparent from an example such as 畅快 *chàngkuài* ("free from inhibition"). Another meaning, as suggested by the example 畅饮 *chàngyǐn*, is "to do something to one's heart's content or to the fullest extent". Examples such as 畅谈 *chàngtán* ("to talk freely and to one's heart's content") and 畅游 *chàngyóu* ("to have a good swim; to enjoy sightseeing") illustrate definitions that cannot be explained in terms of "free" or "uninhibited".

Another illustration of an incomplete definition in *Chinese-English* is 混浊 *hùn zhuó*, which is entered in the dictionary as follows:

> 混浊 *hùn zhuó* muddy; turbid: 混浊的水 turbid water/混浊的空气 foul (or stale) air.

Both are perfectly good examples of 混浊 *hùn zhuó*, but the definition does not encompass the idea of "foul" or "stale" in the second example. The basic meaning of 混浊 *hùn zhuó* is "turbid". It is usually used to describe water or air, but also can characterize eyes, as in *cloudy or unclear eyes*. A qualified definition such as "turbid (of water, air, etc.)" or an expanded definition such as "turbid, thick, stale (of water, air, etc.)" would encompass the broader meaning of 混浊 *hùn zhuó*. The examples need not be changed, but, just as the second example was translated as "foul (or stale) air", the first example, rendered as "turbid water", could be

translated as "turbid (or muddy) water."   In this way the four
adjectives, "turbid", "muddy", "foul" and "stale" could be efficiently related in two examples.

Confusion can also arise with definitions cast too broadly.   One
example from *Large English-Chinese* demonstrates the problem.   Under
the entry *crap* the second definition (with translations of the
Chinese provided) reads:

蠢话 (foolish talk);   大话 (bragging);   废话 (nonsense);
谎话 (a lie);   蹩脚货 (inferior goods);   贱货 (inexpensive
goods);   废物 (trash)   讨厌的东西 (disagreeable things)
with the following examples: *giving us that crap that he has to help his
old man.   Pull crap.   He doesn't give me any crap about moral responsibility.
She will fill up the column with some of her crap.   There's a lot of crap theory
floating around.   ...   Every country is burning all the crap it can dig up.
Like cars and TV sets and washing machines and the rest of that crap.   Can we
go to lunch when this crap is finished?*   The confusion caused by such a
rambling entry is obvious.   The definition needs to be grouped into
at least three separate sub-senses such as: "nonsense (of talk,
etc.);"   "lies, excuses" and "inferior or disagreeable things."   A
more structured definition not only gives the user a better understanding of the word, but also might save him or her from unnecessary
embarrassment.

3.   Problems with examples

The second problem with the use of examples has to do with the
nature of the example itself.   The primary purpose of an example is
to demonstrate the use of a word in its natural environment.   An
example can be either a few words, a sentence pattern or a complete
sentence.   If an example is used correctly it can take the burden
off a definition by showing various ways the entry can be translated
in context, indicate typical modifiers, and illustrate points of
usage (e.g., if the entry collocates with certain verb).   If an
example is used ineffectively, it can at best waste space and at
worst, distort the definition.

One shortcoming of the *Large English-Chinese* is the inclusion of
examples that do not exemplify the use of the entry.   Examples
such as *have a snooze in a silk dressing gown* under *dressing gown*, *a half-*

eaten turkey drumstick under *drumstick, she sat sipping on egg creams* under *egg cream, I like going on escalators* under *escalators* and *An extravagant person has extravagant tastes and habits* under *extravagant* do not in any way add to the user's understanding of the headwords.   Similarly, if an example merely restates the definition it does not exemplify usage.   (cf. Drysdale, this volume - ed.)   The example *Dry docks are used for repairing or building ships* under *dry dock* is more a defini-tion than an example.   Finally, many words, particularly technical terms, if properly defined, do not require examples.   The examples for technical terms in *English-Chinese* such as *drawbridge, dressmaking, drop curtain, duffel coat* and *electro-convulsive therapy* are superfluous. The staff of *Large English-Chinese* are proud, and rightly so, of their citation file of approximately 500,000 items.   A degree of restraint must be exercised in the inclusion of examples.   Examples should be used to augment, not replace, definitions and should serve a definite purpose.   When selecting examples from citation files, dictionary makers should avoid what may be called the "because it's there" syndrome, that is, the inclusion of an example for no other reason then that it is in the file.

4. Problems with the placement of examples

The third problem with the use of examples concerns their place-ment in the dictionary.   Care must be taken not only in the selec-tion of good examples, but also in their proper placement.   The proper placement of examples facilitates the look-up process and adds a "naturalness" or "fluency" to the dictionary text.   The placement of examples in *Chinese-English*, like most features of the dictionary, generally is executed expertly.   Examples follow the definition and precede compound entries which are set off by a diamond sign (◇).   The division between an example and an entry word is sometimes vague, however; the example under 图 像 *tú xiàng* "picture; image" is 立 体 图 像 *lì tǐ tú xiàng* (elec) "stereo-picture" and under 天 平 *tiān píng*" balance; scale" is 分析天平 *fēn xī tiān píng* (chem) "analytical balance".   In neither case is the example listed as an entry word in the dictionary (i.e., under the character 立 *lì* for "stereopicture" or 分 *fēn* for "analytical balance").   The drawback in considering such words as only examples is that, in doing so, the look-up process becomes more difficult.

To illustrate the difficulty, the process would be like looking up
stereopicture in an English dictionary under *picture* and *analytical
balance* under *balance*.   To make the look-up process more efficient,
examples of this sort which are, in effect, entry words should best
be listed as such.   One rule of thumb that might be used to decide
whether or not dual listing is necessary is to decide if a subject
label is needed.   In the two examples above the subject labels
alert the user as well as the lexicographer to the special technical status of the terms.   If an example merits a label it merits
listing as a headword.

Dual listing of example and headword is one solution to the
problem of the placement of certain examples.   However, if not
handled carefully, the solution itself becomes a problem.   Questions arise in *Chinese-English* when words are listed both as examples
and entries, but the English translation differs.   The use of the
entry 并举 *bìng jǔ* "develop simultaneously" is illustrated
by the example 土洋并举 *tǔ yáng bìng jǔ* which is translated as
"employ both simple and sophisticated methods; employ both indigenous and foreign methods."   This example is also listed as a
separate entry, but it is translated as "use both indigenous and
foreign methods; use both traditional and modern methods."   Note
the verb *employ* in the first translation and *use* in the second.
Also note the use of the adjectives *simple/sophisticated* and *indigenous/
foreign* in the example, versus *indigenous/foreign* and *traditional/modern*
in the headword.   Although both renderings are acceptable, needless confusion results from this disjointed translation.

5. Problems caused by the absence of examples

The fourth and final problem concerns the absence of examples.
Like a picture, an example can be worth a thousand words of definition.   As the above discussion has shown, examples can supplement
and extend the definition, often with great economy of means.   An
extra burden is placed on the definition without an example.
Furthermore, in definitions lacking examples it is more difficult for
a user to bring to bear his or her knowledge of a word in context to
help clarify meanings.   For instance, what better way to illustrate
the use of *absent-minded* than to include the almost universally
understood *absent-minded professor?*

One of the most impressive features about *New English-Chinese* is its tens of thousands of examples of usage. To appreciate the wide range of the examples one need only look at words such as *abundance* with four examples, *charge* with over thirty examples, *of* with over fifty examples and *set* with well over one hundred examples. However, a number of entries that merit examples either lack them or have unsatisfactory examples. One way to approach the question of which words merit examples is to look at what might be called the "complexity" of a word. The "complexity" of a word may be indicated by the number of definitions required to define it properly. The more complex a word the greater the need for examples. Some complex words in *New English-Chinese* that do not have examples are *accentuate* (with seven definitions); *consummate* (with eighteen definitions); *embarrass* (with fourteen definitions); *glint* (with twenty-one definitions; *grotesque* (with fifteen definitions); and *lionize* (with twelve definitions). The number of definitions and sub-definitions needed to treat these and similar words should alert the lexicographer to the need for examples.

Definitions whose examples are inadequate or unsatisfactory are only a slight improvement over definitions without them. It can be especially difficult for the bilingual lexicographer to strike a balance between too many and too few examples. One way to achieve this balance is to consult native language informants and monolingual dictionaries, such as *Webster's Third New International Dictionary* and *The World Book Encyclopedia Dictionary* if English is the source language. Native language informants were not available to the makers of *New English-Chinese* because of the chaos of the Cultural Revolution. It is obvious that they drew heavily upon *Webster's Third* and *World Book*. Some of the entries in *New English-Chinese* with inadequate examples include: *achieve* with one example reading *The working class understands that it can achieve its own final emancipation only by emancipating all of mankind,* while *Webster's Third* for the same entry has three examples and *World Book* has six; *rite* with one example reading *the rites of hospitality,* while *Webster's Third* has nine examples and *World Book* three; and *ritual* with one example reading *ritual murder,* while *Webster's Third* has thirteen examples and *World Book* eight. The number of examples in *Webster's Third* and *World Book* should have signalled the need for more examples for such words in *New English-Chinese*.

6. Conclusion

Examples are vital to any general language bilingual dictionary.   When used in concert with a well-constructed definition,
examples illustrate the use of an entry in its natural environment.
Although examples cannot take the place of a definition they can
demonstrate, in an efficient manner, points of actual usage not
easily conveyed in a definition.   All entries do not require
examples.   For those that do, especially complex words, examples
should be selected with care and serve a definite purpose.   Without examples, the burden of understanding the meaning and use of a
word rests heavily on the definition and the dictionary user.
With examples, both the dictionary and the dictionary user are
richer.

Ton Broeders

THE TREATMENT OF PHONOLOGICAL IDIOMS

1. Introduction

The main purpose of this paper is to demonstrate the need for the
representation of the accentual pattern of English idioms in learners' dictionaries, a point raised earlier in Broeders and Hyams
(1984). My approach will be as follows: after a short illustration of the nature of the problem and a brief review of the principles underlying the marking systems that are already being used,
notably in the *Oxford Advanced Learner's Dictionary of Current English*
(OALDCE) and the *Oxford Dictionary of Current Idiomatic English* Volume 2
(ODCIE 2), I will argue that, although the accentual pattern of
many idioms is at least theoretically predictable, accent marking
is nevertheless necessary for the foreign learner, and propose an
alternative marking system which is both theoretically sound and
user-friendly.

2. The nature of the problem

If an idiom is defined as a combination of words whose meaning
is not predictable from that of its individual constituents, then,
for present purposes, a phonological idiom can be defined as an
idiom whose accentual pattern is not predictable either. A look
at a number of prominent dictionaries shows that while the semantic
unpredictability of idioms is fully recognised by dictionary makers,
the unpredictability of the accentual pattern of many of these
expressions is apparently much less obvious. As a rule, the problem is ignored altogether. Where this is not the case the treatments that are found are at best only partial and always inadequate.
The nature of the problem is fairly easily demonstrated. In the
following expressions, the syllable carrying the main or nuclear
accent is always capitalised:

> (1) a pain in the NECK   (2) a FINE kettle of fish
> (3) NOW you're talking   (4) now you're eXAGGerating
> (5) search ME   (6) KISS me
> (7) you can say THAT again   (8) you can say that aGAIN
> (9) the bird has FLOWN   (10) the BIRD has flown

A comparison of these expressions shows two things. The first is that (1) and (2), which are both complex noun phrases containing a postmodifier, nevertheless differ in the position of the main accent. The second point that is worth noting is that the position of the main accent in the idioms (3) , (5), (7) and (9) differs from that in the non-idioms (4), (6), (8) and (10). A first tentative conclusion might therefore be that semantic idioms differ from otherwise identical (or closely similar) non-idioms in the position of the nucleus. However, there are at least two problems with this conclusion. The first is that it is contradicted by (1): *a pain in the neck* is a semantic idiom but it has the same pattern as, say *a pain in the chest*, which, as far as I am aware, is not idiomatic. The second problem is that even when our conclusion does seem to be valid we have no way of knowing *how* the accentual pattern will differ, i.e. to what element the nucleus will go if it does not have the position it has in the non-idiom.

3. Current practice

There are three dictionaries which claim to cater for the needs of the foreign learner in this area. They are *OALDCE*, *ODCIE* 2 and the *Longman Dictionary of English Idioms (LDEI)*. The main problem with the treatment in the first two of these is that it is based on a misunderstanding of the principles underlying accent placement in English. Thus, *OALDCE* (Third Edition, p.xiv) says that "... the principal stress usually falls on the last 'non-grammatical' word of the combination", which, incidentally, also makes for a particularly unrevealing notation in the case of noun compounds, with the regular pattern as in *BANK clerk* consistently being marked, while the exceptional pattern as in *town CLERK* is unmarked. Strangely enough, the subsequent replacement of J. Windsor Lewis by A.C. Gimson and S.M. Ramsaran as pronunciation editors in the revised Eleventh Impression of *OALDCE* (1980) has left the notation system basically unchanged. In the front matter of the second dictionary, *ODCIE* 2, we find: "In any idiom, one word is always more strongly stressed [...]. In most cases this is the last 'full' word (i.e. noun, adjective, verb or adverb) in the phrase or clause ..." (1983:liii). The truth of the matter, however, is that the rules for accent assignment in English are rather more complex than

these two dictionaries would lead us to believe.   A successful
attempt at formulating such rules can be found in Gussenhoven
(1984:69), whose SAAR (=Sentence Accent Assignment Rule) shows
quite clearly that in SV sentences which are entirely [+focus],
i.e. do not contain material that is represented as "given" information, the main accent goes to S, as in

> (11) the CHAIRman has resigned
> (12) your SHIRT'S been ironed
> (13) the BEAver has escaped

It is worth noting that this point apparently also escaped the
notice of Quirk et al. (1972:940-941), who after stating that "The
rule is that *in any unit marked as new, the nucleus assumes ... final position"*,
find themselves compelled to resort to "general cultural norms" to
account for the position of the nucleus in

> (14) the KETTle's boiling
> (15) the MILKman called

"In a domestic context", Quirk et al state, "the one thing to an-
nounce about kettles is that they are boiling, just as the milkman's
activities are limited to calling, etc.   The point, with all three
examples, is that given the subject and given the situation, the
predicate follows as a foregone conclusion" (1972:941).   This,
then, is apparently supposed to explain the "givenness" or "semi-
givenness" - the terms are theirs - of *boiling* and *called*.   But the
vacuity of this argument becomes obvious if one considers a sentence
like

> (16) the MILKman didn't call

Now (15) and (16) have the same accentual pattern.   Surely, things
have come to a strange pass when the exact opposite of an event
which is said to be a foregone conclusion is also a foregone conclusion.

4. An investigation

In order to investigate whether there are such entities as
phonological idioms we can now look at a limited number of idioms
arranged according to their syntactic structure and determine to
what extent SAAR is capable of accounting for their accentual pattern.

4.1. SV patterns

The first type is that exemplified by (9) *the bird has FLOWN*, an
SV pattern. For the purposes of SAAR, sentences are analysed as
combinations of Arguments, Predicates and Conditions. Although
these are basically semantic concepts, they roughly correspond to
grammatical constituents, at least in the cases discussed below.
Thus, Arguments are typically constituents that function as subject
or object, while Predicates correspond to syntactic predicates and
Conditions to adverbials. *The bird has FLOWN* is therefore analysed
as an A P pattern. For our purposes, SAAR is as follows:

(a) *P A* [PA]
     A P [AP]   (ordered)

(b) [ ]→ [AP/PA], (In [AP/PA], accent A)

According to SAAR (a), an *A P* sequence will form a domain, to which
SAAR (b) will assign an accent, which, according to the condition
stated, will be associated with A:

(17) the BIRD has flown

At least, this is what happens when all the material in the
sentence is presented by the speaker as being [+focus], i.e. as
information that the speaker presents as his "contribution" to the
conversation. Note that the entirely italicized symbol *A P* is
[+focus]. When we turn to the idiomatic version *the bird has FLOWN*,
we must assume that we are dealing with a pattern A *P*, in which A
is [-focus], i.e. information which the speaker presents as common
background knowledge between himself and the hearer. In this case,
SAAR (a) does not apply and the main accent goes to P. Compare
(18) and (19):

(18) Princess DI's pregnant
(19) Princess Di's PREGnant

In (18) all the material is [+focus], while in (19) the speaker
assumes the hearer to be aware of the fact that *Princess Di* is "given"
information in the sense that she had already been established as
the topic of the conversation, or, alternatively, had recently
entered into a marriage in which she was generally expected to bear
children sooner rather than later.

It would appear therefore that idioms of the type *the bird has*

FLOWN are rule-governed. The problem is, however, that in these cases, unlike in (18) or (19), the foreign learner has no way of knowing that the Argument is [-focus]. For that to be the case he would have to be fully aware of the fact that *the bird* here stands for, say, the person the speaker is looking for (his "quarry"), and is therefore "given" information.

The [-focus] status of the Arguments in the following SV idioms can be accounted for in the same way:

(20) the penny DROPPED   = "the remark was understood"
(21) the mind BOGGLES   = "I can't comprehend this"
(22) the plot THICKens   = "the affair becomes more confused"
(23) where the shoe PINCHes = "where the difficulty is situated"

(24) and (25) can also be accounted for by SAAR

(24) all HELL broke loose
(25) till the COWS come home

Note that these SV sentences are similar to (10), the non-idiomatic *the BIRD has flown*. In other words, the sentence is entirely [+focus], or *A P:* a domain is formed and the accent is assigned to the Argument. It appears therefore that SV-type idioms are entirely regular from a phonological point of view so that, strictly speaking, the term phonological idiom does not apply to them. However, because of the semantic opacity of most of these combinations it is extremely difficult for the foreign learner to decide which constituents are + or - focus, so that the accentual pattern cannot really be said to be predictable to him.

4.2. SVC patterns

Here are some examples of idioms fitting an SVC pattern:

(26) THAT'S more like it
(27) THAT'll be the day
(28) THAT'S the stuff

Their accentual pattern is adequately accounted for if we assume that the semantic Predicate, i.e. *is more like it, will be the day, is the stuff* is [-focus]. *That* is [+focus] and will therefore be assigned an accent according to SAAR (b). Again, it appears that accent assignment is regular and predictable as long as it is realised that the Predicate is [-focus]. Note, by the way, that if the entire sentence is [+focus], SAAR would also generate *THAT's more like it.* However, it appears that if the Argument is not lexically filled, AP domain formation does not take place (Gussenhoven 1984:29). Hence we get *that's corRECT.* Domain formation does not occur either in what Gussenhoven calls definitional sentences. Compare (29), which is definitional, and (30), which is not.

> (29) milk is ANimal
> (30) the MILK is sour

4.3. SVOC patterns

A third type is the SVOC pattern in:

> (31) paint the town RED
> (32) keep your EYES peeled

Note that these idioms differ in the position of the nuclear accent. If we compare them with non-idiomatic SVOC patterns, it appears that their accentual pattern is as in (32): *he got his proFESSor annoyed, he pushed the DOOR open, he's dyed his HAIR blue.* Since these can be used in response to a question like *What did he do?*, all the material - except the subject - can be interpreted as new information and is therefore [+focus]. So, for the purposes of SAAR, we are dealing with a *P A A* structure. After domain formation has applied, this will yield [*P A*] [*A*], and the nuclear accent will go to the final Argument: *he got his professor aNNOYED.* Nevertheless, this is not what we find. As Gussenhoven (1984:39,105) suggests, combinations like *get annoyed, push open, dye blue* would seem to behave like single semantic Predicates. SAAR will therefore operate on a *P-A-P* pattern, in which case the nuclear accent, after domain formation has applied, correctly moves to the object Argument. The same would seem to apply to SVOO patterns like *(What did he do?) he gave the CAR a wash,* where *give a wash* behaves like a single semantic Predicate, unlike *give a bike* in *(What did he do?) he gave his son a BIKE.* It appears therefore that (32) has the regular pattern, while (31) is marked. Again, the explanation lies in the [-focus] status of one of the constituents. If *the town* is [-focus], SAAR applies to a *P-A-P* structure, and the result is *paint the town RED.* So what is unpredictable about (31) is not the position of the nuclear accent, but the fact that *the town* (and *paint?)* is presented as given information, and is therefore [-focus].

It is worth noting that in their recently published *Comprehensive*

Grammar of the English Language Quirk et al (1985:1365) suggest that

(32a) I am painting my LIVing room blue

is to be interpreted as having marked focus *only*, i.e. that *blue* is [-focus]. They also claim that in

(32b) I am painting my living room BLUE

"... *all* of the information ... may be new." In other words, the suggestion is that (32b) could be used in response to a question like *What's happening?* The truth of the matter is, however, that (32b) would require a context in which *painting* and/or *my living room* can be presented as given. The following combinations could occur:

(a) with *painting* as well as *my living room* [-focus], (32b) could be used in response to *What colour are you painting your LIVing room?*

(b) with *my living room* only [-focus], (32b) could be used in response to *What are you doing with your LIVing room?*

(c) with *painting* only [-focus], (32b) could be used in response to a question like *What colour are you painting your ROOMS?* A more likely answer would be something like *I'm painting the 'living room BLUE, the 'bathroom PINK, the 'kitchen WHITE*, etc. Note that in this case domain formation does not apply (Gussenhoven 1984:76-77).

Quirk et al's incorrect observation probably stems from their assumption that "... the intonation nucleus ... occurs on the last appropriate syllable as determined by the prosodic rule in 18.4" (1985:1363). There is further evidence for this on page 1357, where they say that "... some [...] define end focus in terms of the (stressed syllable of the) last open-class lexical item of the last clause element ...". What is striking here is the absence of any explicit commitment to this definition on the part of the authors as compared with the clear stand they took in Quirk et al (1972: 940-41). Nevertheless, it is clearly their adherence to the "last open-class item" principle that obscures so much of the discussion of focus in the 1985 grammar.

4.4. SVOA patterns

This type is illustrated by:

(33) have a TONGUE in one's head
(34) have many IRons in the fire

Again ignoring the subject, the pattern is P A C. These expressions are comparable to non-idiomatic sentences like:

(35) put a TIger in your tank
(36) he's got a RAdio in his car
(37) she's got a KNIFE in her bag

On the other hand, superficially similar structures like (38) and (39) have an accented Condition.

(38) he's got a house in FRANCE
(39) he's got two sons at uniVERsity

Gussenhoven accounts for this difference by saying that adverbs denoting the general time-space orientation of a proposition are statutarily [-focus]. Again, the pattern can be accommodated by the theory, but the idioms will probably not be recognized as belonging to this type by the foreign learner.

4.5. Other patterns

(40) she certainly LOOKS the part

In SAAR terms, this is A *C P* A, with *the part* [-focus], i.e. "given information" in the sense that it refers back to (part of) an earlier statement.

(41) search ME
(42) you could have fooled ME
(43) you're telling ME

What is interesting here is that an element which is normally [-focus], i.e. a (personal) pronoun, is here [+focus]. The pattern is *P A*, but there is no domain formation in this case, so that both P and A are assigned an accent.

4.6. Phrases

Here are some examples:

(44) a NASty piece of work
(45) a FINE kettle of fish
(46) a WHALE of a time
(47) at the BEST of times

In the above examples we are no longer dealing with clausal patterns but with noun phrases. In complex NPs, the main accent is assigned to the lowest head noun of the phrase that is ⌈+focus⌉: *the girl at the top of the TREE*. However, if *tree* was ⌈-focus⌉ we would get

(48) (No, I'm talking about) the girl at the TOP of the tree

Or, if the [-focus] head is preceded by a ⌈+focus⌉ premodifier, the accent will go to that premodifier, as in (49):

(49) (I mean) the GREEN car

Idioms like (44) - (47) must therefore be analysed as containing a [-focus] head. The accent then goes to the next higher [+focus] head or, failing that, to the [+focus] premodifier.

There are also idioms whose accentual pattern is less easily accounted for:

(50) get on like a HOUSE on fire
(51) there's nothing TO it
(52) what are friends FOR?

These are cases that as yet SAAR seems unable to come to grips with.

4.7. Noun + Noun and Adjective + Noun combinations

Finally, there is a very large group of idioms consisting of noun + noun or adjective + noun combinations whose accentual patterns can pose problems. Examples are:

(53) (look on) the BRIGHT side
(go off) the DEEP end
a BIG shot
(like) NObody's business

(learn) the HARD way
(it's) a GOOD job
GREY matter
daylight ROBbery

The regular pattern here would be as in (54) for noun + noun combinations, and as in (55) for adjective + noun combinations.

(54) POST office
(55) a tall ORder

Because of the large numbers involved, it would seem essential that these are adequately treated. The best dictionary here is the *Longman Dictionary of Contemporary English (LDOCE)*, which, however, does not indicate the accentual pattern of these combinations when they form part of larger units, as in *look on the BRIGHT side.*

On balance, we can say that although it is frequently possible to account for the accentual patterns of idioms - in which case the term phonological idiom is not, strictly speaking, appropriate - it is nevertheless clear that the focus distribution which is so important for the assignment of the main accent is often far from obvious, especially for the foreign student.   A notation which is based on purely theoretical principles will therefore not be adequate.   It would, for example, leave both (25) and (20) unmarked, because they are theoretically predictable.   A further complication arises from the fact that there is frequently a difference between the accentual patterns of unrehearsed, spontaneous speech that SAAR seeks to account for and the patterns found in reading styles.   Thus, an entirely [+focus] newspaper headline like

　　　(56) prime minister resigns

would usually be read

　　　(57) prime minister reSIGNS

as opposed to the unrehearsed [+focus]

　　　(58) the prime MINister has resigned

As a result, idioms that are found in dictionaries are also likely to be pronounced with a "reading style" pattern, unless the speech style pattern is explicitly indicated.

5.   The notation

In view of these considerations, the notation that I prefer is a pragmatic one.   In fact, I should like to refer to the policy of *LDEI*, which I have been fortunate enough to be able to revise on this point.   What the convention amounts to is that an accent mark is put before the accented syllable of the word in which the main accent falls whenever this word is *not the last content word*.   Note that this convention, unlike those of *OALDCE* and *ODCIE* 2, implies no claims about the "normal" position of the accent.   In addition, accent marks are also used whenever the position of the main accent might not be immediately clear to the foreign user.   Three cases can be distinguished here:

(a) expressions like *the penny 'drops*

(b) expressions containing a compound noun like *take pot 'luck*

(c) expressions with a transitive phrasal verb with a non-pronominal object like *let the 'side down, put one's best foot 'forward*

6. Conclusion

I have tried to demonstrate that many idioms have accentual patterns which, although they can frequently be shown to be rule-governed, are not normally predictable to the foreign learner, precisely because he will be insufficiently familiar with the meaning and use of the idioms. A look at existing dictionaries suggests that there is an insufficient awareness of the nature of this problem and a lack of theoretical insight into the principles underlying accent assignment on the part of the pronunciation editors of these dictionaries. Compared with the highly sophisticated treatment of grammatical patterns in the learners' dictionaries, the treatment of accentual patterns is still decidedly sketchy and both theoretically and practically misguided. One would hope that, for the sake of the learner and his non-native teacher alike, this state of affairs will soon be remedied.

BIBLIOGRAPHY

1. Dictionaries

Atkins, B.T., et al. (1978). Collins Robert French Dictionary.
   London and Glasgow: Collins. (Collins-Robert).
Avis, W.S., Scargill, M.H. and Gregg, R.J. (1979). Canadian Junior
   Dictionary. Toronto: Gage. [^{1}1977] (CJD).
Bailey, Nathan (1721). An Universal Etymological English Diction-
   ary. London: E. Bell et al.
Bielfeldt, H.H., et al. (eds.) (1982). Russisch - Deutsches
   Wörterbuch. Berlin: Akademieverlag.
Bielfeldt, H.H. and Lötzch, R. (eds.) (1983). Deutsch-Russisches
   Wörterbuch. Berlin: Akademieverlag.
Boch, R. (1985). Dizionario francese-italiano italiano-francese.
   2nd edition. Bologna: Zanichelli. [^{1}1978] (Boch).
Burridge, S. (1981). Oxford Elementary Learner's Dictionary.
   Oxford: Oxford University Press. (OELD).
Carver, D.J., Wallace, M.J. and Cameron, J. (1974). Collins English
   Learner's Dictionary. London and Glasgow: Collins. (CELD).
The Charlie Brown Dictionary. (1974). London and New York: Hamlyn.
Cockeram, Henry (1623). The English Dictionarie: or An Interpreter
   of Hard English Words. London: E. Weaver and N. Butter.
Cowie, A.P. and Mackin, R. (1975). Oxford Dictionary of Current
   Idiomatic English, Vol. 1: Verbs with Prepositions and Particles.
   London: Oxford University Press. (ODCIE 1).
Cowie, A.P., Mackin, R. and McCaig, I.R. (1983). Oxford Dictionary
   of Current Idiomatic English, Vol. 2: Phrase, Clause and Sen-
   tence Idioms. Oxford: Oxford University Press. (ODCIE 2).
Diccionario Ideográfico Polígloto. (1960). Madrid: Aguilar.
Dizionario Garzanti francese-italiano italiano-francese. (1966).
   Milan: Garzanti. (Garzanti).
Dubois, J., et al. (1980). Dictionnaire du Français Contemporain
   2nd edition. Paris: Larousse. [^{1}1966] (DFC).
Dubois, J. with Dubois-Charlier, F. (1978). Dictionnaire du
   Français Langue Etrangère, Niveau 1. Paris: Larousse. (DFLE 1).

Ferrante, V. and Cassiani, E. (1973). Dizionario moderno italiano-
francese francese-italiano. Turin: Società Editrice Internazionale. (Ferrante-Cassiani).

Ge Chuangui, Lu Gusun and Xue Shiqi (1975). A New English-Chinese
Dictionary. Shanghai: People's Publishing House.

Gove, P.B. (ed.) (1961). Webster's Third New International Dictionary of the English Language. Springfield, Mass.: G. & C.
Merriam. (W3).

Hanks, P. (1979). Collins Dictionary of the English Language.
London and Glasgow: Collins. (CED).

Hazon, M. (1961). Grande dizionario inglese-italiano italiano-
inglese. Milan: Garzanti. (Hazon).

Hornby, A.S. with Cowie, A.P. and Windsor Lewis, J. (1974). Oxford
Advanced Learner's Dictionary of Current English. 3rd edition.
London: Oxford University Press. (OALDCE 3).

Hornby, A.S., Gatenby, E.V. and Wakefield, H. (1963). The Advanced
Learner's Dictionary of Current English. 2nd edition. London:
Oxford University Press. [[1]1948] (OALDCE 2).

Hornby, A.S. and Reif, J.A. (1985). Oxford Student's Dictionary for
Hebrew Speakers. Tel Aviv: Kernerman Publishing. (OSDHS).

Hornby, A.S. with Ruse, C.A. (1978). Oxford Student's Dictionary of
Current English. Oxford: Oxford University Press. (OSDCE).

Hornby, A.S. and Svenkerud, H. (1983). Oxford Engelsk - Norsk
Ordbok. Oslo: J.W. Cappelens Forlag.

Imbs, P., et al. (1971-). Trésor de la Langue Française. Paris:
Centre National de Recherche Scientifique.

Johnson, Samuel (1755). A Dictionary of the English Language.
London: W. Strachan for J. and P. Knapton et al.

Kirkpatrick, E.M. (1980). Chambers Universal Learners' Dictionary.
Edinburgh: W. & R. Chambers. (CULD).

Kirkpatrick, E.M. (1983). Chambers 20th Century Dictionary.
Edinburgh: W. & R. Chambers. [[1]1901].

Lloyd, S.M. (1982). Roget's Thesaurus of English Words and Phrases.
Harlow: Longman. [[1]1852].

Long, T.H. and Summers, D. (1979). Longman Dictionary of English
Idioms. Harlow and London: Longman. (LDEI).

Longman Dictionary of Applied Linguistics. (1985). Harlow: Longman. (LDAL).

Macmillan Learner's Dictionary (1983). London: Macmillan.

Morris, W. (1979). The American Heritage Dictionary of the English Language. 2nd edition. Boston, Mass.: Houghton Mifflin. [[1]1969]. (AHD).

Murray, J.A.H., Bradley, H., Craigie, W.A. and Onions, C.T. (1884-1928). The Oxford English Dictionary. A New English Dictionary on Historical Principles. Oxford: Clarendon Press. (OED).

Onions, C.T. (ed.) (1944). The Shorter Oxford English Dictionary on Historical Principles. 3rd edition, revised with addenda. Oxford: Clarendon Press. [[1]1933] (SOED).

Procter, P., et al. (1978). Longman Dictionary of Contemporary English. Harlow and London: Longman. (LDOCE).

Procter, P., et al. (1982). Longman New Universal Dictionary. Harlow and London: Longman. (LNUD).

Ragazzini, G. (1984). Il nuovo Ragazzini. Dizionario inglese-italiano italiano-inglese. 2nd edition. Bologna: Zanichelli. [[1]1967] (Ragazzini).

Robert, P., et al. (1977). Dictionnaire Alphabétique et Analogique de la Langue Francaise. Le Petit Robert. 2nd edition. Paris: Société du Nouveau Littré. [[1]1967].

Robert and Signorelli (1981). Dictionnaire français-italien italien-français. Dizionario francese-italiano italiano-francese. Milan: Signorelli. (Robert & Signorelli).

Skey, M. (1977). Dizionario inglese-italiano italiano-inglese. Turin: Società Editrice Internazionale. (Skey).

Summers, D., et al. (1983). Longman Active Study Dictionary of English. Harlow and London: Longman. (LASDE).

Sykes, J.B. (ed.) (1982). The Concise Oxford Dictionary of Current English. 7th edition. Oxford: Clarendon Press. [[1]1911] (COD).

Woolf, H.B., et al. (1973). Webster's New Collegiate Dictionary. 8th edition. Springfield, Mass.: G. & C. Merriam Co. [[1]1898] (W8).

Wu Jingrong (1978). A Chinese-English Dictionary. Beijing: Commercial Press.

2. Other literature

Aitken, A.J. (1973). Definitions and citations in a period dictionary. In: McDavid and Duckert (1973:259-265).

Aitken, A.J. (1983). DOST and the computer: a hopeless case? In: Zampolli and Cappelli (1983:51-63).

Al, B.P. (1983). Dictionnaire de thème et dictionnaire de version. In: Revue de Phonétique Appliquée 66/67, 94-102.

Al-Kasimi, A.M. (1977). Linguistics and Bilingual Dictionaries. Leiden: Brill.

Al-Kasimi, A.M. (1983). The interlingual/translation dictionary: dictionaries for translation. In: Hartmann (1983c:153-162).

Allen, J.P.B. and Widdowson, H.G. (1974). English in Physical Science. London: Oxford University Press.

Allen, S. (1983). Språkdata Lexibase System. An integrated view of a lexical project. In: Zampolli and Cappelli (1983:51-64).

Amsler, R.A. (1984). Machine-readable dictionaries. In: Williams, M.E. (ed.): Annual Review of Information Science and Technology. Asis: Knowledge Industry Publications 19, 161-209.

Ard, J. (1982). The use of bilingual dictionaries by ESL students while writing. In: ITL Review of Applied Linguistics 58, 1-27.

Arntz, R. (in press). Mehrsprachige Terminologiearbeit und internationale Terminologieangleichung. In: Snell-Hornby, M. (ed.): Übersetzungswissenschaft-eine Neuorientierung. Zur Integrierung von Theorie und Praxis. Tübingen: Francke.

Barnhart, C.L. (1962). Problems in editing commercial monolingual dictionaries. In: Householder and Saporta (1962:161-181).

Bartholomew, D.A. and Schoenhals, L.C. (1983). Bilingual Dictionaries for Indigenous Languages. Mexico, D.F.: Summer Institute of Linguistics.

Baxter, J. (1980). The dictionary and vocabulary behavior: a single word or a handful? In: TESOL Quarterly 14, 3, 325-336.

Beaugrande, R. de and Dressler, W. (1981). Introduction to Text Linguistics. London: Longman.

Béjoint, M. (1981). The foreign student's use of monolingual English dictionaries. A study of language needs and reference skills. In: Applied Linguistics 2, 3, 207-222.

Bensoussan, M. et al. (1984). The effect of dictionary usage on EFL test performance compared with student and teacher attitudes and expectations. In: Reading in a Foreign Language 2, 2, 262-276.

Bergenholtz, H. and Mugdan, J. (eds.) (1985). Lexikographie und Grammatik. Tübingen: Niemeyer. (= Lexicographica. Series Maior 3).

Black, A. (1986). The effects on comprehension and memory of providing different types of defining information for new vocabulary. Cambridge: MRC Applied Psychology Unit.

Bloch, M. (1971). Use Your Dictionary. Tel Aviv: Karni Publishers.

Bloch, M. (1985). Use Your Dictionary as a Learning Tool. Tel Aviv: Tcherikover Publishers.

Bolinger, D. (1968). Aspects of Language. New York: Harcourt Brace and World.

Braecke, C. (1981). Het verklarend handwoordenboek als leermiddel voor gevorderden: grammaticale informatie in twee Engelse edities. In: Woorden in het Vreemde-talenonderwijs. Amsterdam: Vrije Universiteit Uitgeverij, 17-31.

Broeders, T. and Hyams, P. (1984). The pronunciation component of an English-Dutch dictionary. In: Hartmann (1984: 165-175).

Bujas, Ž. (1975). Testing the performance of a bilingual dictionary on topical current texts. In: Studia Romanica et Anglica Zagrabiensia 39, 193-204.

Burridge, S. and Adam, M. (1985). Using a Learner's Dictionary in the Classroom. Oxford: Oxford University Press.

Catford, J.C. (1983). "Insects are free"; reflections on meaning in linguistics. In: Language Learning 33, 5, 13-32.

Cherchi, L. (1985). Aux deux bouts de la chaîne: propriétés transitoires de l'acquisition et de l'activation du lexique. In: Les langues modernes 3, 4, 39-46.

Cousin, P.-H. (1982). La mise en équation des entités lexicales françaises et anglaises dans un dictionnaire bilingue. In: Calleri, D. and Marello, C. (eds.): Linguistica Contrastiva. Rome: Bulzoni, 255-277.

262

Cowie, A.P. (1978). The place of illustrative material and collocations in a learner's dictionary. In: Strevens, P. (ed.): In Honour of A.S. Hornby. Oxford: Oxford University Press, 127-139.

Cowie, A.P. (1981). The treatment of collocations and idioms in learners' dictionaries. In: Applied Linguistics 2, 3, 223-235.

Cowie, A.P. (1982). Polysemy and the structure of lexical fields. In: Nottingham Linguistic Circular 11, 2, 51-64.

Cowie, A.P. (1983). The pedagogical/learner's dictionary: English dictionaries for the foreign learner. In: Hartmann (1983c: 135-144).

Cowie, A.P. (1984). EFL dictionaries: past achievements and present needs. In: Hartmann (1984:155-164).

Cowie, A.P. (1986). Strategies for dealing with idioms, collocations and routine formulae in dictionaries. Paper presented at the Workshop on Automating the Lexicon, Grosseto, 18-23 May.

Cowie, A.P. (in press). Collocational dictionaries - a comparative view. In: Murphy, M.J. (ed.): Proceedings of the Fourth Anglo-Soviet English Studies Seminar. London: The British Council.

Cruse, D.A. (1982). On lexical ambiguity. In: Nottingham Linguistic Circular 11, 2, 65-80.

Delisle, J. (1980). L'analyse du discours comme méthode de traduction. Ottawa: University of Ottawa Press.

Dineen, F.P. (1967). An Introduction to General Linguistics. New York: Holt, Rinehart, Winston.

Dubois, J. (1981). Models of the dictionary: evolution in dictionary design. In: Applied Linguistics 2, 3, 236-249.

Ellegård, A. (1978). On dictionaries for language learners. In: Moderna Språk 72, 3, 225-242.

Engels, L.K. et al. (1981). L.E.T. Vocabulary List. Leuven: Katholieke Universiteit.

Fillmore, C. (1978). On the organization of semantic information in the lexicon. In: Farkas, D., Jakobsen, W.M. and Todrys, K.W. (eds.): Papers from the Parasession on the Lexicon. Chicago: Chicago Linguistic Society, 148-173.

Fox, M., Bebel, D. and Parker, A. (1980). The automated dictionary. In: Computer 13, 7, 35-48.

Galisson, R. (1983).   Image et usage du dictionnaire chez les
    étudiants (en langue) de niveau avancé.   In: Etudes de lin-
    guistique appliquée 49, 5-88.

Gorcy, G. (1983).   L'informatique et la mise en oeuvre du Trésor
    de la Langue Française, Dictionnaire de la Langue du 19e et du
    20e Siècle (1789-1960).   In: Zampolli and Cappelli (1983:
    119-144).

Götz, D. (1984).   The Art of Speaking.   In: L.A.U.T. Series B,
    100, 19.

Grosjean, F. (1982).   Life with Two Languages: an Introduction to
    Bilingualism.   Cambridge: Harvard University Press.

Grzegorek, M. (1984).   Thematization in English and Polish: a
    Study in Word Order.   Poznań: Wydawnictwa UAM.

Gussenhoven, C. (1984).   On the Grammar and Semantics of Sentence
    Accents.   Dordrecht: Foris Publications.

Güttinger, F. (1963).   Zielsprache: Theorie und Technik des
    Übersetzens. Zürich: Manesse.

Halliday, M.A.K. (1967-68).   Notes on transitivity and theme in
    English.   Journal of Linguistics 3, 37-81, 199-244; 4, 179-215.

Hartmann, R.R.K. (1976).   Über die Grenzen der kontrastiven Lexi-
    kologie.   In: Moser, H., et al. (eds.): Probleme der Lexi-
    kologie und Lexikographie.   Düsseldorf: Schwann, 181-199.

Hartmann, R.R.K. (ed.) (1979).   Dictionaries and their Users.
    Exeter: University of Exeter.   (= Exeter Linguistic Studies 4).

Hartmann, R.R.K. (1982).   Das zweisprachige Wörterbuch im
    Fremdsprachenerwerb.   In: Wiegand (1982:73-86).

Hartmann, R.R.K. (1983a).   On theory and practice.   In: Hartmann
    (1983c:3-11).

Hartmann, R.R.K. (1983b).   The bilingual learner's dictionary and
    its uses.   In: Multilingua 2, 4, 195-201.

Hartmann, R.R.K. (ed.) (1983c).   Lexicography: Principles and
    Practice.   London: Academic Press.   (= Applied Language
    Studies 5).

Hartmann, R.R.K. (ed.) (1984).   LEXeter '83 Proceedings.   Tübingen:
    Niemeyer.   (= Lexicographica.   Series Maior 1).

Hartmann, R.R.K. (1985).   Vocabulary learning and German-English
    lexicography.   University of Exeter: Mimeo.

Hatherall, G. (1984).   Studying dictionary use: some findings and proposals.   In: Hartmann (1984:183-189).

Hausmann, F.J. (1977). Einführung in die Benutzung der neufranzösischen Wörterbücher. Tübingen: Niemeyer.

Hausmann, F.J. (1981).   Wörterbücher und Wortschatzlernen Spanisch.   In: Linguistik und Didaktik 45/46, 71-78.

Heath, D. (1982).   The treatment of grammar and syntax in monolingual English dictionaries for advanced learners.   In: Linguistik und Didaktik 49/50, 95-107.

Heath, D. (1985).   Grammatische Angaben in Lernerwörterbüchern des Englischen.   In: Bergenholtz und Mugdan (1985:332-345).

Heath, D. and Herbst, T. (1985).   Wer weiss schon, was im Wörterbuch steht?   Plädoyer für mehr Wörterbucharbeit im Englischunterricht.   In: Die Neueren Sprachen 84, 6, 580-595.

Heger, K. (1969).   Die Semantik und die Dichotomie von Langue und Parole.   In: Zeitschrift für romanische Philologie 85, 144-215.

Herbst, T. (1984a).   Adjective complementation: a valency approach to making EFL dictionaries.   In: Applied Linguistics 5, 1, 1-11.

Herbst, T. (1984b).   Bemerkungen zu den Patternsystemen des Advanced Learner's Dictionary und des Dictionary of Contemporary English.   In: Götz, Dieter and Herbst, Thomas (eds.): Theoretische und praktische Probleme der Lexikographie. München: Hueber, 139-145.

Herbst, T. (1984c).   A proposal for a valency dictionary of English.   Paper presented at the AILA Congress, Brussels, 5-10 August.

Herbst, T. (forthcoming).   Von Fehlern, die vermeidbar wären - Ein weiteres Argument für mehr Wörterbucharbeit im Englischunterricht   In: Zöfgen, E. (ed.): Wörterbücher und ihre Didaktik. Bielefelder Beiträge zur Sprachlehrforschung.

Hönig, H.G. and Kussmaul, P. (1982).   Strategie der Übersetzung.   Ein Lehr-und Arbeitsbuch. Tübingen: Narr.

Householder, F.W. and Saporta, S. (1962).   Problems in Lexicography.   Bloomington: Indiana University Press.

Howlett, D.R. (1983).   The use of traditional and computer techniques in compiling and printing a dictionary of medieval Latin from British sources.   In: Zampolli and Cappelli (1983:153-160).

Huang, G.F. (1985).   The productive use of EFL dictionaries.   In: RELC Journal 16, 2, 54-71.

Hultin, N.C. and Logan, H.M. (1984). The New Oxford English Dictionary Project at Waterloo. Dictionaries 6, 182-198.

Ilson, R.F. (1984). The communicative significance of some lexicographic conventions. In: Hartmann (1984:80-87).

Ilson, R.F. (ed.) (1985). Dictionaries. Lexicography and Language Learning. Oxford: Pergamon Press. (= ELT Documents 120).

Ilson, R.F. (1986). British and American Lexicography. In: Ilson, R.F. (ed.): Lexicography: an Emerging International Profession. Manchester: Manchester University Press and the Fulbright Commission, 51-72.

Ilson, R.F. (forthcoming). General English dictionaries for foreign learners: explanatory techniques in dictionaries. In: Lexicographica, 2, 6-12.

Jain, M.P. (1978). Review article: Longman Dictionary of Contemporary English. In: Indian Journal of Applied Linguistics 4, 1, 86-104.

Jain, M.P. (1981). On meaning in the foreign learner's dictionary. In: Applied Linguistics 2, 3, 274-286.

Johansson, S., Leech, G.N. and Goodluck, H. (1978). The Lancaster-Oslo-Bergen Corpus of British English. Oslo: University of Oslo.

Kay, M. (1983). The dictionary of the future and the future of the dictionary. In: Zampolli and Cappelli (1983:161-174).

Kempson, R.M. (1977). Semantic Theory. Cambridge: Cambridge University Press.

Kipfer, B.A. (1982). Bibliography of computer applications in lexicography and lexicology. Dictionaries 4, 202-237.

Kipfer, B.A. (1984). Workbook on Lexicography. Exeter: University of Exeter. (= Exeter Linguistic Studies 8).

Kipfer, B.A. (1985). Dictionaries and the Intermediate Student: Communicative Needs and the Development of User Reference Skills. University of Exeter: Unpublished M.Phil. dissertation.

Knowles, F. (1983). Towards the machine dictionary. In: Hartmann (1983c:181-193).

Krashen, S.D. (1982). Principles and Practice in Second Language Acquisition. Oxford: Pergamon Press.

Kromann, H.-P., Riiber, T. and Rosbach, P. (1984a). "Active" and "passive" bilingual dictionaries: the Ščerba concept reconsidered. In: Hartmann (1984:207-215).

Kromann, H.-P., Riiber, T. and Rosbach, P. (1984b). Überlegungen zu Grundfragen der zweisprachigen Lexikographie. In: Wiegand, H.E. (ed.): Studien zur neuhochdeutschen Lexikographie, Vol. 5. Hildesheim - New York: Olms, 159-238.

Kruse, A.F. (1979). Vocabulary in context. In: English Language Teaching Journal 33, 3, 207-213.

Kühn, P. and Püschel, U. (1982). "Der Duden reicht mir". Zum Gebrauch allgemeiner einsprachiger und spezieller Wörterbücher des Deutschen. In: Wiegand, H.E. (ed.): Studien zur neuhochdeutschen Lexikographie, Vol. 5. Hildesheim - New York: Olms, 121-151.

Labov, W. (1972). Sociolinguistic Patterns. Philadelphia: University of Pennsylvania Press.

Labovitz, S. and Hagedorn, R. (1981). Introduction to Social Research. 2nd Edition. New York: McGraw-Hill. [1 1971].

Lado, R. (1979). Language and thought: effect of translation vs interpretation. In: TESOL Quarterly 13, 4, 565-571.

Lakoff, G. and Johnson, M. (1980). Metaphors We Live By. Chicago and London: University of Chicago Press.

Lamy, M.-N. (1985). Innovative practices in French monolingual learners' dictionaries as compared with their English counterparts. In: Ilson (1985:25-35).

Landau, S. (1984). Dictionaries. The Art and Craft of Lexicography. New York: Scribner's.

Laplanche, G., Michiels, A. and Moulin, A. (1982). Computer-produced and computer-marked vocabulary tests based on LDOCE. In: Lutjeharms, M. and Culhane, T. (eds.): Practice and Problems in Language Testing. Leuven: Katholieke Universiteit.

Le Dorze, G. and Nespoulos, J.L. (1984). Processus de la lexicalisation. Modèles psychologiques et leur application à l'étude de l'aphasie et de la traduction. In: Méta 29, 1, 68-80.

Leech, G. and Svartvik, J. (1975). A Communicative Grammar of English. London: Longman.

Lemmens, M. and Wekker, H. (forthcoming). Grammar in English Learners' Dictionaries. Tübingen: Niemeyer.

Lentz, L.T. (1981). An integrated computer-based system for creating the Dictionary of the Old Spanish Language. In: Linguistica Computazionale 1, 19-42.

Lewis, R., and Pugmire, M. (1980). How to Use Your Dictionary. Cambridge: National Extension College.

Luscher, R. (1975). Deutsch 2000. Grammatik der modernen deutschen Umgangssprache. München: Hueber.

Lyons, J. (1977). Semantics. 2 vols. Cambridge: Cambridge University Press.

McDavid, R.I. and Duckert, A.R. (eds.) (1973). Lexicography in English. New York: New York Academy of Sciences. (= Annals of the New York Academy of Sciences 211).

McDonough, S.H. (1981). Psychology in Foreign Language Teaching. London: George Allen and Unwin.

MacFarquhar, P.D. and Richards, J.C. (1983). On dictionaries and definitions. In: RELC Journal 14, 1, 111-124.

Marckwardt, A.H. (1973). The dictionary as an English Teaching Resource. **In: TESOL** Quarterly 7, 369-379.

Marello, C. (forthcoming). Dizionari bilingui italiani. Bologna: Zanichelli.

Martin, M. (1984). Advanced vocabulary teaching: the problem of synonyms. In: Modern Language Journal 68, 2, 130-137.

Martin, W.J.R., Al, B.P.F. and Van Sterkenburg, P.J.G. (1983). On the processing of a text corpus. In: Hartmann (1983c:77-87).

Meara, P. (1980). Vocabulary acquisition: a neglected aspect of language learning. In: Language Teaching and Linguistics: Abstracts 13, 4, 221-246.

Meara, P. (1983). Vocabulary in a Second Language. London: Centre for Information on Language Teaching and Research.

Mitchell, E. (1983). Search-Do Reading: Difficulties in Using a Dictionary. Aberdeen: College of Education. (= Formative Assessment of Reading - Working Paper 21).

Moulin, A. (1983). The pedagogical/learner's dictionary: LSP dictionaries for EFL learners. In: Hartmann (1983c:144-152).

Müller, K.A. (1983). Das Longman Dictionary of Contemporary English: nutzbar im Fach Englisch für Juristen? In: Mitteilungsblatt des Sprachenzentrums der Universität Augsburg 9, 53-63.

Niedzielski, H. (1984). Semantic considerations of set and some of its French equivalents. In: Hartmann (1984:242-252).

Nuccorini, S. (1984).   I "Learners' Dictionaries" e i loro utenti:
note su un particolare tipo di testo e su un particolare tipo
di destinatario.   Paper presented at the 8th AIA Congress,
Siena, November.

Ogden, C.K. (1944).   The ABC of Basic English.   London: Kegan
Paul.

Omaggio, A.C. (1983).   Methodology in transition: the new focus
on proficiency.   In: The Modern Language Journal 67, 4, 330-
341.

Opitz, K. (1979).   Technical dictionaries: testing the requirements of the professional user.   In: Hartmann (1979:89-95).

Országh, L. (1969).   Wanted: better English dictionaries.   In:
English Language Teaching 23, 3, 216-222.

Palmer, F.R. (1981).   Semantics: a New Outline.   2nd edition.
Cambridge: Cambridge University Press.   [[1]1976].

Petersen, P.R. (1983).   New words in Danish 1955-75.   A dictionary compiled and worked out in a traditional way and managed and
typed via computer.   In: Zampolli and Cappelli (1983:179-186).

Pfister, M. (1983).   Présentation du Lessico Etimologico Italiano:
possibilités d'établir des index lexicaux et morphologiques
par ordinateur.   In: Zampolli and Cappelli (1983:187-200).

Picchi, E. (1983).   Problemi di documentazione linguistica.
Archivio di testi e nuove tecnologie.   In: Studi di Lessico-
grafia Italiana 5, 243-252.

Plante, P. (1983).   Le système de programmation DEREDEC.   Mots 6.

Ponten, J.-P. (1975).   Kontrastive Semantik und Bilinguale Lexikographie,   In: Funke, H.G. (ed.):   Grundfragen der Methodik des
Deutschunterrichts.   München: Hueber, 210-217.

Quémada, B. (1983).   Présentation du programme.   In Zampolli and
Cappelli (1983:13-31).

Quirk, R. (1973).   The social impact of dictionaries in the U.K.
In: McDavid and Duckert (1973:76-88).

Quirk, R. and Greenbaum, 5.   (1973).   A University Grammar of
English.   London: Longman.

Quirk, R., Greenbaum, S., Leech, G. and Svartvik, J. (1972).   A
Grammar of Contemporary English.   London: Longman.   (GCE).

Quirk, R., Greenbaum, S., Leech, G. and Svartvik, J. (1985).   A
Comprehensive Grammar of the English Language.   London and New
York: Longman.

Rey-Debove, J. (1971). Etude linguistique et sémiotique des dictionnaires français contemporains. Mouton: The Hague.

Richards, I.A. (1943). Basic English and its Uses. London: Kegan Paul.

Rudzka, B., Channell, J., Putseys, Y. and Ostyn, P. (1981). The Words You Need. London: Macmillan.

Ruhl, C. (1975). Primary verbs. In: Makkai, A. and Makkai, V.B. (eds.): The First LACUS Forum 1974. Columbia, S. Carolina: Hornbeam Press.

Ruhl, C. (1979). Alleged idioms with hit. In: Wölck, W. and Garvin, P.L. (eds.): The Fifth LACUS Forum 1978. Columbia, S. Carolina: Hornbeam Press.

Ščerba, L.V. (1935). Preface. In: Sezeman, D.V. (ed.): Russko-Francuzskij Slovar'. Moscow.

Schmitt, P. (in press). Die "Eindeutigkeit" von Fachtexten: Bemerkungen zu einer Fiktion. In: Snell-Hornby, M. (ed.): Übersetzungswissenschaft - eine Neuorientierung. Zur Integrierung von Theorie und Praxis. Tübingen: Francke.

Scholfield, P. (1982). Using the English dictionary for comprehension. In: TESOL Quarterly 16, 2, 185-194.

Selltiz, C., et al. (1976). Research Methods in Social Relations. 2nd edition. New York: Holt. [1 1951].

Sinclair, J. (1985). Lexicographic evidence. In: Ilson (1985: 81-94).

Snell-Hornby, M. (1983). Verb-descriptivity in German and English. A Contrastive Study in Semantic Fields. Heidelberg: Winter.

Snell-Hornby, M. (1984). The linguistic structure of public directives in German and English. In: Multilingua 3, 4, 203-211.

Snell-Hornby, M. (1985a). Dynamics in meaning as a problem for bilingual lexicography. Paper presented at the International Conference on Meaning and Lexicography, Lódź, 19-21 June.

Snell-Hornby, M. (1985b). Translation as a means of integrating language teaching and linguistics. In: Titford, C. and Hieke, A. (eds.): Translation in Foreign Language Teaching and Testing. Tübingen: Narr, 21-28.

Sora, F. (1984). A study of the use of bilingual and monolingual dictionaries by Italian students of English. In: Papers on Work in Progress 12, 40-46.

Stein, G. (1979). The best of British and American Lexicography. In: Dictionaries 1, 1-23.

Stein, G. (1984). The English dictionary: past, present and future. Special lecture given at the inauguration of the Dictionary Research Centre. Exeter: University of Exeter.

Steiner, R.J. (1984). Guidelines for reviewers of bilingual dictionaries. In: Dictionaries 6, 166-181.

Stock, P.F. (1984). Polysemy. In: Hartmann (1984:131-140).

Swan, M. (1985). A critical look at the communicative approach, 2. In: ELT Journal, 39, 2, 76-87.

Sweet, H. (1899/1964). The Practical Study of Languages. London: Dent. [re-issued London: Oxford University Press].

Tannen, D. (1982). Ethnic style in male-female conversation. In: Gumperz, J.J. (ed.): Language and Social Identity. Cambridge: Cambridge University Press, 217-231.

Tomaszczyk, J. (1979). Dictionaries: users and uses. In: Glottodidactica 12, 103-119.

Tomaszczyk, J. (1981). Issues and developments in bilingual pedagogical lexicography. In: Applied Linguistics 2, 3, 287-296.

Tomaszczyk, J. (1983). On bilingual dictionaries: the case for bilingual dictionaries for foreign language learners. In: Hartmann (1983c:41-51).

Tomaszczyk, J. (1984). The culture-bound element in bilingual dictionaries. In: Hartmann (1984:289-297).

Ullstein, B. (1981). The dictionary war. In: The Bookseller 13 June, 2056-2060.

Underhill, A. (1983). Use Your Dictionary. 4th impr. Oxford: Oxford University Press. [[1]1980].

Ungerer, F., Meier, G.E.H., Schäfer, K. and Lechler, S.B. (1984). Grammatik des heutigen Englisch. Stuttgart: Klett.

Urdang, L. (1979). Meaning: denotative, connotative, allusive. In: Hartmann (1979:47-52).

Vannerem, M. and Snell-Hornby, M. (in press). Die Szene hinter dem Text: "scenes-and-frames semantics" in der Übersetzung. In: Snell-Hornby, M. (ed.): Übersetzungswissenschaft - eine Neuorientierung. Zur Integrierung von Theorie und Praxis. Tübingen: Francke.

Werner, R. (1982). Das Bild im Wörterbuch. In: Linguistik und Didaktik, 49/50, 62-94.

West, M. (1953). A General Service List of English Words. London: Longmans, Green.

Whitcut, J. (1979). Learning with LDOCE. London: Longman.

Widdowson, H.G. (1978). Teaching Language as Communication. Oxford: Oxford University Press.

Widdowson, H.G. (1979). Explorations in Applied Linguistics. Oxford: Oxford University Press.

Widdowson, H.G. (1983). Learning Purpose and Language Use. Oxford: Oxford University Press.

Wiegand, H.E. (1977). Nachdenken über Wörterbücher: aktuelle Probleme. In: Drosdowski, G. et al. (eds.): Nachdenken über Wörterbücher. Mannheim: Bibliographisches Institut, 51-102.

Wiegand, H.E. (ed.) (1982). Studien zur neuhochdeutschen Lexikographie, Vol. II. Hildesheim-New York: Olms.

Wiegand, H.E. (1984). On the structure and content of a general theory of lexicography. In: Hartmann (1984:13-30).

Wiegand, H.E. (1985). Fragen zur Grammatik in Wörterbuchbenutzungsprotokollen. Ein Beitrag zur empirischen Erforschung der Benutzung einsprachiger Wörterbücher. In: Bergenholtz and Mugdan (1985:20-98).

Yorkey, R. (1969). Which desk dictionary is best for foreign students of English? In: TESOL Quarterly 3, 3, 257-270.

Zampolli, A. (1983). Lexicological and lexicographical activities at the Istituto di Linguistica Computazionale. In: Zampolli and Cappelli (1983:237-278).

Zampolli, A. and Cappelli, A. (eds.) (1983). The Possibilities and Limits of the Computer in Producing and Publishing Dictionaries. Rome: Linguistica Computazionale.

Zgusta, L. (1971). Manual of Lexicography. The Hague: Mouton.

Zgusta, L. (1984). Translational equivalence and the bilingual dictionary. In: Hartmann (1984:155-164).